"I WISH I COULD GIVE MY SON A WILD RACCOON."

Eliot Wigginton, who started *Foxfire* magazine with his ninth- and tenth-grade English classes in 1966, still teaches high school in the Appalachian Mountains of North Georgia and, with his students, guides the activities of The Foxfire Fund, Inc. His students now are expanding their efforts to include not only the production of the *Foxfire* magazine and books, but also the creation of television shows for their community cable TV station, a series of record albums of traditional music, and a furniture-making business.

Hundreds of public schools, some with the assistance of IDEAS—a Washington-based private foundation—have integrated the *Foxfire* concept of education into their curricula.

"I *wish* I could give my son a *wild raccoon.*"

edited with an introduction by
Eliot Wigginton

Anchor Books
Anchor Press/Doubleday
Garden City, New York
1976

Contents

Acknowledgments

Assisting with this project has been a meaningful experience in many ways. The response to our search for material was overwhelming, and as the submissions began pouring in, we often found ourselves scrambling to keep up with everything. Through it all, we were constantly amazed and gratified at the willingness of so many people to put so much of their own time and effort into getting the interviews together, especially when we could not guarantee that we would be able to use everything that came in. There were so many bright spots, too, in the inevitable correspondence concerning the various details. So many people's letters stepped beyond the business at hand and bridged that gap between polite indifference and a warmer, much more personal confrontation, and to these people I want to extend my own sincere thanks for making some of the initially more mundane duties so enjoyable.

Those people whose material we were able to accept are acknowledged in the following pages, and we hope they already realize our deep appreciation of their contribution to this book, but we would also like to acknowledge those others whose time and effort and contributions made the necessary job of editing so difficult. To them as well go our sincere appreciation and thanks for their work and support.

Jane Anderson, Metcalf Middle School, Exeter, Rhode Island
Loney H. Peacock, Hilltop High School, Chula Vista, California
Brian Crandall, Oneonta, New York
B. Carr, Oneonta, New York

Mary Sisson, Oneonta, New York
Antonio Avanzato, Oneonta, New York
Toni Carson, Oneonta, New York
Cathy Jo Smith, Oneonta, New York
Cindy George, Oneonta, New York
Russell Groat, Oneonta, New York
Dorothy Hendry, Huntsville High School, Huntsville, Alabama
Aidalu Ford, Jess Lanier High School, Bessemer, Alabama
Barbara Perkins, Jess Lanier High School, Bessemer, Alabama
Daisy Chapman, Abrams High School, Bessemer, Alabama
Mrs. Merritt Culp, Dayton, Ohio
Dorothy McPhillips, Kelso, Washington
Ann Freeman, Dallas, Texas
Susan McGettrick, Schenectady, New York
Joanne.Reid, Rockford Public Library, Rockford, Illinois
Rose Anne Hartman, Volunteer Services Program, Kingston, Ten-
nessee
Barry Malm and Mrs. Dorothy Sorge, Firebaugh, California
Barbara Sanderson, Ypsilanti, Michigan
Bonnie Bush, Shepherdsville, Kentucky

We would like to add a special acknowledgment of several student publi-
cations whose applications of *Foxfire* ideas in their own surroundings have
produced strong, individual magazines worthy of reader interest and support both inside and outside their geographical areas.

Log Skidder, Whitefield, New Hampshire
Laulima, Pahala, Hawaii
Folk and Kinfolk, Hamilton, Georgia
Old Timer, Albany, Texas
Tsa' aszi', Ramah, New Mexico
Mountain Trace, Parkersburg, West Virginia
Cityscape, Washington, D.C.
Bittersweet, Lebanon, Missouri
Loblolly, Gary, Texas
Nanih Waiyah, Philadelphia, Mississippi
Spile, Brookline, New Hampshire

—LAURIE BRUNSON

Introduction

I guess Bill Moyers is to blame for all this.

It was through him that I was introduced to a group called Reading Is Fundamental; a group which, believe it or not, gives new paperback books from major publishers to children all over the country on the assumption that they will read them and thereby improve their reading skills.

Amazing—from several standpoints, not the least of which is that the group literally does give the books away—free. Citizens' groups and industries in the local recipient communities pick up the tab, which, thanks to the publishers' generosity, amounts to about fifty per cent of the retail price. Amazing also because it seems to be working. Great numbers of students, many of whom have never owned books before in their lives, have begun reading with enthusiasm, and library circulation has risen greatly. Can we believe the statistics? I think so. I believe them. It's easy for me, as a high school teacher, to see the attraction of the program as far as the kids are concerned. I can hear them now as they crowd around crates of brand-new books: "You mean we don't have to give these back at the end of the year? No fines? Honest?" Yeah, I can see it.

Anyway, what happened was that RIF was having a meeting to decide what to make of the Bicentennial, and, logically enough, considered the idea of sponsoring the publication of a book for kids to help celebrate it. During the course of the discussions, I guess Bill, knowing what we were doing in Georgia with kids and *Foxfire,* must have mentioned my name, and one thing led to another. . . .

So one day I found myself sitting in Washington with Mrs. Robert McNamara, founder and national chairman of RIF, and a staff member bouncing ideas around. I was having a hard time getting excited about either the discussion or the fact that I had ever met Bill Moyers, because, like Ebenezer Scrooge and Christmas, I was not completely enthralled with the Bicentennial which I thought had been responsible for stimulating very few good projects at that point. For my money, it looked an awful lot like the whole thing was careening toward certain doom and hopeless commercialism, and I mostly just wanted to be left alone with my students so we could quietly think about this country in our own way and in our own time.

But there I was on a brilliantly clear Washington day, wanting very much to be out in it; and at some point an idea that I had once very much wanted to do but had repressed as being a nearly impossible task murmured its way back into my consciousness and I mentioned it. "Here's something you might want to get someone to do."

And they thought about it, liked it, and said, "Fine. When can you do it?"

And I said, "You're crazy."

And they said, "Fine. When can you do it?"

You can close your eyes and imagine the rest.

The idea had simply been an extension of the work I had already been doing for ten years with high school students in the southern Appalachian Mountains of North Georgia. There we have spent hundreds of hours taperecording and photographing the older residents of our community, primarily on the subject of their youth and what their families did to survive when they were essentially self-sufficient. During the course of that work, we had found together that most of these people, who had watched eighty or more years go by, had perceptive, often moving things to say not only about the past, but also about our present and future. Though we hadn't thought about it when we started the project, it stands to reason that a person who was fifteen years old when the first airplane left the ground (a fact that still absolutely floors me) and is still alive and active today must have some thoughts about a society that is now seriously contemplating manned space colonies.

Okay. Now what would happen if, instead of limiting our perspective to the southern Appalachians, we stretched a little? What would happen if we had Navajo kids talking with Navajo elders, Chicano kids talking with Chicano elders, Eskimo kids—you get the idea. And what if we then brought the results of all those interviews together into one volume? What would we then have?

This book is one answer to that question.

Work began in April 1975. Through Loretta Barrett, the Editorial Director of Anchor Press and RIF Board member, Doubleday agreed to publish the book and sent a cash advance. With that money, I hired Laurie Brunson, one of my old *Foxfire* students, to work with me. The remainder of the advance was set aside to be divided equally among the persons whose interviews were accepted for publication. All royalties would go to RIF.

I wrote a six-page summary outlining the projected book. It also included a long list of subject areas that we hoped the students that conducted the interviews would encourage their contacts to reflect on at length. The summary read in part, "This book, above all, will be an opportunity for our grandparents to speak their piece from their own special perspective. A forum where men and women from every culture can come together to express, through their grandchildren, their hopes and fears for us as a nation, and their dreams for us as a world."

The mimeographed description was sent to hundreds of adults who work with kids. Their names came from the files we keep on teachers who are advising *Foxfire*-type projects in their own schools, from the RIF files, from the list of adults working with minority students on journalism projects encouraged by the people at the Robert F. Kennedy Memorial Fund, and many others. The end result, months later, was the submission of stacks of interviews from which I selected, and then edited, nearly forty of the best. We knew we couldn't represent every culture (Ralph Rinzler at the Smithsonian had warned me that there were nearly two hundred distinct cultures that made up the population of this country), and one look at Studs Terkel's *Working* warned me that we'd be in over our heads if we tried to get submissions representing even a fraction of the occupations and life styles. Even so, I think the final range here is impressive: from Swedes to Eskimos, from Greeks to Chippewas, from Jews to Mennonites, from firemen to hermits and banjo-makers—all coming together because they have something they'd like to say to young people, and to the rest of us, in 1976. Ada Allen, a black woman in Parkersburg, West Virginia, whose ancestors were slaves, perhaps best expressed their willingness to participate in all this. At one point in the interview, while talking about slavery, she asked the students who were with her if they had never been told about these things before. They shook their heads. In surprise, she said, "I'm sorry nobody has told you all this before. That's pitiful. That's the trouble. People ought to know these things. I believe in telling the facts. People that really know ought to tell you all [instead of letting you get it second- or third-hand, if at all]. That's what's the matter with the schools and the world today."

In the face of the almost overwhelming problems that confront our world now, and in the face of the competition those problems present for our attention, one is tempted to ask, "Why bother? Why listen to any more? Why all the frenetic activity to put a book like this together?"

Well, I can think of a couple reasons. For one, many of the stories that are related here make fascinating reading, if nothing else.

But there's more. One of the biggest rewards for me (and I hope for the reader) as I poured over this material was the realization that despite the culture, despite the personality behind the voice, despite the diverse problems that surround us and compete for our energy, and despite the sometimes awful experiences the speakers have had—and in some cases are still going through—there are definite common threads that unite us into a universal human family. We celebrate many of the same joys and triumphs, we share the same fears and defeats, and we often advocate the same values (note, for example, the similarity between the lesson-bearing tales of Emily Brown, an Eskimo, and Sarah Dupee, a black). And we all hope fervently, if fruitlessly, for a better world, and for a day when we can meet together on common ground to celebrate the joys of our cultural diversity, and to prepare to serve as midwives to a world that will recognize our universality. "It is essential that mankind free itself from the limitations of national prejudice, and acknowledge that the forces that unite it are incomparably deeper than those that divide it . . ." wrote Henry Steele Commager in the January 1976 issue of *Mainliner*. And I believe that.

And there's another reason for a project like this. Listen to Emily Brown talk about the mistakes the early missionaries made with native cultures in Alaska. Listen to Diana Golden talk about what it was like to be a Jew in Auschwitz. Listen to Ada Allen relate again those stories told her by her slave ancestors, and listen to her tell about being "Jim Crowed" in West Virginia. And listen as Stanley Hicks talks about how his land and that of his southern Appalachian neighbors was eased out from under them for a housing development, built by an outside corporation, that he and his neighbors can't even visit.

This is, then, not often a look at the past through rose-colored glasses—a nostalgic tour through the "good old days." In many ways, it is a series of cautionary tales: "We must learn from what's gone before. We must never let this happen again if we are to ever achieve the kind of world that all of us can be happy in."

For the most part, the interviews here were conducted by and with individuals I've never met. Here's a great outpouring of people talking to each other instead of watching television; and though each is an extraordinary person, my suspicion is that each is not necessarily *exceptional*. Every community must have hundreds of them. They are the stuff of which our world is still made—good, sensitive people who *persist* but don't make much noise. Perhaps if we made them move a part of our lives . . .

If there are so many of them, though, why is it that we don't seem to be getting any closer, year by year, to the community of man we all wish for? On September 5, 1975, *Newsweek* published a column by Bill Moyers that I've saved called, "The Meek Must Get Tough." In it, he responded to a letter from one Michael J. Gillman, who, in complete frustration, noted that organized self-interest in this country seems to have completely divorced itself from the common man as it influences policy making, attitudes, and change. Moyers comments on the apparent truth of this observation and concludes, "Everybody seems to be winning except the people. It is enough to tilt a nice man like Michael J. Gillman toward pessimism. It is also enough to undo further the slender threads of community that hold this disparate society together. The unbridled pursuit of organized self-interest may have been tolerable when there was a continent to be tamed, but in a highly complex society, if everyone starts elbowing everyone, everyone gets a black eye. In such a society, the meek will inherit the earth only if they get tough about it."

The meek? Bill will be the first to notice that the interviews in this book are predominately from those very citizens. It is skewed. I admit it. Personal prejudice, I suppose. Perhaps the next man in my situation will stick to representatives of self-interest groups. Meanwhile, the people here, by and large, like the rest of us, are the ones that traditionally get stepped on. The ones whose only defense is what's left of their own dignity after the rape. And what's their future?

Not much. At least not in a world filled with elbows. And yet, in the act of submitting to these interviews, they may have made a contribution greater than any they imagined. For it is important here to remember that the individuals who shared the stories of these elders—their defeats and their fears and their triumphs and their hopes and their prayers—were very young. In some cases, they were only ten or twelve years old. And it is likewise important to remember that this book does not represent simply a one-shot project involving scores of young people, but that this sort of thing is happening on a regular basis in hundreds and hundreds of other communities and public schools.

Inevitably, some of those students, who are all now about the business of shaping their individual philosophies, are going to emerge with their hands on the levers of power. With the memory of stories like these ringing in their ears, they may well stride into our next century with a sensitivity, and with a quiet, smiling, unobtrusive, individual, rock-hard determination that will not only rob the enemy of some of its potential recruits, but may rattle as it has never been rattled before the cage of intimidation that that self-serving and selfish enemy would trap us in.

The meek, Bill, through our children, may *yet* inherit the earth.

—ELIOT WIGGINTON

"And His name is Silam Inua."

EMILY BROWN

Emily Ivanoff Brown was born February 1904 in the Eskimo village of Unalakleet, Alaska. Her father, who ran a trading post, was half Russian and half Yupik. Her mother was a full Eskimo—an orphan raised in the orphanage in Unalakleet.

As a young girl, Emily moved with her family to Shaktoolik, where her father hoped to take advantage of the gold rush throngs heading for Nome.

When Emily was eleven, her parents became worried about the fact that there was no school in their village and sent her to the Chemawa Indian School in Salem, Oregon. She stayed there for nine years and was so much older than the other girls that they called her "Grandma." But in those nine years, she finished grammar school, high school, and two years of practice teaching. On graduation, she signed a contract to teach school at Kotzebue, Alaska, as one of the very few native teachers in the territory.

In 1930, she decided to broaden her education and moved to Seattle to attend a nursing school there. It was there that she met and married the redheaded Robert Brown from Rochester, New York. They returned to Alaska, where they had three sons. In 1938 she helped support the family by teaching again, this time at her old home town of Shaktoolik (where she was fired—but immedi-

ately reinstated—when she told her classes an Eskimo ghost story on Halloween). After the tragic death of her husband in 1941, she continued to teach, raising her sons with her parents' help and attending the University of Alaska at Fairbanks during the summers. She received her bachelor's degree there in 1964.

A three-year bout with cancer forced her to retire from her thirty-year teaching career, so she returned to the University of Alaska, where she won her Master's in 1973. Now, at seventy-one years of age, she is based there in the Department of Native Languages writing a long series of books about her native culture, trying to preserve as much of it as she can. If she feels her age, she won't admit it. "I don't sit around and nurse my wounds!"

—NOLA BEAVER, NICK NICHOLS, CHAR MCNEILL,
PRIMO RODRIGUEZ, KIM POST, AND RAY MCBRIDE.
PHOTOGRAPHS BY RON INOUYE.
—ELIOT WIGGINTON, ADVISER TO FOXFIRE.

OUR PEOPLE for thousands of years have believed in a spiritual God who they think lives in the sky. And every time they need advice, they go up on a knoll—a higher place—and raise their arms like this and talk to Him in that manner. They bring their problems to Him. And His name is Silam Inua. And the meaning of that word is the owner of the universe—the whole world: the earth and what's in the sky. He is the owner of the universe.

The Eskimo people teach their children to respect Silam Inua. The elders are the teachers of the Eskimo people because they're learned people who know how to live. The women teach the girls how to sew and cut the patterns for boots and parkas, and the young men learn how to become great hunters. When a young man catches his first *ugruk* [bearded seal], he doesn't claim that *ugruk*. It is a *more* that the whole community has a festival. They cut it in small pieces or cook the whole thing in the center of an outdoor fireplace and eat it, and then they'll go and bless that young hunter like this: "We hope that when you're out hunting, Silam Inua will make lots of animals to appear before you so you will catch enough to let us eat." And they save the bones, and during the festival they take the bones and put them back in the sea through a hole in the ice so Silam Inua will bless them. They weren't careless people. They didn't throw the bones all over everywhere like some people do at present time.

And they use some parts of the animals for decoration, too. The bladder

Emily Brown

of the *ugruk* or any animal is one part. The hunters tell their wives to save the bladders, and then during this festival they blow them up and paint them different colors and hang them on the wall right by the young hunter. And then after the festival, the people take the balloons and put them down in the sea again, and they have little ritual and they say, "Silam Inua will return these animals someday and give them for us to eat." It's a beautiful culture.

And the children learn this. Sometimes it's hard. When my brother first caught *ugruk,* he was quiet. And the whole village took the whole thing and ate it all. Nothing for his mother. And when he went to bed, Momma heard him crying. And she went to him, "What's the matter? Why are you crying?"

"I got that *ugruk* for *you.*" He didn't like the community eating it.

My son did the same thing. When he first caught white goose, I invited the old folks of our village and I made pillows for them from the feathers. I was trying to pass on the tradition to him. He didn't appreciate it [laughing] and he cried. He said, "Mom, I caught that goose for you and you gave it away."

And I had to talk to him. And now he gives things which he catches away to old folks. It's still clinging to him. He learned from this. And it's funny; he's a real good hunter. I can't help but believe that has something to it—that Silam Inua blesses the people who give things. That's true. A person who is selfish is usually old and cranky, and doesn't give anything away. We have beautiful culture. Beautiful. I could never write it to show the people how our ancestors lived. They were considerate people.

But they never wasted any parts of the animals they caught. Sometimes they used whalebones for sinkers in their nets. And what they couldn't use was cleaned up and returned to the waters, or to the kitchen midden in town and covered with ashes—not just scattered all over the place. They were real clean people, and they had great respect for animals. We learn so much from animals. Our ancestors learned how to pick nonpoisonous plants by watching what the animals ate. That was the origin of how we knew which were good plants and which were bad. So they won't let animals be mistreated.

I might tell you a legend. They have a taboo that the children should not abuse birds and animals. If you do, something terrible will come to you to repay what that animal suffered through his mistreatment. So one time these two brothers were out snaring ptarmigan, and when they came up to see their snares, they saw a live ptarmigan that was caught in one. And so the older brother said, "I wonder if it would fly if we plucked the feathers."

They got so curious that the younger brother held the ptarmigan and the older brother plucked all the feathers. And then they threw it up in the sky and it came down kerplunk and killed it.

And so a year or two afterwards, both boys got sick and the shaman couldn't cure them. And he kept telling them that they must confess: "Have you done something to someone? Have you mistreated an animal?" And they wouldn't tell. And they suffered this disease and they wouldn't eat and they were starving. But they never died. They were suffering. They were being punished. Finally the youngest boy confessed. And after they confessed, they both died. And that's a lesson.

Eskimos were raised with these taboos. These are laws and advice they give to their children. How to conduct themselves as members of a community. They are laws that a person must not do. Like you must not kill anyone. If you do, then you or a member of your family will be killed also to balance the evil that has been done by your family. And that's what taboo means—laws that you must not break.

I'll tell you a story about a man who killed another man in Buckland, Alaska. This really happened. When he killed this man, he knew he or one of his family members would die. And he didn't want any of his children to be killed. What he did was when everyone went to bed, he told his two sons, the youngest one and the oldest one, about this law—and he said, "I have broken the law of our community. If they don't kill me, they're going to kill one of you, so you're going to escape."

He got his kayak ready for survival—food and whatever they needed on the way—and he sent them out. He told them which way to go to Unalakleet, my village, and they left. And their father was killed because it was the law.

And they traveled and went to an orphanage. They would be considered orphans now because they left their home for good. They could never return for their father told them not to. And they grew up at that orphanage at Unalakleet. And when the youngest one became old enough to handle dog teams—twelve or fifteen years old—he became our minister's dog-team driver, and even saved the minister's life once when some drunk men were going to kill him. And that boy's name was Ojyock. That means rock. And he was my mother's uncle.

There are many of these taboos or *mores*. Eskimo people love their children. When they get a baby, the baby is always in the warmth of the mother. Never apart. We don't have any cribs. The baby always goes with the mother no matter where she goes. And that brings love to the baby.

And so it is a *more* that when you have a baby and you are going to eat your food, don't eat it alone. Bring your little child or baby and pantomime feeding it, too, while you are eating. The way you should do it is not think only about your hunger, but think about your baby's hunger too. After you chew the food up good in your mouth, then take a little piece of that food and put it up to the baby's mouth, and then eat it yourself [until he is old enough to eat with you]. This is Eskimo psychology. If you don't do this, the baby will have a feeling that he is being neglected.

There is a very, very old legend about that called "The Diapered Ogre Baby." One time the chief's daughter-in-law forget to feed the little baby by miming, and you know what happened? The chief who was living in the same igloo knew what had happened that particular night, so he told his wife to get his knife handy because he knew something would happen.

So they went to bed, and while they were sleeping, the baby began eating its mother. You could hear a smacking sound—eating something, you

Standing: Ray McBride, Nola Beaver, Nick Nichols, Emily Brown, Char McNeill; seated: Kim Post, Primo Rodriguez

know. And he looked across the room, and the baby had turned to ogre—a baby animal.

And so the chief was responsible for his subjects, and he climbed up to the window in the top of the igloo and took his megaphone and told the people to flee as fast as they could from the village because his grandchild had turned to a little animal with big mouth and big teeth, and it had just killed its mother by eating her breasts. She had bled to death.

And so the people went out and ran away from the predicament they were in. They didn't have any control over it. It crawled on its stomach with a little diaper on, you know?

And there lived in this community an orphan, and he was trained to run fast. He was the fastest runner in the community. And he went with the group of people who were fleeing over the mountains. And when they were halfway through this group of mountains, the chief stopped the people and told them to rest a little bit. And he said, "I left my knife in my igloo and I need it." Knives at that time were very hard to make and they were precious to the people. "Whoever goes back to get my knife can marry my daughter and become the leader after I die."

And this boy volunteered: "I'll go."

And he ran all the way back to the village.

When he came near the village, he waited while the ogre baby went from house to house. He was now near the last house. And the boy ran as fast as he could and jumped through the window up in the ceiling of the igloo and found the knife. But by that time the ogre baby could smell the scent and chased him over the mountains crawling and crying, and so the race was on for either life or death. And he was so exhausted when they were about halfway to the end of this ridge that he took his mittens off and dropped them, and the ogre baby stopped to eat them. That gave him a chance to get ahead, but the ogre baby began gaining again. And so he took his parka off and tore the right side sleeve off and dropped it. And he tore his parka as he ran, and the ogre baby ate it piece by piece and still was overtaking him.

About that time he saw a caribou trail that led to the mountains on the other side. And so he went on the caribou trail and he knew that he had to do something. Otherwise he would be overtaken. And he noticed that the snow was soft at the foot of the mountain where there's usually more snow that's deeper, and so he decided that he would run as fast as he could and jump into the snow and cover himself with the snow. And the ogre baby was coming down now, following him, but going slower as he had lost the human scent which had mixed with the caribou scent. So the boy jumped into the deep snow and covered himself and he waited. He could hear the baby coming, but he was quiet. And then it stopped—and stopped crying—it was smelling around. But it went on following the caribou trail.

And he waited and waited until he couldn't hear the baby crying way off, and then he got out and shook himself free of snow and walked to the people. They were right across the bay now. And of course when he got there the people shouted and they were glad that he was safe, and he became a famous young man. And he married the chief's daughter, and when the chief died, he became chief.

And that's the way we teach the children. We have legends that represent how you could be good, and we have legends on the other side like this one. If you're forgetful of the teachings, you suffer the consequences of being so forgetful and careless. This is the children's education. It is also the basis of our literature—teaching the children how to be good and what bad means by these stories.

And we had wonderful festivals. In the fall of the year, we had one like Halloween. When a person dies, then the next baby that is born in that village is named after that person. They think that the spirits don't die. The spirit must go to a little baby and live again. And in the fall they have a festival called *dugummaaq*. These babies that were named within that year are visited by the dead persons' relatives. They paint themselves like spirits —it's what you might call the representation of the spirit of that dead relative that is visiting them. And the baby's parents will give the "ghosts" gifts like boots or parkas or food—Eskimo ice cream or dried meat—something like that.

It's like trick and treat. Momma said she used to hide and hide and hide because she was afraid of the spirits. There must have been a lot of crying in the homes! They had to do this as part of their education—to respect their cultural festivals.

I was named after my mother's cousin. Her name was Emily—her Eskimo name was Ticasuk. And when I became older, my mother told me what it meant. That means a hollow in the ground. And I cried when I was a little girl. Big tears rolled down my cheeks because I was so disappointed. Every time I saw a hollow in the ground, I would walk around it. I didn't want to walk into it because it was my name! And then my mother told me not to cry—that it was a beautiful name. You see, the four winds on this earth, when they blow from the north or south or east or west, they bring the wealth of the earth and they lodge into that hollow, and that's *mine. Now* I think it's a beautiful name. But sometimes my mind doesn't always work the way I want it to, and sometimes I think that it is hollow! But no person is perfect, no matter how successful you are; but when you do the best you can, your mind will help you.

And then we have another festival near Christmas. This is a very long

celebration. It's a week long. They invite all the people from a neighboring village, and then the host community takes care of these villagers. And they have dancing and drama. My mother's dance was depicting how her ancestors made their living. My grandfather's way of making a living was that of a trader. He'd go through with his sailboat—his umiak—and sell things and buy things in exchange. And so my mother used to dance when she was a little girl. They would drum for her, and by rhythmic motions and miming, she would be a sailboat. That means, "My ancestors made living this way." And she'd dance. Oh, it's just beautiful, I think.

And we had expert dancers and those who could mime and tell stories, and they prepared for that festival, too. The best food was saved for the guests, and they'd treat them royally and they'd give gifts to each other, and they'd exchange their legends. It would take them a whole year to learn to do a specialized act of any drama. If they made a mistake when they were tested by the elders, they'd put this particular drama away for next year. They do not perform just halfway. The drama must be perfect. They were not careless. They were particular people. They performed whatever they were going to show to their guests before they arrived. They didn't want to put a shame to their society by making a mistake. They gave a perfect performance. And the food preparation must be perfect. They're perfectionists when it comes to doing a program in front of their friends that they have invited.

And then the missionaries came and told them not to do any dancing because this was the work of the evil spirit. But they were wrong. It was not. The festivals were beautiful. You see, the missionaries had no interpreters and they didn't study our culture before they set up their schools. They did the damage not knowingly. And though the missionaries have destroyed our beautiful traditional customs—in my case I'm sorry that they did—I do not blame them, because they didn't study first about the way we lived and it took them years to know how they not knowingly destroyed our tradition.

Our Eskimo language is the simplest language that you could learn and study, but our natives now communicate in English. *Now* the education department in Alaska says we're going to do research and save the languages of the Alaskan native peoples. But it's a little bit too late. It's funny. It doesn't seem logical for students to study their own language that they have forgotten. Because they've had to learn English as their first language, they've forgotten how to manipulate their mouths. They sound like babies when they talk Eskimo language. It has been written out now in English language alphabet, but the letters don't match our sounds. You can't make the word sound right by reading the English spelling. That's why it sounds different. It's mixed with the English and we have to conform to the sounds of "T" and "H" and "G"—they're not really our own sounds. You can understand them, but it doesn't sound natural.

And it all happened because the U. S. Government gave an order back in 1912 to establish schools here and tell teachers in Alaska that the native language should not be spoken by native people. "Teach natives English language so they can become civilized and be educated." They wanted us to become civilized as fast as they could go with us. They didn't realize the mistake that they were making. And when I was a teacher, I had to enforce it because our principal would say, "When they talk Eskimo, give them a demerit and put it on their record and punish them after school. Make them clean the school building." It was a very difficult time. The parents were unhappy because their children would come home and tell them that they were detained instead of going home after school. I used to feel sorry for the kids. It was so easy to forget, you know, and talk Eskimo language. It's natural for them to speak. And then we'd have to go out in the yard and watch them—remind them, "Remember, speak English language!" And that was done all over Alaska.

And that's how the Eskimo children forgot their language. And now they're spending millions of dollars to restore that lost art—that oral language. And that doesn't seem right for white men to have done this—to erase our cultural traditional things. But the damage is done, so . . .

And so we changed from our tradition to the white culture. And that's funny too. They want us to be white, and then they won't let us. They are the dominant culture, and they have cliques and won't let us in. We have to suffer socially. They can never put their nose down. It's always up this way. They make friends with you when you're alone, and you think they like you, and then you see them at party and they won't even speak. They're embarrassed to be seen associating with you. It happens to me. At a party here, one of my instructors and his wife wouldn't come near me. Why are they like that? They don't want to rub elbows with native people? Is it pride in them? I guess you can't erase that.

We try hard to fit the pattern of their lives, but at heart we're still Eskimos, and so we get confused. What do they want from us?

Let's just be what we are and not be fakes like that.

And let's help them see who we are. Because of the fact that outsiders don't know how we lived in the past, they think we're just primitive people. Our way of life has never been written as it should be, and so this is my last work. This has been my purpose after I retired from teaching—to try to retrieve and preserve the beautiful literature we have that is practically unknown. I'm doing an encyclopedia that will be written by Eskimos themselves who know their culture, and this is what I'm going to leave for my grandchildren when I pass away. I want to leave something that they can learn from about my culture and respect their own people thereafter.

You can help in this. Get an education so they respect you and listen to what you have to say, and then help us. The way of education, it's up to

you. You either succeed or you don't. I succeeded because I was persistent. I came to college every summer for eleven summers, and I got my Master's degree in 1973. And that was something for me because I had to work hard. Coping with English language is very hard. Every time I was in school, I enrolled in the hardest English subject because I wanted to learn. I had will that no one could take away from me. I wanted to succeed and I worked hard, and you can do the same, too. Try to be an example to others. Go on and conquer. Be like a soldier. Conquer your fears. Your best friend is a dictionary. I wore out a whole dictionary getting my education.

What you need when you go to school is bulldog tenacity. When the bulldog bites, he doesn't let go. And so when you bite education, don't let it go. Keep it in your mouth. There's always a channel up here in your head to put it away in. And when you need that wisdom or that education, it will unfold in your life.

You know, when you make up your mind to do something good, you can *do* it. Whatever you do in life, when you try to do something nice for your people, you will never regret it when you get to be my age. You will be thankful that you have that something in your life. That good or bad, it's like a plant. If you have done something that is good, it comes up as a fruit. But if you have done something that is not good, it comes as a thistle—a weed. That comes from my mother. That's the way native people believe.

And that's my message to you folks. You can teach others to do things for other people. Selfish people don't do anything. Just work to make money— save. Whenever you do a kind deed to other people, you will get the same treatment in your life when you become helpless person. And that's the way life is. Our life is very important. God gave you His soul so you could be part of the community and your family. What must you do to do something with your life? You know how to answer that question. Are you going to be a drunkard? What are you going to be? Are you going to try to do something within your power to be a good example for your people? You think it over. Make up your mind.

And be consistent! Don't be like a jellyfish that goes when the tide changes. Are you going to be that kind of fish? No, you're not, because you're human. God gave us good brain. It's a computer. And it will show you how to do things if you ask the Lord to help you. I relied largely in my life on God's help. He saved my life several times. I was going to have a major operation. I had cancer. I died at the operating table. But before I went under, I asked the Lord, "Lord, I am not ready to see you yet. Please let me live for a little while longer." And you know, He did. They had to massage my heart when my breath was gone. I was dead for four or five minutes. I was almost dead for good, but God let me live. Our soul has to go back to God because He lent it to us. And you know, God always tells you when you're going to do something wrong. A person who is weak will accept the bad. The Holy Spirit does not want to live in a soul where it is dirty. Do you like to live in a dirty house? The Holy Spirit doesn't. And this is all true.

Now this is a Christian attitude, but I have learned. I always thank the Lord in the morning and I ask Him, "Lord, help me to plan my day to Thy glory, not mine." And He leads me to do something for somebody else. I think it's a beautiful life.

An Eskimo life is something like that. They love to do things for others. They love to give things away that they make themselves. And they were happy people years ago. Happiest people. That's why they have such wonderful smiles. The white man smiles from the lips, but the Eskimo smiles from the heart. They're not pretty physically, but they have beautiful personalities. We have a lot to learn from Eskimo and Indian cultures.

That's one reason I show my appreciation to my parents—because they let me know what value means: value of education, your birth, your heritage, and the way you should live with your neighbor. These are values. And a man who has wisdom knows what's of value, and as you grow older you can spot what's of value too. Value of life is the most significant value. You can destroy yourself if you do not obey laws—if you do not love your neighbor—and if you take drugs and drink. These are very detrimental to your mind, and you don't survive when you get older. Then the government has to take care of you. You are a nuisance to the citizens of your country. You're not loyal to your country. You destroy yourself.

The main thing is to identify who you are, and be sure to find out what type of work you love to do. Then you can expand your ability and serve the Lord and humanity at the same time.

"I could just see myself hanging on top of that pole."

LLOYD MAYS

Lloyd Mays was born May 8, 1908, in Decatur, Texas. His parents were William and Mary Mays. His father, a farmer, died of TB when Lloyd was eight years old. Lloyd's three older brothers supported the family until they got married. Then, at the age of eighteen, Lloyd had to quit school and start farming to support the family.

He quit farming thirty-four years ago when a doctor told him he was allergic to dust. Since then, Lloyd has been working in the oil patch. At the age of sixty-seven, he still puts in a hard day's work.

He and his wife live eighteen miles from Albany in a trailer surrounded by oil wells where he "pumps" the lease. A pumper looks over the lease and sees if the wells are all working to their potential, and, if not, sees to it that they are fixed. In addition he fixes leaks and makes repairs.

Last Christmas a tragic fire destroyed the Mayses' home and all their possessions. They escaped with only the clothes they had on. Lloyd's wife is an invalid and it must have been very hard for her.

"I could just see myself hanging on top of that pole."

Lloyd had to just "start over" as he put it. He was at about the age most men retire and all he had was a pair of borrowed glasses and a fruit jar full of pennies, but he has worked hard to rebuild.

—CHARLES HOLSON, JIM LAW, JAMES BALL,
CATHY TEINERT, AND BETTY KEY.
—WINIFRED WALLER, ADVISER TO OLD TIMER.

I WAS BORN in Decatur, about fifteen or twenty miles north of Fort Worth. Moved from there up to Olney. Then, when I was eight years old, my dad died. I had three brothers older than I was, and, of course, after my dad died, they took over until they got married. And then I went to school. Well, I guess I was about eighteen when I had to quit school and go to work. My older brothers had all gotten married and we didn't have anyone to do the farming so I had to do it. I had three brothers and my sister [left] I had to support. I got part of the ninth grade.

When I first went to work, I was working on an old spudder. Have you ever seen a cable tool [a spudder]? Just like you was picking something up and dropping it, see, and mashing a hole in the ground. You drill four or five foot, and then you got to run a baler in there, see, and bale this mud out. A rotary has got a pump that blows it out, see. If you drill fifty foot with a cable tool a day, you done a pretty good day's work. But sometimes you drill three or four hundred foot a day with a rotary drill, see? When I first went to work I was working on an old spudder. Well, this driller was running the baler and the cable. Well, when it hits, the cable will wad up on the floor, you see, and this cable went right around him and then the baler started in the hole. That cable cut his head off right below his ear and I was standing there, and his head rolled plumb across that floor. Gol-l-ly bumb! It was just me and him out there working.

The main thing is that the man that you're working with has got to know what he's doing. Now a lot of people, they get out there and don't pay no attention to what they're doing see, and they get reckless. If you'll notice, most every accident is carelessness.

One time I thought my clutch was slipping. I was standing there watching it, to see if it was slipping or not, and had this rag in my hand, an old rag so you could wipe your hands off, and this belt caught this rag and pulled my old arm plumb around and plumb over that clutch. I don't know if you can see it for my whiskers but it poked a hole in my face right there. But it happened that it didn't hurt me too bad. That was just careless, see. And another time I was trying to put on some belts and bumped up against this switch and my hand caught in this belt and it cut the ends of my fingers off. But I never have been hurt very bad working in the oil field so far. It's been close, though.

I was pulling a well down here by myself and had the rods laying on a horse down there and when I'd start back in the hole, I'd catch that elevator and sort of push them out of the way. I had on a pair of them old cloth gloves and when I pushed that thing over, the end of that rod went right up in that glove and, boy, it started taking me up that pole and I couldn't get to my clutch, see; done pulled my feet off the ground, and about that time that old glove come off. You know how hard them old canvas gloves are to pull off. How that thing come off, I don't know but if it hadn't, it would have taken me plumb to the top of the pole, boy. Ha ha—I could just see myself hanging on top of that pole. Weren't nobody around there nowhere, see. Boy, I got out there and sat down for a long time before I worked any more, too. But I guess if there'd been anybody else there, more'n likely he'd a'just done watched it anyway. Like an old boy that was helping me right before I got one of those fuse testers to put them fuses in electric boxes, you know. Anyway, this old boy had a switch on the side of this old box where you pull it down to test a fuse, see. I'd stick a fuse in it and he'd turn it on, and if it didn't go, we'd know it wasn't no good and we'd put another one in there. And I put a fuse in there and he didn't pull that switch off, see. Gol-l-durn! Instead of him pulling that switch off . . . Boy! And it was a-shaking me! Finally it knocked me out and I fell, and when I fell, why it pulled my hand loose. Course that killed the electricity. Where I had my hand on the side of this box it burned a big blister on my hand. He said, "I just froze, I don't know what in the world I was thinking about." All he'd a'had to done was just pull that switch down, see, but he just stood there looking at me. He said, "I couldn't no more pull that switch off than Adam." Boy, I got to where I won't fool with that dad-gummed electricity. I been shocked too many times with it. Makes you kinda gun-shy. When you don't know anything about it, boy, you better leave it up to the electricity guy.

And never work with anybody that's reckless or anybody drinking. Now take anyone drinking, they'll get you hurt because their mind can't function right, see, and they can't quite think quick enough and they get reckless. In the old days they kept whiskey all the time. My dad had it sitting on the table and I never thought nothing about it. You hardly ever seen anybody getting drunk or slipping around drinking. We just used it just for medicine. If you had a sore throat or something, he might give you just a teaspoon or so of whiskey and the next morning you'd be all right. [If someone came in drunk,] I just tell them to go home. I'd figure that they's going to get hurt, see, so I'd just tell them to go home and come back tomorrow when they felt good. Course it's their business what they do when they get off, but I don't allow them to drink [on the job], and I let them know it when I hire them.

[Oil's a rough business. If someone isn't getting hurt, then something else is getting messed up, like the land or the water.] Like they went to pumping this salt water back into this oil sand to make it make more oil. Course if there's a well over yonder that's in the same sand, well, this salt water is going to go over there, too.

The way they got it now, when they start to run pipe the Railroad Commissioner is supposed to be out there and see that it's done right, you see; but a lot of times he don't even come around. The oil field people could help more than the government could by just being honest. They could take care of it theirselves, see, if they would do it. But there's a lot of them, see, that say, "Oh, just so that I get a dollar." That's all they care! They don't care if it's done right or not. These new wells that I work on right down here—that old pipe that they run in there has holes in it, see; and the Railroad Commissioner should have been there and made them run new pipe in it instead. I've tried to explain to the boss. Course there's just lotsa guys just get by any way they can. Won't even pay no attention to what the Railroad Commissioner tells them. I've had things happen, like a leak happen of a night, see, and maybe water'd be running plumb to the creek by the time I got down there next morning. And first thing you know you got an acre of ground killed. I feel like I've just done the best I could, by golly. But the company is the main one, see. I knew it wasn't right, and the Railroad Commissioner would have me shut 'er down, see, and the boss would come along and start it up again, the sucker. Course I was working for him and I had to do what he told me to, see? I've seen lotsa good [water] wells ruint just by salt water. They've let it go so long now that it's done ruint half the country. Now if they'd-a started a long time ago and make them take care of this water like it ought to be, why, they wouldn't of had all that pollution and stuff. They're trying, but I'm afraid it's too late for most of it.

Course there's a lot of these old wells that they plugged, see, but they don't plug them right. Ruined this dad-gummed little old creek down here. If they could find all these old wells and plug them, but the trouble of it is that a lot of these old wells, they don't know where they's at.

Used to be when I first moved out here, I could be around any of these creeks, see, and I could stop and get me a drink but, boy, it'd make you sick now if you tried to drink some of it. Even these earth tanks around, they don't taste right, do they? It don't take much salt water to ruin it.

I tell you when I first moved up here, I could go down there to the river and I never would take no drinking water with me. I could drink that water down there then, see? But, boy, you can't now! Now that's how bad it's got

Jim Law, James Ball, and Lloyd Mays

since I've been here. And all the pecan trees, boy, I could go down there and take a tow sack and get all the pecans I wanted, but now there's not any pecan trees down there; no trees or nothing. That's what I hate about the dad-gummed oil field. It's ruining a lot of water, do you know it? We got to do something about it or I don't know what's gonna happen. First thing you know we're not gonna have any water or anything is what I'm afraid of. We've drilled 1,400 foot and never have gotten any fresh water. It's all salt water, see? It's from the ocean. The elevation out here is 1,550 foot. When you drill down and get down even with the ocean, by golly, you hit that salt water.

They got to get all this salt water shut off someway, but that's gonna be hard to do, boy! Only way they could do it is just get everything shut off for sure, you see, and course the streams and things would finally clean up all right; see, it would rain and finally clean them up.

But a lot of guys, I don't know, they won't pay no attention to it. They just let it leak in the creek. In a way, it's helped me. I've had a job. But I'd rather had a job somewhere's else than to ruint all this water and land—the fish and everything else, see?

I can't figure out [why ranchers allow this to happen], can you? Boy, if I had a ranch I don't believe I'd let them drill. In the long run the person that's got the land don't make much anyway; not enough to fool with ruining their water and stuff and their grass. Naw, if I had a ranch, I don't think I'd want it. I'd rather make a living off my cattle than ruin my land, hadn't you?

Mostly what's the matter is too much politics. I know a bunch of honest guys that's went into politics that's turned out to be regular crooks, by golly! They'll feel obligated. You take a big company, now, they'll say, "Well, if you'll help us, why we'll help you." In other words, "If you scratch my back, I'll scratch yours," see? "If you'll help us, why, we'll help you get elected," see? Then when they get in office, well, they'll feel obligated to this company. Course they're gonna help them every way they can. First thing you know they'll do anything for a dollar, see, just to make a little money.

And I think these old congressmen and senators—I think if we'd get rid of them and get some young guys up there, by gollies, that might help a little bit, don't you? That's the way I feel about it, shore enough! I think they've had it long enough. They did the same thing over and over all the time, you see? Get some young guys up there that have a different idea about things.

Like population. Since I was just a small kid, when you talked about two or three thousand people, boy, that was a bunch of people, but now you talk about millions. I was just watching a ball game here the other night and they's fifty to sixty thousand people there! Used to you go to a ball game, why, if there's a hundred and fifty people there you'd think it's a big crowd! Well, I don't know how you gonna control it. It's gonna be hard to do.

If I could stand dust, I'd still be working on a ranch. But that dust give me the asthma. Used to be, like when you was farming, when you got your crops laid by you didn't have much to do, see, so they'd go visiting. Now most people have got to put in so many hours a day working they can't. Then, used to, they was busy but back then you could take off when you wanted to. Now you got a boss that's following you around and you got to do what he wants you to do. Back then, you wanted to go visit your neighbor, you'd just take off and go visit him for half a day. But now you're working for the other guy. Seems like you enjoyed life better before. Now I might be wrong, but it seemed like you did.

And most of the boys that worked for me, most of them, I think were pretty good friends. We always got along, seemed like. Friends are the main thing, boy! I don't know if I got any enemies or not. I guess I have, but I don't want to if I can help it. I want everybody to like me and get along with me, don't you? You got to have friends and neighbors to survive. You can't live by yourself. You've got to have friends, boy, to get by. I try to make friends if I can. Most especially anybody I'm working with.

Course being out away from town, seems like, makes you enjoy people more. The reason I live out here—I'd rather work than to drive out here and back. Boy, you take and drive out here and back every day—I'd rather work as to drive! And I just like the country, hear the coyotes howling and things like that. It seems like you're more free and seems like the air's cleaner. [And then there's always things happening like that antelope.]

I wish you'd seen that antelope! Boy, she was really a good pet. It belonged to [my neighbor]. She raised him for a pet, see. He'd come up there in the yard, and seemed like he liked just old cold light bread. Come right up where we was pulling a well. You'd think that machine'd scare it, see, but it'd butt right into you when that old boy'd be wrenching rods; just stand there and butt on him. And then he'd go lay down in the shade of the machine when he was through. People'd come by there where we was working and see that antelope out there and they didn't know what was happening. It was small, and finally I guess it was grown, about two or three years old. He'd foller just like a dog behind the pickup. But I think those old boys drilling that well down there got it. I don't know whether they took it home with them or killed it and cooked it. I couldn't say that they got him but it disappeared right after they came out here, now. Just listening at them talk about going out and killing deer give me a pretty good idea that they'd do a thing like that. Just talking to them you can tell pretty well what kind of guys they was because they talked about killing on other people's land. Sneaking on people's places to hunt, see? Well, you know if they'd do that, they could do something else, don't you?

I had some pictures of it, but I lost them when our house burnt up. I lost a lot in that fire. Wasn't valuable, but it was to me. One thing I missed was my mother's old striking clock. Pictures, things you can't replace, Mother's picture. Course the main thing was *we* got out and wasn't burnt or anything. There were lots of things that I lost that I wouldn't have liked to lose but still, I'd rather lose that than my life any time. Course we lost everything else as far as that goes. I came out with a pair of pants and my house shoes and a undershirt. I never noticed that I didn't even have my shirt on and it was raining and freezing. But I thought, "Well, I'm just gonna have to forget about it. I can't just let it get me down. I just have to start over again." Boy, people was good to us; they helped us every way they could. The next morning after the fire I went back to work. But I lost my glasses, see, I have cataract lens. Well, when I was [going to my neighbor's] I thought something's funny that I couldn't see very good, see? My wife said, "You're gettin' off the road!" I never noticed my glasses till then. They burnt up, see, in the house. I had a friend who had his eyes operated on the same year that I did, see, and I called him and he had an extra pair of glasses and I got by with them till I could get me some more made. I came out and picked up a few things around the house. I had a quart fruit jar of pennies that was sitting in a drawer and I knew just about where they was at; well, I found those!

I was twenty-three years old when I got married. My wife, she was working in a cafe at the time and I was working on this ranch and we was going to this cafe to eat our lunch and that's where I got acquainted with her. I think it's better to go ahead and get married [young]. I don't think if you go ahead and get married you'll come as near getting into trouble as you

Jim Law, Lloyd Mays, Charles Holson and James Ball

will running around is the way I feel about it. She'll make you stay at home, see?

I don't have any [children]. I had stepchildren but I felt just like they was my own and they was good to me. Just two—one girl and a boy. He come up missing and we never found him. They claim that he jumped off in this river, see, but gol-ly bumb, we searched that river for two weeks and never did find him. He'd just got married.

[Now that women's lib,] I don't know, but I just don't like it. I just don't see it. I think they should see to their families first. You take lots of families, both the husband and wife works and the children don't ever see them but at night and sometimes they don't even see them then. Lots of them, they don't even know who their dad and mother is hardly! You got to have that motherly love, is the way I look at it, 'cause if they don't, I don't think the children will respect their parents. You got to sit down and explain things to them and talk to them. Now, you take a little child, if you don't talk to it and love it, well, it don't know if you love it or not. If you bring up a child young like you want it to live, it'll usually live that way. Lots of them go back on their raising, but most of them will do pretty good. You got to talk to them and love them and explain to them what you want them to do and explain to them the value of things, but you got to give that love first. Then you've got to spank them to make them realize what they're doing wrong. My dad, when he told me not to do something, boy now, I didn't do it! And I loved him just as good as I believe any child could love their parent.

When I was in my twenties, I thought I knew more than the President! But I guess all teen-agers are thataway. There's a certain age, see, where they think, "Well, now, I've done learned it all now." I think experience will teach them. Experience is the best teacher you can have, I think. I think all you can do is talk to them, see, and explain and they'll know what to do. I don't think you should just set rules for them. I don't think it's right. I think they should have their freedom just same as anybody else; but explain to them, and I don't think they'll go wrong.

What I'd give them for advice is to go to school and learn all they can. Education, I think, is what creates jobs. You don't have to have money to be successful. Course money helps a whole lot, but there's a lot more to success besides money. I'd go to school, boy, all I could.

And the first thing is to live right. Serve God, you see. Well, you're gonna live right if you do that and I think you can prosper more thataway by living right and doing the right thing, by golly. And I think you'll make more than you will by trying to cheat somebody out of a dollar. I think honesty is the best policy, by golly. If a man is as good as his word, he'll be all right, I think. If your word's not any good, well, I don't think you are either, do you?

The reason I don't care if I have a whole bunch of money or not is because when you die, you're sure not gonna take it with ya. Course it's all right to have money, by gosh [depending on how you use it]. If I had a whole bunch of money I'd open me an orphans' home somewhere. Take care of these kids, you know, that don't have any way of taking care of theirselves. Don't have any parents or anything like that. That's the only thing that I would want money for—just for something like that. Help somebody.

I'm satisfied with what I've done. I guess if I had it to live over, I'd live the same way because I feel like that I've done all that I can, to my knowledge. So I feel satisfied with what I've done with my life. Oh, there's been a few things I've done wrong, all right—I guess everybody's done things that they wished they hadn't done. But still, I'm pretty well satisfied with what I've done.

And I don't think it'd be any better to bring the past back. You hear people talking about old times. All it does is let the young people know how they used to live, is all I can figure out. If we had to go back to the old times, I don't know how we'd get along, do you? Course we would, but it would be a slow go!

"I've been Jim Crowed."

ADA ALLEN

Ada Allen's father's ancestors were slaves in Southern cotton fields. She herself was born in Parkersburg, West Virginia, where she still lives today. Her father worked for a local stoneware pottery factory hauling and grinding clay.

Ada had seven brothers and four sisters, most of whom married and had families. An exception was Ernest, who still hasn't settled down long enough to marry. "Ernest said he wasn't old enough to get married. And he's seventy-nine. He just hoboed all over the country. He never had no stopping place."

Ada has spent most of her life in Parkersburg with the exception of four years when she was an eleventh-floor maid in a boardwalk hotel in Atlantic City. She and her husband had one adopted daughter.

Despite the fact that she has often been "Jim Crowed," she has traveled extensively on short excursions. The fact that sometimes, because of her race, she hasn't even been allowed to buy a sandwich in a town she was passing through hasn't dampened her enthusiasm for the world around her. "Wherever you go, I don't care how big the place is or how small it is, there's always some good there if you're looking for it."

*Her advice to young people is short and to the point: "I'd tell
them to quit this foolishness and this dope and this carrying on and
straighten up and fly right. That's my motto."*

—PEGGY LIEVING, CINDY TERRY, MARK TRAVIS, TERRYE EVANS,
JENNY JOHNSTON, AND DREMA LEMLEY.
—KENNETH GILBERT, ADVISER TO MOUNTAIN TRACE.

I WAS BORN out here in Potter Junction—Emerson Avenue. My
pop worked for Donaghho Pottery [famous in West Virginia for its
stoneware]. He ground the clay they made those jars with.

Mr. Donaghho was a great fiddler. Always played the fiddle. And Pop
worked in that clay that made those jars. Came right out of that hillside.
And they had a little crank truck then and these men would haul this; dig
the clay out of the bank. Then they dump the clay down to make the jars.
There wasn't no machinery, y'know—just horse and buggy days. And my
pop, then, he ground up clay with a horse. It walked around in a circle.
And then my pop filled these large boxes of clay. After he made those, he
had to take the wheelbarrow and wheel it into the other part of the plant
where the men there made the big, tall jars. [The jars were so] tall they'd
have to stand up on this bench and reach down in there to finish them up.
And then they'd take these jars into the kettle. They had these big kettles
where they glazed the jars. My pop glazed the jars after they made them.
Then they put them in these large kilns to burn.

Then they had the Mendenhall gang. They did all the hauling and ped-
dling around all over the country, taking them to the different places to sell.
And they were all our neighbors in them days. They all lived right out
there. And all those cottages out up along the side of that hill were for the
men that did the pottery. Now where the creek runs—right on the edge—
there was a cabin. The Hendershots lived there. And she sewed. Had a
dress made then for fifty cents. That's the truth. And right across from there
was the Dudley slaughterhouse. It had been there for years. When my pop
was a boy, he used to work for the Dudleys. Worked on the Dudley farm.

Then there was Mr. Johnson's general store with the hams and bacon and
all that stuff hung on the outside. And Freeman's blacksmith shop was
there. Our house is still standing. We lived there until the floods came and
everybody had to move out.

I must tell you all that you're well blessed. You're lucky to have what you
have. You ought to be thankful. When we used to come down Sand Road
there wasn't no houses or nothing up there. Just the mosquitoes and the

Ada Allen

snakes. We had to walk [through] there to Sumner School on Avery Street; and after that we'd come home. We were burning oil lamps then.

I went to school at Sumner but I didn't finish. My mom and pop, they kind of got disabled and I had to stay home and help with the family. Sometimes I worked for Mr. Watson for ten cents an hour. And then we had hogs and pigs. The different neighbors saved their garbage and heated it all and fed it to the pigs.

And where the pottery stands, well, we had an old man that lived down in the lower part of town—Third Street. Just almost no man's land in them days. Everything below Third Street was the rough end of town. And this old man had a livery stable. He had horses, but he let them just half starve to death and die. And any time one of these old horses would die, why you'd see him coming up the Sand Road with the thing all covered over. He buried them right up there at the graveyard.

In the winter, we'd all skate on Martin's Pond. That's where they made the ice for people. They'd put it in icehouses and put sawdust on it to keep it for the summer. They had icemen to peddle over the town. [Everybody had iceboxes instead of refrigerators] and they'd have to bring the ice to us.

And on those winter days—all that snow—we wore long underwear. You didn't see no nakedness in them days. The first day of May, that was the day for us to take off our underwear. When the first day of September came, we had to take our summer stuff off and put on the long underwear. It covered you all up. We wore bags of asafetida to keep away the diseases. And I don't care how we went or where we went or how we were dressed, we never took that bag off till summertime. We'd be so glad when May came to get off them shoes and stockings and go barefooted.

And, of course, we went to church—the A.M.E. Church on Clay Street. The last street light we had was on Nash Street, so from there you know what we did? We carried a lamp. Pop walked in front and Mom walked in the back with us kids.

Then on the twenty-second of September we always had Emancipation Day over at the amusement park on Blennerhassett Island. The boat that used to take us down the river was the *Valley Belle*. And [on that day] everything to eat and drink was free. They had baseball games and a dance. Then they had this platform and they would speak on the day and explain Emancipation Day. Oh, it was a good day then. Course slavery wasn't good [but I think it's good to remember—to remind the young people how far we've come]. You know slavery days, the first slaves landed at Jamestown, Virginia, down on the St. James River. Then they opened the cotton fields of Alabama and Mississippi and sent the colored women and their children and men to the cotton fields and kept them as slaves. Lots of them got separated. All Pop's people were separated and he never saw them again.

And so there were our colored women out in the cotton fields picking cotton. They had this master over them, you know. And when they wanted help in the mansion through the daytime, well, this here old slaveholder would go out and look over the cotton fields and he would pick out a colored woman and then he would take her up to the mansion and make a servant out of her to wait on them and their children. He was just like a lot of men looking over pigs and things. Just pick them out. And when they got them in the house and got them fixed up for servants, the women waited on them. Then the white men, the masters of the house, they wasn't satisfied; and, of course, they would take them and use these colored slaves up in the big house and have children by them. And the white man, he placed other colored people on the slave blocks and sold them, you see. And right today in Natchez, Mississippi, the old slave block stands right there as a memory where they sold my people. Right there in Mississippi. I went through there when I was down South.

And, of course, they made the children by these colored women, but they were all sold, don't you see? And so then they begin mixing. The white man, he sold his colored children to everybody so we are all so mixed up, really, that nobody knows who they are. Don't you see my point? And right now you see all colors of babies. You don't know who they are or what they are. But, that's what it started from.

And then, Grandma Brock. Did you hear of her? I bet you didn't. She was a slave and she was the oldest colored lady here in Parkersburg. Died at 103. Grandma Brock was sitting in Richmond when Grant stepped in and took Richmond. She said Lee surrendered right there. And she said it was really pitiful. And when he surrendered, all the slaves all ran out to thank Grant and meet him they were so happy over this. And so Grandma Brock said that these old misses of the homes just filled their aprons full of this confederate money—couldn't spend it no place, but down there—and they came out and just pitched this money out in the streets and they surrendered there. And she said they said, "Come on, niggers, you are all free now." And Grandma Brock said it was pitiful. She said they shouted and they cried and they did everything. And she said as many of them Yankee soldiers as could took the colored women and their babies in their wagons and drove them to a free place where they could get out and breathe. The Yankee soldiers did that.

Grandma Brock had a sister. They were both slaves. She said her sister was just scared to death of the bosses when they lived on the plantation. She said there was one mistress of the house that was real nibby and she was always meddling with the colored slaves. Every night this old mistress came out knocking on slave doors. "Who's in there, who's in there, who have you got in there?" And she said her sister was scared to death.

Mom Brock wasn't afraid, you know, and she said to Serino, her sister, she said, "Now, Serino, I am gonna get rid of that old sister. I am gonna fix her."

And Serino said, "Mary, for God's sake, they will kill us all!"

She said, "Well, now I want you to keep your big mouth shut because," she said, "I am going to get rid of her. I am going to hurt her for coming around here." She said they would work like dogs in that house and wait on all of them and then every night she would come a-knocking, you know, to see who was in their slave house.

So don't you know that night everything was as quiet as a grave. She said here come the old woman and she said she told Serino, "Don't you breathe. Don't even breathe, and stay in here."

When she came to knock, she said, "Who's in there, Serino? Who's in there, Mary?" And she didn't say a word only to say we are all right, and she said she went on. Now on the way they had a cellar—one of those old-fashioned cellars outside, you know. And Mom Brock said she went around the house and hid in the dark and fixed a trap for her. And said then that here she come around, and don't you know she fell a-sprawling over this cellar. She said she screamed bloody murder, and slaves ran out and the people up in the big house all ran out. And she was a-hollering, "I am

Front left: Terrye Evans; Back left: Peggy Lieving, Mark Travis,
Cindy Terry, Kenneth Gilbert, adviser

dead!" Well, Grandma Brock was the maid up there that waited on her. And so don't you know then they called the doctor and they taken the old lady up to the house and put her in bed and so here is all the servants around and the doctor waiting on her. And Mom Brock said she was standing back and said after every minute she said [to herself], "I wish she would have died." But she said she just put on that long front and just waited on her. Dressed herself up, you know, and went right on the job the next morning. And said she had to wait on her most of the time. And said every time she asked for something, she would look at her and say [to herself], "I am sorry you didn't die." And she said after that the old lady lived about six weeks and she died. And Grandma Brock said she didn't shed a tear. All down in her was, "Thank God."

My mom, she knew Aunt Hattie Lacefield in them days, and she was a slave. She lived all through it. Finally she came to our house and stayed quite a while with us. And she told us how she was treated and everything. She said on this particular evening when she was going up to milk the cows, why, this little white boy that belonged to the people called her "nigger," so she slapped him. And he ran back to the house screaming and they all came out and he told them what happened; so the first thing the old slaveholder said was, "Well, Hattie, you be ready in the morning because we are coming out to take you down and whip you for hitting the boy."

And Aunt Hattie said she prayed and she sang and she prayed, but she didn't say anything. You couldn't say anything because she would have been killed right there, you see.

And said the next morning bright and early she was all dressed up in her uniform standing there at the stove and she had this big cup of water on the stove, and said she was singing asking the Lord to help her and guide her. About eight o'clock here came this man. Well, he had this blacksnake whip in his hand. You've seen the pictures. And she said he knocked on the door. Said, "Hattie, I come to take you down to give you your whipping."

And she said, "All right." And she said she just kinda stepped back and reached on the stove and got this cup of boiling water. And said when he started to reach for her to grab her and drag her out, she just let him have this cup of water. Then she had to take to the woods and hide in the woods for ten or twelve days before they could get her out of there. Her husband, Uncle Al, he would slip her something to eat in the evening after dark. Those big logs you see a big hollow in? That's where she slept for ten days. Finally they managed someway, somehow, to run off. They ran on down to one of those undercover places where they were sending the slaves to be free. They got in there and finally landed in Pennsylvania or Ohio. That's how they got away. It's just pathetic, you know. But it's true. It's true. I know what I'm talking about.

Thank goodness when I was a girl that had all changed. At least in Potter Junction people were kind. Mr. Donaghho, the pottery man, he loved all of us and we loved him. He was a wonderful person. People here loved people and cared for them. You didn't see all this malice. In them days, it was just a regular neighborhood of people. Colored and white, all of them right there together. Everybody didn't know you as color. Color has nothing to do with whoever you are. It's the insides, what's in you. I don't care if they're white as snow. It's what's underneath that counts, isn't it? I see that and I think of it. [But it wasn't that way everywhere, I found out.] I was in Louisiana one time, New Orleans, we had to have Jim Crow in those days. Everything separate. I wasn't Jim Crowed because we had a special train made up in Cincinnati. [Instead of] not allowing the colored to ride in the same car, we didn't go that way. We had a special train. I was with the ladies of the church. And we went first class!

I've had such a lovely time that I don't begrudge anyone. But I'll tell you, it pays to go places when you're young. I've done a lot of traveling. See, when you was young in them days, on traveling excursions you could go to Atlantic City, Washington, and Baltimore for ten dollars a round trip. For sixteen days. And stop in all them places. I worked for a Neal family about eighteen years. I was in one family all them years. They're all dead now. And when August would come, I'd have to have my vacation. Why, I'd go to Atlantic City for sixteen days. If I hadn't gone then and seen things, I'd still be sitting right here, looking at the walls. So I thank the Lord I could go some places and be able to get up and get around. I've had a heart condition now for twelve years so I can't any more. But I've had a good life, I've no regrets. It's been wonderful. I loved that traveling, of course, but being colored made a difference in those days. "No, you can't do so-and-so —the colored can't." I was sorta handicapped. There were some towns where a colored person couldn't buy a sandwich.

Once I was coming from Washington to Parkersburg. I was the only colored one on the bus. [We stopped in a] town, and there was a sign there: "This place up here for the white and this place down here for the colored." Now, that was here in West Virginia. So all the white people went on up to the dining place where it was cool and everything, you know. I had to go in this barbecue place. They had tables around, and this poor boy that waited on me, he acted like he was scared to death. I felt sorry for him. I went to the counter and said, "I would like to have a glass of iced tea and a sandwich of some kind," because I hadn't ate anything. So he went in back and fixed me the iced tea and a sandwich. And I was sitting at one of these tables. And so here drove this great big car from Texas. I was sitting there by myself. So these two white men came in and alls they needed was a whip, you know. They had these broad-rimmed hats on. I never did see such mean-looking white men. And instead of them going on up tending to their business, why they came over to my table. They tried to get my attention, but I never opened my mouth. And so they went to the counter and said, "What you got, boy?" You know, this smoking and carrying on. Showing off. I never let on. Didn't say nothing. I couldn't say anything. So then they walked over to my table and said, "Fix me up whatever she's eating!" So then they came back, you know, and stood over me and slapped a glass down. And they had this bottle of whiskey. And so they sat down at the other table just like we are sitting and slapped this whiskey down on the table and said, "Have a drink!" I never, I never let on. In the meantime, there was a white gentleman come in. He sat there at the end of the barbecue counter and he seen everything. I didn't know what was going to happen. But then finally them two dudes went out and got in the car. I hadn't looked at them yet. And so after, this white gentleman, he walked over to my table. He says, "Lady, don't you get off the bus in any more of these places. Now," he says, "I've been everyplace. But," he says, "I've never seen or been anyplace that I've seen a colored lady or a white lady either ever sit up under what that man did you." And he said, "I felt sorry for you. But I couldn't say anything. If I would have said anything, probably we both would have been killed." He said, "The best thing you can do when you get to these places is don't get out of the bus. It isn't safe."

Well, now when I got to Winchester, Virginia, I just had to go to the restroom. And I got off and went on in the place and this colored girl met me and she said, "Where are you going?"

"Well," I said, "I would like to go to the restroom." And she was scared to death, of course. I was feeling sorry for them. They couldn't help it, because they were under that jursidiction, you understand. And, there wasn't any use of my starting something to make it harder for them. It was hard enough as it was without me starting a commotion. So she said, "Oh, it's way up there. You'll have to go way up there."

When I come on out and the bus was leaving Winchester, this poor colored boy come to the door and stood there. I said, "Well, I don't want to bother you very much, but," I says, "I would like to have a drink of water." And I says, "All I want in this damn town is a drink of water."

He just acted like he was scared to death. He walked way around down someplace and brought me a tin cup of water, and says, "Keep it." Now that's the way I was served. And I wasn't in Mississippi, either. Right here between Washington and Parkersburg. Now that's how it was. Oh, I've had quite an experience. I've been places where I've been all dressed, you know, and look up and here would be a sign, "This side white, this side colored." There's a lot of Jim Crow business here in this town even today. I've been Jim Crowed. It's just lately we got places that we can eat here.

It's been hard to get jobs, too. A lot of plants didn't want no colored people over there. DuPont or none of them. What jobs there was was bad. When the Chancellor Hotel was built, and from the time it was built, my brother, Ernest, ran the shoe-shining stand downstairs. That's the only kind of colored they allowed in there—ones with those kind of jobs. And I walked in there one day before they even allowed colored people, and some of them looked at me like I was simple—walking in that hotel. And I never let on like I'd seen it 'cause I was going to see guests that was from California. And I didn't even look at them or ask them anything. I didn't even go to the desk 'cause I knew where I was going. And there was such a stretching of necks, saying I should have come over and asked somebody. But I didn't. No, I didn't. That's the way I've always been.

When I moved to this neighborhood I was the only colored person here, but I've lived here about twenty-five years, I guess. They never did allow colored people [to buy on these] streets. We had to buy undercover. When we got this house, we rented to a white family before we ever moved in it. They didn't want no colored people in the neighborhood. But the years I been here, I never had one fuss or fight with anybody. All the cussing and damning that's been going on, they've all been white. When the school merged you'd have thought the town was going to have a riot. There was one lady, I thought she was going to die. She was warning the colored chil-

Ada Allen's home

dren not to like school here. Oh, she come running with her dress halfway above her knees, "Oh, Mrs. Allen, Mrs. Allen, what's the world comin' to? All these colored children mixing with the white children!"

I told her, "You don't know if you're my sister or my aunt. Because," I said, "we're all so mixed up [racially] nobody knows who they are anyway." My pop, in his time, he said he didn't know who he was because he was so mixed up. I never paid any attention to it. I lived that way all the years. Never had any words with anybody. So that's the way I've lived; the only way you can live. And wherever you're going or wherever you may be, why, it pays to have the respect for people, and respect for yourself. That's the main thing.

And I never did stoop to low stuff. All the money you see and all the finery never has crossed my mind. There's no jealousy in my blood.

And now another thing. I've been in all these places. But you know in all my days, I've never drank anybody's liquor, no whiskey, no beer, no nothing. And I've never played cards. But one thing about me, I've always been broad-minded. Because everybody knows what they's going to be. And it's up to them. If you want to be somebody you can do it. If you want to be a nobody, then nothin' from nothin' leaves nothin'. I don't care how good-looking you are, how pretty you are, whatever. It pays to carry yourself and have respect. It really pays.

I played with white people all of my life. Never thought nothing about it because I never thought there was anybody born any better than myself. I don't care who they are or what color they are.

That's my motto every time. And you know I am not mad at anybody. I am just speaking the truth.

And my colored people, I don't care how colored they are, how bad off they are, or how they look. You never hear me run them down. Don't you see my point? Because I have seen so much of the hard times that our people have had to come up against, and look what they have had to face to come up here as far as they are.

One thing about me, I don't condemn people. It's within you what you're going to do and what you're going to be. Mom used to tell us, "Every tub has to sit on its own bottom, and every soul has to answer to its own soul's salvation."

And one thing I'll never forget my pop told me. He says, "Ada, wherever you go, wherever you may be, have the respect to respect yourself, and have the respect for other people, but just one thing: Don't let nobody run over you." And I've done that and had a wonderful life. I've never been ashamed of being colored because I had nothing to do with it.

I've pulled a long ways and I'm proud of my life. I really am. I had a grand time.

"We started walking all around the mountain collecting snails."

KATINA ANDROS

Katina Nick Andros was born in 1905 on Lily Island off the coast of Greece. She says she "came with tears" because her mother had hoped for a boy. Boys didn't require wardrobes or gold pieces and took less money to raise! Her father, Theodore Vardemes, ran a lumberyard and the family lived comfortably until after World War I, when food became very scarce on the island. Katina attended local schools through the seventh grade.

With the idea of helping his daughter have a better life, Katina's father announced her engagement in 1929 to a Greek man living in the United States. She had never met him before. The wedding took place in Greece and afterward the couple traveled to the U.S. by ship. We asked Katina if she had any memorable feelings upon her arrival at New York and she said, "No, I was down in the bottom of the boat being sick." They settled in San Antonio, Texas, for three years, then moved to Houston, where they had a son Mike and twins Chrissie and Theo. At the age of five Mike died of polio; within six months Theo was also lost to this disease. Two years later the husband abandoned the family, leaving Katina penniless with a little daughter.

For two years Katina worked as a domestic for other Greek families. Her daughter recalls how her mother used to buy live sheep, slaughter them in the garage, and "use everything but the hoofs." Katina became an American citizen and was "very proud."

Two years later Katina met and married Nick Matthew Andros, a Greek captain in the merchant marine who had left home at age eleven to become a sailor. Later he captained tankers for the Pure Oil Company and continues to love the sea today.

In 1958 Katina returned to San Antonio with Nick and has lived there ever since. She learned to drive at age fifty-two, loves to fish and crab on the Texas coast, is considered a pillar of the Greek Orthodox community, and "cooks for any affair." Chrissie, now married to Dan Anthony, a Texas restaurateur, says of her mother, "There's nothing she hasn't done—except maybe hang wallpaper." After our first interview, Mrs. Andros said she was going outdoors to cut the grass.

—CHRISTY WALKER, RHONDA NARRO, MYSSIE LIGHT, JOHN SANTOS, SCOTT HARRISON. PHOTOGRAPHS BY GEORGE SANTOS.
—NAOMI SHIHAB, ADVISER, TEXAS COMMISSION ON ARTS AND HUMANITIES.

IN THE OLD COUNTRY, especially after the First War, people were very poor. After the war my father sold lumber on credit; people have no jobs, no money, we broke. We starve. We eat all we have, we use all the gold pieces lying around, and then each father wants to find some way to send his kids out of that place to a better life. That's why they made me marry that man who was thirteen years older than I was. And I came to United States so I can have a good life and help the folks in the old country too; but instead of helping them, sometimes I wanted to help myself. We were poor here. My first husband didn't want to work. If he found a daytime job he want a nighttime job; if he found a nighttime job he want a daytime job. So at first there was no way to have a good life.

I didn't want to marry him. I liked somebody else. He was here in the U.S. and he sent his picture to me and write on the back, "This is my face, if you like. If you don't like, send it back." So I called my father and showed him the picture and said, "Read this! What the devil made him say that? No schooling? No one taught him how to write? He have no better sense? There must be a lot of ways to ask a girl to marry you, not just, 'This is my face.'"

I had never met him before.

After my father received the picture, he announced to the local people that his daughter was going to be engaged. He was happy. He thought he had found his daughter's luck. All the old people congratulated him. So when I didn't want to marry that man and I didn't like the way he propose to me, my father couldn't send a telegram and say, "Don't come," because he'd already announced it! He thought it would shame him if I didn't get married. In those days, over there, such a thing would give a girl a bad name. They would say, "Well, maybe she already has somebody." In those days you weren't supposed to look at a boy. You hold your eyes to the ground or they think you streetwalker already. So my father sacrificed my early life and saved his name.

Two and a half years ago I went back to Greece. During the Second War I slaved over here. My hands were big pink skins because I tied boxes full of clothes and sent them over to the old country. I helped save a lot of families. For many many weeks I sent boxes. American people were giving me clothes to send. I had one whole room full of clothes. And when I went over there to visit, all those people knew I was there and no one even came to tell me hello.

When I first came to America I was afraid to go outside and mix with American people because I thought they wouldn't like me. But they were always very very friendly. They would help me if I didn't know something. Sometimes now I go to the store and I don't know the name of something and they help me. I can go anywhere in United States and I'm not scared. But over in Greece I'm scared.

The political system? In Greece if you want to be a mayor you have to buy a lot of people to vote for you. Everybody gives a lot of favors. So nobody cares much who's going to run. Democracy was born over there but they keep it better over here.

With marriage, for example, the way they do it here they give a little bit of freedom to the kids to think for themselves and that is better. Because over there, for example, if mothers are talking, they make the kids go away and play. They keep us dumb. But here one thing I like is the freedom, and one thing I don't like is there's too much! In the past five years things have been going the wrong way. Kids go out and they don't tell their parents what they're gonna do, who they're going with, who their friends are. The main thing to do is if you have a friend, or if you're a girl and you have a boyfriend, bring him to your mother, to your father. Find out who his folks are, what life they lead. If your folks live a nice life you probably gonna be

Katina Andros

nice. But if you see your father drunk, your mother smoke and drunk and marijuana, well, you're gonna go a worse way.

In the old days kids grew up, they never stole, they never did bad things; but now it's the same over there as here, only worse. But I like better United States. Here if I get on a bus and want to sit down, a young one will get up and give me the seat, but over there now they let old people stand up. They don't do anything. They used to have respect but they don't any more. I think this country is better on that. [But you have to stay *with* kids to teach them that respect.]

I don't think it's good to leave the kids with somebody else. They won't get the mother's and father's ways, the ways *you* would like to raise them. If you get a baby-sitter, you don't know how she'll raise them. It ruins the family to have someone stay in for you. You can have your grandmother, an

Top (left to right): Christy Walker, Rhonda Narro;
Bottom: George Santos, Myssie Light

aunt, but no strangers. Don't trust strangers with kids. In the nights I used to help Chrissie with her homework. She always came home and found her clothes ironed, the beds made, the dinner ready on the table. She never did find her mother going anywhere.

You should be able to rely on your parents. Before you do anything, instead of asking your friend about it, go to your mother, father, and ask them. The mother is like the chicken, you know. If the chicken sees anything scared, she covers it up with her feathers. And if you ask your mother she's gonna cover you up like the hen covers up the little chickens. And she'll give you better advice to straighten up yourself. And don't trust strangers in this. There's nobody else who's gonna give you the advice your momma's gonna give you. Nobody. Maybe sometimes she hits you, like I did one time to Chrissie; maybe sometimes she's mad. But she's gonna turn around and tell you the right thing.

Like education. I think education is important. Education helps you all the time, no matter how young you are, no matter how old you are. If you don't have education you're not going any farther. The more education you have the more brains you develop.

I only went to the seventh grade. My father got very sick then, and I had to help with the business in the lumberyard. Without me the family could not go on. I wanted to go farther in school but my stepmother said to my father, "If you let her go to school I'm gonna divorce you." My stepmother wanted me to work and learn dressmaking so I could make a trousseau for my two sisters. So they took me from the school and I went to the dressmaker. For a year I had night dreams about school. I would cry all night. But my stepmother said, "No, you're not going."

I like to learn things. If I see you do something I like, I want to learn it. My father taught me this: everywhere you go, if someone asks you if you know something, like if you know how to cook a certain food?—you say, "Well, so-so." Ask for the other person to tell you how he does it. If he does it better than you, cop something from him. If he does it worse, tell him what to do better.

From 1940 to 1955 the U.S. was perfect for anybody to live in. Since 1955 it has gotten very difficult for many people to live. Especially if they don't have a steady income. Now we have hard times here just like in the old countries. These days you have to mark down how to spend your dollar if you want to live. All over the world we're under the same blanket. People started wanting too much luxury. Too many things, too many things. The TVs came out. At first you had one TV, small; then you not satisfied with one, you have to have TV in each room because you like one program, someone else like another program, she have her own TV, you have your own TV. That is the reason.

Clothes! We used to have one dress for the summer, one for the fall, one for the winter, one for the spring. Four dresses for the year. Now you have ten dresses each month and you don't have enough! You go to my closet and you'll see twenty dresses hanging up and they are twenty dresses I never wear! People want too many things. That's why we have a hard time. I don't care. As long as I'm clean and have enough to cover me up on my bed and food, that's all I need. What you say is, "Gimme for today and not for tomorrow." The next day you start again. I don't care if my friends change dresses every Sunday. I never did pay any attention to no one. I live the way God gives me to live. And I'm satisfied. The way you're raised from the beginning does this. It's not important, you know, to have lots of money; it's just nothing, nothing, nothing. It's important to be healthy, to work, and to have a good night's sleep, a good life, that's what.

Religion is important to me. I was raised Greek Orthodox. To me and to my family and to all Greeks, religion is very important. We pray. We always pray. The first thing we believe in is the Father, Son, and Holy Spirit. When I get sick I have a certain name to pray to, a certain saint. And the things I pray, the things I ask for, they come to me with no hard time. But you have to *believe* it. You have to know they *do* help you.

I'm gonna tell you something that happened to my life. I told you how for years during the war we have no bread, no flour, no oil on the island. What we could raise on that little island was not enough for 35,000 people. On the last day of August everyone was starved to death. Everywhere you could see kids just crying. It was terrible. A bishop came out of the church and told another old man to go from door to door on the island to give everyone a message. In those days nobody had any radios to know what was going on. So the message was this: everyone on the island was supposed to meet at the waterfront so we could pray. And we all came and we prayed for five hours, from eleven in the morning to four o'clock that afternoon. We were out in the hot sun praying and sweating to death. It was terrible. Before we walked home and spread out from street to street, we lit candles and carried them with us. And then it started raining, the hardest rain of our lives. After the rain stopped we found snails crawling into our homes. Thousands of them, thousands and millions! So we started walking all around the mountain collecting snails, and a blind lady who knew me by my walk came and said, "Katina! Let me walk next to you and tell me if I pick up rocks or snails!" So everyone was collecting and for two months we had enough snails, the whole island, 35,000 people, to eat and live on. We put them in baskets, bushel baskets, and we put thyme, a spice, in there with them and they would eat the thyme and throw up the things they ate in the mountains and that was the way we cleaned them out. Then we ate them ourselves. We could cook them different ways and that was the answer to all the prayers. The people knew that. Sure. Who could deny it?

It was a miracle. We had four kinds of snails coming from underground. The rain drew them out, see. The island wrote in its newspaper about how we lived on the snails. And then soon the wild greens started coming out. And we could cook and eat. We were saved.

They taught us in the church to say prayers to yourself, every day, every minute. Every hour every day is for the prayers. Don't ever stop. Do it while you do everything.

Life is harder for everyone because they don't do that much now. That's why God is making so many bad things right now. We are not doing right. It's not only in America, it's in every nation right now.

In the morning I get up, wash my face, and then I say in Greek, *"Proto Theos,"* which means, "First God and after, me." You always say, "First

Left to right: Katina Andros, Christy Walker, Naomi Shihab

God." Like if someone is leaving you say, *"Proto Theos,"* then, "I'll see you in two months." First God, yes. I never let Chrissie go out of the house before she made her cross! *Then* I start my housework. Today my grandson is coming over and I'm already cooking some meat and macaroni. I have to feed my old man too. In the evening I crochet. I make bedspreads and things. And then sometimes we go fishing down at the coast. If my husband don't get to see water once a month, he drives me crazy in the house. I still like to go fishing, yes. The coast here is not the same as the coast back home. The smell is different. Over there we have clean water. Over here it's muddy. Over there the edge of the coast is rocky and the water is so clear you can see thirty feet down. The biggest fish I ever caught was a three-and-a-half-pound flounder.

A lot of things happened to me, you know, but it would take days and days to tell them.

"Go ahead. Don't look back. Straight ahead."

ANTHONY TROIANO

Mr. Anthony Troiano, Sr., was born in Foiano di Val Fortore, Benavento Province, Italy, December 27, 1897. He is seventy-eight years old.

Anthony and a sister embarked on a boat for America in January of 1913, leaving their parents and other relatives behind. He was sixteen years old and very optimistic of his future. He came to the United States wanting to improve his financial condition and someday have his own family. He felt he was only "to gain not lose" by coming here. He took up residence in Enfield, Connecticut, where he has lived ever since.

He was able to find work in and near Enfield. His first job was in Bigelow Sanford, a carpet mill. Then, when the Government was putting in Route 5, he was able to find employment driving a truck until he had to have an appendix operation. He had his operation and learned to be a welder for the Gas Light Company, of Springfield, Massachusetts.

Then around 1931 he was again unemployed. By that time the Depression existed and jobs were scarce. He now had a wife to support and they were expecting their first child. With money saved

*he opened his own auto shop. He repaired radiators and did body
work. His first day open he made seventy-five cents. He remained
in the car business and now is the owner and operator, along with
his two sons, of Troiano and Sons' Gas Station, Garage and Oil
Company.*

*Anthony didn't have much of an education. In Italy he went as
far as the fourth grade. Once in America, he wanted to learn some
type of trade, so he took correspondence courses and learned sheet
metal welding, English, and basic math.*

*He married an American-born woman, October 6, 1927, named
Anna Tina. They had three children, Anthony, Jr., Frank, and
Teresa. For hobbies he plays the violin, reads, listens to opera music,
tends his garden, in which he grows grapes to make wine, and
grows other fruits and vegetables.*

*Anthony Troiano, Sr., has had good fortune coming to the United
States and is a very happy man today. His ambition was to work
hard to get ahead, and he will tell you as he told me, "Work hard
and be honest, you can't do nothing without work hard."*

—MARIE E. YOUNG.
—DENNIS CORSO, ADVISER FOR ENFIELD HIGH SCHOOL
SOCIAL SCIENCE LAB, ENFIELD, CONNECTICUT.

WHEN I CAME to America, all the way I was thinking that I
wanted something, to start my own business from the beginning. My own
business so I can create a good family. I started work in the shop, Bigelow
Sanford, carpet carrier. Then in a few weeks I asked to work the looms, too.
Used to have two looms so I learned to take good care of the looms and to
learn my trade. And I would get seventy-five cents a day, four and a half
dollars a week. In two weeks I make five seventy-five. When I go home to
my sister I say, "Oh, look, look! Look at my pay!" I thought that was big.
Since then I take it home and I watch my looms and all the time I never
have no trouble and I get a raise over there to nine dollars and a half a
week, to ten dollars, ten dollars and a half, and up to eleven dollars a week
after six months. And I get vacation, not paid at that time.

Then I did other things from 1917 to 1930. So in 1930, Depression had
started. I was ashamed to look for a job, you can't find nothing anywhere;
so I decided to start my own business. I had a lot of encouragement. I had
a few dollars saved so I got my own business. My line of work was welding

sheet metal, radiator repair, and painting the car, body work. And I did it alone. No partner, never ever. I never wanted nobody. I started my own! So, first day I started my business I make seventy-five cents. And I started my business with seventy-five cents a day, same as when I started working Bigelow Sanford Company. So I will never forget the day. It's the record of my life. I started my own business with seventy-five cents a day. 1934, I built my own building. That is the day I started at 777 Enfield Street. Now I don't know what I get a day!

In the past you started slow in business and you get a little big. When you get big, you got to have a lot of encouragement to go ahead because there is more power, more competition; but if you want to handle your business with a lot of courage, never worry about anything. Go ahead. Don't look back. Straight ahead.

Now I am very happy with my business and I thank God for the success I've been having so far. My hope is that my children stick together in the business, both them and me. If they stick with me it will be wonderful for them, but if they separate it will be a disaster. Because there is not much power then. There's got to be unity.

America is a beautiful, beautiful country. To be beautiful, you got to be good yourself. You got to work hard and be honest. I thought America to be a wonderful country for the future all times. Anybody come over here and asks me, I tell them, "Good country if you want to work hard." Some young people now don't work so hard but if you teach them right off, I think you can teach them to be good. A lot of people want to waste time and do nothing, but if you supervise them, you can educate them not to waste the time.

And you can teach them to go to school, and to make friends. School is a beautiful thing for anybody. I believe in education and to read and write. It is a wonderful thing if you go to school and use what you go to school for. And the best thing in the world is to have a friend. If you got a friend you don't make an enemy. I don't believe in fighting and making unhappiness. And I don't believe in war. War brings a lot of disaster to the people for nothing; brings a lot of suffering, a lot of disabled men and in the end we gain nothing. I'm against war. Nobody gains because people lose their husbands, sons, cousins, and there is a lot of suffering.

I'm not afraid of death; we're going to die anyway, today, tomorrow, any day.

Q: What is your favorite possession?

A: What I like most . . . peace in the family.

Anthony Troiano, Jr.: No, that isn't a possession. What do you have that you think the most of?

A: PEACE IN THE FAMILY!

"I'd rather be a cowboy than anything."

JACK PATE

Jack Pate was born December 29, 1903. It was only fitting that he took his first breath of life in the town of Fort Griffin, which was on the Western cattle trail. Born in cattle country, Jack has been a cowboy all his life.

Jack was reared in Shackelford County, Texas, and was the son of a trail driver. His grandfather was also a stockman. He was part of a large family, having four sisters and five brothers. He "graduated" from school in the ninth grade but contends that he is still going to school. "I went to that school of knocks most of my life."

Ranch work began as soon as Jack could ride a horse. He first worked alongside of his father for some of the large ranches around his childhood home. These ranches were owned by the Matthews, Reynolds, and Nail families. Next he worked on the Bright Ranch, which is located north of Sierra Blanca, New Mexico.

In the early 1940s, Jack ran wagons, tending to the cattle on the Stafford and McKeller ranches in New Mexico. These ranches covered 200,000 acres of land. Later he worked for Mr. and Mrs. H. A. Thompson, also in New Mexico. As foreman, Jack worked on

*the Jones Ranch for twenty-five years. He still considers this beauti-
ful New Mexico ranch his home.*

*In 1927 Jack married Margaret MacMillian. She passed away in
1965, leaving him with their seven-year-old adopted daughter, Susie
Marie. These two then "batched" for the following eight years until
he married Etna Poer. Jack was sixty-nine years of age at the time.*

*Over the years, the Pates have reared many beside Susie. These
include three nephews and an orphan called Willie, who later was
killed in Vietnam.*

*At this time Jack and his wife are residing in Albany, Texas, the
county seat of Shackelford County. He hasn't slowed a bit, and still
works days on the surrounding ranches. In fact, on his seventieth
birthday he began the tedious task of breaking a colt. Asked if cow-
boying has kept him young, Jack replied, "Well, I'm not old! Yeah,
I guess so. I think living outside and eating cow meat and gravy
keeps you young."*

—MICHELLE HARRIS, NANCY DURHAM, MARYANNA GREEN,
JIM WALLER, PAUL STRIBLING.
—BARNEY NELSON, ADVISER TO OLD TIMER.

I'VE BEEN RIDING more or less all my life. I was just like all
kids. I was always doing something I shouldn't-a done. I used to run off
from school and things like that. The first day's work I ever drew wages for
in my life, oh, I was probably nine. All I did was hold cuts [cattle that have
been cut from the herd for some reason]. I got a dollar a day. I was in the
money! I helped them five days and that five dollars looked like five big
bicycle wheels to me.

My parents never tried to keep me from being a cowboy. They wanted
me to go through school, and I didn't do that but it wasn't their fault, it was
mine. I went to school out there on Diller Flat. I got through the ninth
grade. There was nine of us kids. I'm the only outlaw in the outfit.

When I was about sixteen years old [I started working full time]. I
worked here when I was a kid when they were cleaning up the fever ticks
in this country—about the time of World War I. Course, I wasn't but about
fourteen years old but the boys, most of them, went to the army and my
dad, he helped everybody, and, course, I had an old horse or two and I
went and helped them, too. Course, I was in the way, I imagine. My dad
was an old trail driver. [My grandfather came to this country as a pioneer

settler] and of course they fought the Indians out of this country. I was working for thirty dollars a month. Just cowpunching fever.

I was busy all the time but—well, I'd prowl them hills just like an old coyote. I had two or three ponies, and I was big enough to ride and I knowed that country. I used to gather wild plums in plum time and, oh, such stuff as that. I don't know why a rattlesnake didn't bite me. I've thought about it since, but I didn't think about it at the time.

I'd rather be a cowboy than anything. I'm not sorry. If I had it to do over, I'd probably do it again. I've worked for good people. I guess when I went to New Mexico was when I shore enough took over an outfit. I run a ranch at Magdalena, New Mexico, that belonged to Mr. Jones, and another one in Moore County [Texas]. I had a home at both places and they was 302 miles apart and I run both of them.

Course they wasn't any trucks then; everything was on the train, and we shipped at Kent most of the time and there was a lot of hoboes. That was back in the Depression time. Those people were out of jobs, couldn't find a job and just drifting over the country riding the T.P. One summer I was in camp and at what we called the "Deep Wells," right next to the railroad tracks, and we fed a good many hoboes there—boys that was hungry and between jobs, you know. Always, anybody come along hungry, we fed them. In a way it's tradition with ranch people—it's been that way as long as I can remember. Those people never bothered us—most of them was just boys trying to get somewhere and wanted to go to work; and, ever' once in a while, one of them boys would take a notion he wanted to work with us and we'd get some pretty green hands.

I run a wagon a lot in New Mexico. That outfit finally built up to where they had three ranches. They furnished me a chuck wagon and about eighty-six saddle horses, and I think we had about twelve head of mules.

I had a good cookie at the time. He was a good cook but he was a character. We'd get in around a town and he was sure liable to get drunk on me. One time he got drunk and got back to the wagon, finally got back home, and we was camped and just had our bedrolls out on the porch about November or December; I smelled that coffeepot and I heard old Lilo moving things around in the kitchen and I said, "Lilo, what's the matter with you?"

He said, "You know what I've done?" He said, "Went and volunteered for the army." But when he went up for his physical he couldn't pass it. We just had beef and beans and that Br'er Rabbit syrup, you know, but he was a good bread cook. And everybody liked him. He always had time to do anything for you. He always took good care of his team and he didn't want anybody fooling with them. He worked for me about thirty years.

I like to be with a good bunch of cowboys. You take a good bunch of

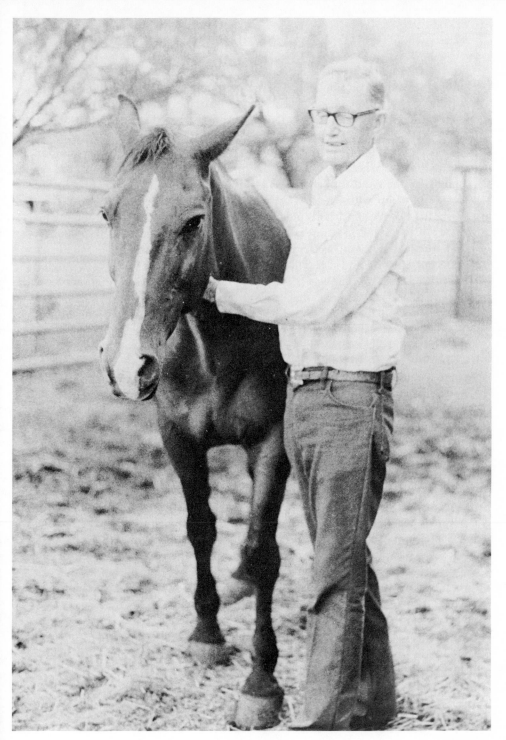

Jack Pate

cowboys branding or gathering cattle—it's all fun. A lot of them are always pulling something on someone. There's not many dull minutes. But I'm a little funny about that picking on anybody. Anytime you see me picking on somebody it's somebody I like. If it's some old boy I like, I might do anything to him; but if it's some old boy I don't know or somebody that might not take a joke right, I just leave them alone. We pulled nearly anything on one another. Pushed an old boy off in the cold water in a tank and he caught me then and rubbed my hair full of cockleburs. One old boy I used to stay in camp with, there wasn't anything I wouldn't do to him, but he was a big booger and I had to do everything I could to stay even. One winter we was staying in camp and just had a little old shack with no roof on that we stayed in, and we had a hole dug in the ground outside where we done our cooking and fire building, and we had a horse that we wrangled our other horses on that was pretty mean to buck. We took turn about cooking breakfast, and the one that cooked breakfast always throwed some hot ashes under old Dusty to try to get the man wrangling horses bucked off. We didn't do that horse much good. That boy roped me one time and threw me down and I let him think I'd forgot it for about a week or ten days. There was a little old gate that was torn down that we always come in to come to the house. One night one of us would turn out the horses and the next time the other—we took turn about doing everything. So about the time he got to the gate, I stepped out there and threw a stewer full of water on him. He made a run at me and I'd tied me a baling wire up about chest high from one post to the other . . . I stayed on the hill that night. But we had a lot of fun. We'd pen up a bunch of horses and flip heads or tails to see who rode first and one'd pick for the other.

We made most of our own fun all the time. We used to pitch horseshoes, play cards a little. Never did play poker much. We used to play poker for pecans a lot—we didn't have much money. I wound up with two big cake sacks full of pecans one time. But I never did win any money playing poker —I never did play poker for money. We used to play baseball a lot, or get together and have a rodeo once in a while. We used our old horses that we rode. Take them over there and buck them at them shows and take them back home and go to working cattle on them.

[We had good times, but it was really hard work, too. Especially in winter.] In the wintertime the snow would break down the fences on us a lot and always those steers would scatter and go. You'd eat breakfast before daylight and you might eat dinner long after dark, too. We've laid out lotsa cold nights. I remember one night we laid out and I heard the next day that it was twenty-nine below that morning. We had just stretched a tarp across from one tree to another to kinda break the wind off us.

It's easier like they do it now. I know there's been lots of times in my life that I never laid down on a bed that had springs on it—slept on the ground or on the floor if I was in a house, but most of the time on the ground. I finally got me a little seven by seven teepee tent. I'd just roll my bed up in it for cold and for rain. I've rolled my bed up and got my slicker on and sit down over it like an old hen, too, to keep it from getting wet. I tell you, when a bed is wet in cold weather, it's pretty rough sleeping.

We always got up early. We used to get up four-five o'clock, especially if we was out with a wagon. If you didn't have somebody holding the horses —a night hawker—you'd have to go out and wrangle them. We didn't work from headquarters or nothing. When you was branding outside it would take a lot of help. I've seen twenty or twenty-five boys with that wagon. You had to have help to hold the calves, and then you had to have flankers and men to drag them.

I guess I enjoy branding more than any because I always enjoyed roping. Catch them by both hind feet and drag them up to the branding fire and a set of flankers—one of them'll catch that rope and the other one'll catch hold of his tail and just jerk him over. One of them will sit down and hold a foreleg to keep him from getting up and the other one will hold his heel so he can't kick. I tie them on. I like to tie. I don't want something getting away. If I'm roping outside, I tie all the time. A lot of time if I'm riding a horse that's not gentle that I think is liable to get in a jam in branding and dragging calves—I dally. But as long as I'm riding a gentle horse I tie.

And if we were gathering cattle in the fall in rough country, it wasn't nothing to ride that horse forty-fifty miles. We had plenty of horses, took care of them, kept them shod, and they got hardened to it.

Some horses are stubborn and disagreeable and it doesn't make any difference what you try to do with them, you can't get along with them. Once in a while you find people like that, too. I used to ride a gray horse a long time ago that I called Polka Dot that I just loved like a person, and I've had several since. I've worn out more horses than a lot of people have —ride them till they went to getting stiff where they was dangerous and old, and then turn them loose and set them free. Let them die at the ranch, you know. I didn't sell them.

That old horse I used to ride named Champagne—an old bald-faced horse—I think he was thirteen years old. He wasn't the gentlest horse you ever rode but he went on and made one of the best horses I've ever seen. I could take him and I'd head or heel either one on him, rope calves on him, or take him to a cutting, and I tell you, it wasn't over till he got done. He was a real horse. And a deer hunter shot him right through and through one evening. That was about the hardest lick I ever had in my horse business.

Michelle Harris, Nancy Durham, Jack Pate, Maryanna Green,
Jim Waller, Paul Stribling

I've never went and roped or took any part in rodeos since and that's been about fourteen years ago. He was a real horse. I couldn't hardly speak to a hunter for two years. He was right in his prime.

[Those horses were something.] Once I was out trying to get everything done I could [because] the forecast said [a storm] would hit about eleven that night. We worked and put a bunch of cows and baby calves in the barn. I was packing hay to some cattle in Franklin Canyon, about two miles from the house, to feed some yearlings. About the time I got there that storm hit. You couldn't a-seen your hand. It would just pack that snow in the fork of my saddle and you couldn't took a stick and packed it any tighter. That old horse just headed towards home and had to angle right into it. Sometimes that old horse couldn't stand it and he'd turn around with his head away from it and there'd come a lull in that wind and he'd turn around and start again. I knew I didn't know the way but I knew he did. A boy down below me there, who worked on a ranch down south of Santa Rosa, he was out horseback, too, and he didn't make it in. He got off his horse and backed up against a tree to get out of it and that's where they found him.

That storm we had seventy inches in twelve days and we already had snow on the ground. Our cars was sitting at the end of the house and it covered them up. A horse can't do anything when that snow gets up above the point of his shoulders. You've got to break a trail for him. And them cattle snowed in, you take these old blue spruce or pine and they'll get in there and tromp out a place and stay there. Well, that snow gets piled up around them and you've got to find them and pack that hay in there to them. I've had them stay in them kind of places two or three weeks. I lost a good many little calves [but no cows]. But them people down below me on the flats—we had hay stacked out in the meadows and in barns and everywhere, you know, but we hadn't had a bad winter since '64 or '65 and they'd got careless and I'll tell you, them people lost a lot of cattle. They dropped feed out of them helicopters for the cows, but those antelope died in piles there on them flats.

That storm's when I lost all my good looks. The next morning my old face was swelled up, the hide all come off and I had to take a hot towel to get my eyes open. It wasn't funny.

[Then there're always accidents to make things hard.] I got hung to an old gray horse one time and I thought he was going to kill me. He fell with me and the saddle horn caught on the inside of my leggins—broke that string and pulled my boot right up to the saddle horn. He finally pulled my leggin's loose. Why he didn't kill me, I don't know. He kicked knots on me and then kicked 'em off, but he never did kick me in the head. I got into the hospital on Thanksgiving night and stayed there until the second of February and went on crutches about eight months. He was a gentle horse but he got scared. That was the first horse that ever made me afraid of a horse. It was a lesson to me. Later I got in another jam that was another lesson to me. I had a horse fall with me and when he quit rolling, I had a leg caught plumb up under him and he had both hind legs straightened out wedged down in the fork of a mesquite and he couldn't even touch the ground with his front feet. He couldn't get up and I couldn't get out from under him. Them broom weeds was just as high as they are right now and I stayed there until Talmage Palmer found me. And I thought about all the mean things I'd done until old Palmer found me, too. Never broke a bone in me. But that was a lesson to me. I never have stayed by myself and broke horses since. Never stay by yourself and ride them kind of horses.

Another job that was to do sometimes was hunting bears that were killing stock. A bear will whip all the dogs in the country. You take an old bear with cubs—she'll go up a tree and take them cubs up a tree and she'll come down and you can't get enough dogs around here to whup her. Bear is a lot more dangerous than a mountain lion. Course, a bear is gonna get away from you if he can. I'm not much of a killer, but if a bear gets to killing calves or killing goats . . . One time we had a little bunch of goats at the ranch and an old bear come through there and killed thirteen just for fun, you know. I took a couple dogs and put him up a tree and I killed him, but I never killed anything I didn't have to for some reason.

I had some good dogs and I used to also go hunt wild cattle for people. They was Catahoula and Border Collie—good dogs. I found one bull that was so big I couldn't handle him. I later got him but we killed him loading him. He had took up in what we called Ortega Springs and you couldn't get a vehicle in there to haul him out with, and he was too big to neck to something. That old bull, I imagine, was six-seven years old. He was a Hereford bull, a sharp-horned bull, probably weigh 1,400 pounds. I let them dogs chew on him till I seen that he wasn't going to come out and I just called them off. And this Mexican boy, we decided we'd get that bull. We found a cow in heat and took eight other cows and calves over there with us. About five or six miles across there, and we spent all day coaxing him back to the corrals and getting them in. Well, we got that bull in on the scales, and we had a *good* set of scales; made out of two-by-sixes and two-by-eights. And that bull seen them gates was locked on him and he just hooked the whole end out of them scales and out of there he went.

Well, we went in and changed horses and we went to work on him again and finally got him back in. We opened the gates, and there was cedar posts there at that gate set in cement. When he went through there I caught him and just jerked my slack and pitched my rope over it. That bull hooked ever' board off that fence; everything that joined that post, he cleaned it up. I got that old bull wrapped up around it and finally got enough wraps on it where I could tie over to the other post. And I went and called Jiggs Potter, and he sent a boy up there the next day with a power wagon with a winch on it and a stock rack on it made of pipe—something he couldn't tear up. So we got the chain hooked around that old bull's horns—course, his old head was sore by then and I was letting the slack off that rope and old Juan was trying to pull it up in there—and he got his nose in there and that old bull jumped just as high as he could and come down and broke his neck. Every cowboy in that country had tried to get that bull. You know, he could kill a horse. He was a sharp-horned bull and you had to watch what you was doing.

Sometimes Willie went with me catching bulls and cattle. That Willie was a little boy that sure wanted to be a cowboy. Willie's mother died when he was just a little old kid and he just took up with me and made that home. Never was a better-hearted boy. We put him through school and he made a cowboy, and I mean a good cowboy, and he was killed in Vietnam when he was twenty years old. I always thought that boy was a wonderful boy.

A short while before he had to go to that army, we went to Sonora to a rodeo and they was having a team roping; and Willie was in-the team roping, the calf roping, and the bronc riding and he won the all-around. They gave him a fancy belt buckle made out of that [turquoise and coral] with two eagles on it. The prettiest belt buckle I'd ever seen. And there was a little old kid there [watching] and I know Willie didn't know who he was; I didn't. I don't suppose we'd either one seen him before or since. He was just standing there with his mouth open looking at him when they was giving him that buckle, and Willie turned around to that little old kid and he said, "Here, son, you can have it. I didn't want one with no damn chicken hawk on it anyway." He'd never seen that kid before.

And this Pete Liles—he was another boy that took up with me when he was just a little old kid and I don't think there's ever been a better boy than Pete Liles. They just took up with me. My oldest sister, she died when [her kids] were just little old kids and I raised them. Susie, too.

Susie's mother was sick and the doctors had told her she couldn't live. Susie was a little baby and my first wife was with me then and she [Susie's mother] wrote my wife a letter and asked her to promise her, if she died, we'd take Susie and raise her. Susie was just a baby maybe two months old and she was in the hospital herself at that time with pneumonia. So we went in there and I paid Susie's doctor bill and we brought her home with us and we kept her until she was about two years old before we adopted her. Her mother didn't die, but she didn't want to take Susie away from us and we didn't have any children of our own so we just adopted her. My wife died then and Susie was just a little tad, and Susie and I batched about eight years. Well, she was pretty tough and she used to ride with me a lot and go with me. When she got a little bigger we roughed it out together. Just like any other cowboy, we made do; we trapped coyotes, skinned skunks, and done everything to keep going. Really of my own I didn't have any, but I raised about four and I think they all turned out pretty good, I don't know why. Naw [one guy] said all kids and dogs took up with me and he didn't know why. I guess they like the horses or something. You know, I say ninety-five per cent of the little boys wants to ride a horse and I guess wants to be a cowboy and I don't know why. I know all the little boys come to my house—you know, with horses around that's the first thing they want to do. It's something you like; you like being out and it's something you grow into. If you start and follow it long enough, I don't believe you'll quit.

Course, you're gambling being in the cow business. Some of them win and some of them lose. It's something you can't help and there's no use to holler about it. Just do the best you can. That complaining won't help you. I'm not much of a hand at it. I don't think it does any good. Just go on and forget about it. I don't hardly worry about anything as long as I have my wife and my friends. It'd be a poor old world to live in if you didn't have a bunch of friends. That's the most valuable thing that there are. You can take money and buy a lot of things, but it won't buy a bunch of friends. If I didn't have friends, I'd be in a heck of a shape.

And my wife's helped me a lot in different ways. She's helped me raising Susie. And we don't have to have anybody to help us brand 'cause we just have a little old outfit—about eighty-ninety cows—and we just go down there and get them old calves and get a pigging string and tie them down and she always vaccinates, sometimes runs the irons—whatever there is to do. Course, we don't get along as fast as some outfits but we can make our own lives together, and that's what makes this a wonderful country. I don't think there's another country in the world that I'd want to be living in today. I don't like these protesters. You talk about these people that don't want to work? I think if they don't want to work, they ought to get their hat and leave. Either love it or leave it—I'm a hundred per cent thataway. Fight for our rights if we have to. I don't think we have to fight wars to keep our freedom, but I think we should if we have to. Maybe we've made some mistakes and fought some wars that we shouldn't have, but I think if it takes a war for us to keep our freedom, I'm a hundred per cent for it. I really did [think Vietnam was a mistake]. That boy told me, "I'm going over and try to help win it." And he didn't last two months. I brought him back and buried him at Ocate.

These mistakes we've made should help keep us out of these wars in the future. I think it should be left up to the people. I think the people should have a right to vote on it. There's things that come up and we've got people up there that's supposed to represent us and I think that people ought to have their say about it before they go into it.

[Maybe we need a cowboy President.] Naw, he'd have to have more education than most cowboys have got, I'd think. Now there was one time one cowboy lived that might have made a President—Will Rogers. If he had run for President, he might have been elected, too. But the average cowboy, he doesn't have the education to be a President. Course I think with the experience he's got, it'd help him. He knows what people has to do to live, and he knows the hardships and the good parts, too. A good President ought to have the education *and* a country boy's experience.

And I think more people ought to believe in God and be taught that right is right and wrong is wrong. Principles—they should be honest and stand up for what's right. They ought to try to raise their children and teach them what's right and what's wrong. And I sure think they ought to fight this dope. I sure don't believe in dope.

And I think a person doesn't believe in God—there's something wrong with him. I don't think it hurts anybody to go to church. I don't go as much as I should but I sure don't think it hurts anybody to go to church. I'll tell you what—a cowboy'll go to church when they get a chance, but a lot of them don't get a chance. You live pretty close to nature when you're a cowboy.

I like early of a morning. I guess it's my favorite time of day. It's always cool and the air is clear and everything and it smells so good of a morning early in the high country. Spring of the year is the best. It's not hot, it's not cold, and that's branding time. It is the climax of what you've been working for. The spring of the year is when you're trying to save your calves and then when they're up big enough to brand, you're checking what you've done and know what you've done.

Yeah, these old doves holler and these old redbirds hollering, and I like to hear these old dogs bark—tree a lion or run them wild cattle either one—it'll grow on you. I like to hear a cow bawl. I don't like to hear 'em bawl when they're hungry, but I like to hear an old cow bawl up her calf of an evening. I like to smell the pines. In the spring of the year you get in those high pines—I think it's a smell anybody would like. That's living close to nature when you're punching cows.

I think sundown of an evening is a pretty time of day too; and the mountains, I guess, is the prettiest sight I ever seen. You get up above ten thousand feet and you can look back across and the sun's going down—especially if you're about fifteen miles from home trying to get in—you'll see some pretty sights thataway. It'll make you like to be a cowboy.

The reason there's not a lot of good cowboys like there used to be is so many more things that boys can make more money at. Instead of following cowpunching for a trade, they follow something else. I never did have much money. You never seen many cowboys with much money. I'd like to have a hip pocket full. Money's not everything but it's a good thing to have. I guess a man could live without any but it would sure be unhandy. If a man has principle and his friends and money to go with at it, he's a real successful man, I'd say. But most important is just be honest, try to help people and do what's right. I think cowboys is as good a class a people as any. They might not have as much money as some but money don't mean everything. It's just whatever you're happy doing. I'll tell you one thing. Most cowboys—if they've got a dollar and you need it—you can shore get four bits of it.

Would I recommend it? Well, really I don't guess I would—but I wouldn't change my own life. Do what you're happy doing. It's poor pay and hard work but I think living outside and eating cow meat and gravy keeps you young!

"Dolphins used to follow the boats."

ELLEN AND CLARENCE PETERSON

The son of a Danish immigrant, Clarence Peterson moved with his family to Bell Gardens while he was still a young boy. At that time the area was a small farming community, and his childhood in the early 1900s is a vivid example of life in premegalopolis Los Angeles. His recollections of the empty beaches and of a rural existence within the city limits are a sharp contrast to the present reality.

Mr. Peterson was still a prosperous farmer in the 1920s and describes the changes that took place during that decade as well as the effects of the Depression in the years that followed. The influx of thousands of people without food, shelter, or money permanently altered the neighborhood and the community almost overnight. The Petersons have seen many changes in their lifetime and think the country will have many more.

—DEBBIE EDENFIELD, KEVIN LEWIS, ROBERT STOUT, LINDA STOUT, SHERRY JONES, FELICIA PUSATERI, CASSANDRA BOINTY,

SHAWN HARRIS, AND JULIE POMPA.
—MICHAEL BROOKS, ADVISER FOR SUVA INTERMEDIATE SCHOOL,
BELL GARDENS, CALIFORNIA.

CLARENCE PETERSON: My father and mother came here as immigrants and they couldn't speak the language. And they didn't have the language help that they are giving the children today. They had to get in there and learn everything the hard way; everything was in English. But even then he felt that he made a right move in moving and in becoming a citizen. There was very little soil in Denmark and other parts of Europe. Denmark has some, you know, but they don't have thousands of acres like they have here. So he wanted to come to America to do better for himself, and to get a better farm.

They worked hard and they farmed up in East Los Angeles, where I was born. [East Los Angeles is now a sprawling Chicano neighborhood.] They farmed for eleven years on rented property, and they had three of the worst dry years when the crops didn't hardly mature. There was just enough feed for our own stock. But they made enough in eleven years to buy this place down here.

ELLEN PETERSON: We really had to work in those days; I got up at four o'clock in the morning. Sometimes I was too tired because I'd read rather late and my father would come and get me and shake me and put me in the middle of the floor and then I'd have to get breakfast and put up lunches and go to school—walk three miles—then come back and either hoe corn or help with the turkeys or do something on the farm.

I had my fair share of canning, believe me. My hands would just be all puckered from sitting in the kitchen all day long canning peaches and apricots and all kinds of things. We had stacks of big half-gallon jars of fruit and we had fruit every morning for breakfast. My parents had big drying areas and they would dry apricots and sell them, you see. We had two big orchards, and we had a lot of apples. We had apples almost all winter until they were either eaten or rotted. And we had quince and we had two different types of apricots, two different kinds of pears, and we had grapes and everything. When the summertime came, we would sit in the kitchen working over the steam of that stove canning all day long. And when Grandma came, she'd help too; we'd sit there all day long peeling that fruit —all day long. And then my mother would have to add the sugar and measure the water and can the fruit. And then when it came to the corn, my mother would put it into a big pressure cooker, what they'd call a coldpack, and by putting the corn into a pressure cooker, you'd eliminate the possibility of poisoning.

CLARENCE: In those days you couldn't go to the corner grocery store next door and buy these things; you had to put things up for the winter.

ELLEN: My mother made her own bread, and many a time I'd help her pounce it down. You'd have your own mix and it would raise way up, and I could come in and help her pounce it down and then have it raise again. Some women would have it raise three times, and that would take away those holes. If you baked it right at first, it would be just full of holes. You'd want nice fine small holes, so you'd have to check on it and keep pouncing it down. Doing it over and over. It's much easier to buy it ready-made. But your homemade bread and homemade cookies are just delicious. They're lots of work. We'd make waffles and we'd make biscuits and pancakes and things like that, too.

And we had six hundred turkeys and Mom sold those, you know, for the market. We had six hundred turkeys on the ranch.

Kids today don't have it quite that hard. I got one dollar a year and that was all that I was given outside of my food, board, and clothes. Then if the mice chewed the grain sacks, I would mend those sacks and I could sell them for ten cents a sack and that was my money. And if the turkeys were injured, which they often were, I would repair and mend them like a nurse. I would sell them at the store and that was my money. But I had to earn it.

CLARENCE: We raised sugar beets. That was during World War I. From 1915 to 1919, we raised about four hundred tons of beets per year— that would make about one hundred twenty-five tons of sugar; and that was one crop that I didn't like. It was one hard crop to raise. A lot of stooping. We had Mexican laborers do the thinning and hoeing, but the irrigating and cultivating and the hauling down to the beet dumps, where they were hauled by rail to the factory, that was quite a chore.

We generally had about six horses, and they were not riding horses but they were draft horses used in farming. And we had to feed them and curry them and harness them for the day's work. We also had around three or four cows; they had to be milked. And then after school, if there were a couple of hours of daylight, we'd hitch up the team and start plowing. No play.

Then the Depression and the Dust Bowl came along to make things harder. That was a crazy time. The women drank in that time; they began when they began to accompany the men into the speak-easies. Before that time they wouldn't have thought of going to a beer parlor, and they didn't smoke in public. They were more refined before as I remember them. Prohibition just changed them completely. It seemed like it made them loose and bold. It made them absolutely different. The skirts were raised, too. They were long before, and then they got these slinky-tasseled short skirts and did the Black Bottom, and the Charleston. That was when the different dances began. Before that time there were waltzes and the fox trot. It was more refined.

Our family wasn't too affected by the Depression. We were lucky. We didn't lose too much because we weren't in debt. And that was the difference; we weren't in debt like some people. My family sold a crop of oranges. We usually signed up with the packing house and the packing house usually sold the oranges for $2.50 a box. They were sold in New York for $2.56 a box. The farmer got six cents a box. We had to fumigate and irrigate and had to buy ladybugs to fight bugs and we had to hire men and go to all that expense and got only six cents a box. For two years it was real bad. It was a wonder that we didn't lose our shirt. But we were lucky because we had some savings and we survived. We didn't make any money but we survived. Right near us, there was an Oxford graduate and he and his brother ran a filling station and he was glad to have it.

Lots of people were in bad shape. On top of everything else, there was the Dust Bowl; people herding in here, coming so thick and with their chickens and washboards and living in tents.

ELLEN: It wasn't easy for those who had been here first. The Okies would come up and ask for water and we'd let them have it. There wasn't any water system here. We just let them pump it themselves, didn't charge for it; they could come over and help themselves. They had it hard, the people that came over from Oklahoma and Arkansas and Alabama and down through there. I give them credit; they brought themselves up by their bootstraps. They were hard-working, nice people as a rule. They got in and worked. They had hardships, no question of that—even more than we did, because they didn't have any well or anything. They weren't established here and they had to start from scratch and build up from a tent first and then up to a one-room house and maybe add a room and that's how they grew. Having children in those conditions was really rough. You know, they grew a lot of their own vegetables to get by, so I give them that credit.

Speaking of water, it's funny now. We dug wells for the house; one was 110 feet deep and the other was 440 feet deep. The 440-foot well is now under the Super A Market. After I married Mr. Peterson, the Governor came by and saw if we were pumping water out of these wells. If we were pumping water, we'd have to pay for it because Los Angeles claimed they owned all of the water rights. In the early days there were riparian rights which were the water rights. If you bought the land you had a certain amount of water. You were entitled to them; no one tried to cut you off. But here after twenty years, L.A. felt they owned all of the water and if we were pumping from our well, we would have to pay Los Angeles for the water.

So many things like that have happened to change things. Used to be that the skies were blue and we had no smog, and there are so many flowers that are missing now that I knew as a child. We had many wild roses and maidenhair ferns along the river. And we had even those square-stemmed ginseng flowers and flying Dutchmen and all kinds of wild flowers which you never see any more. We had weeping willows and lots of cattails and just lots of beautiful blackbirds with red spots on the males' wings. You see those now, but not like we saw them. It was really nice for the children because they would enjoy that and would go down there and picnic. Now, of course, instead of the river we have concrete channels which keep the river from flooding over the property. In the old days there were no true river beds. Sometimes the trees fell down and then it would push the water out of the flood channel and flood all over the property and would make new channels which would be very destructive to the crops. I was in on the 1937 flood and in on the 1938 flood. We saw the bridge go out in 1937 and we saw the big houses go down the Los Angeles River. When I lived in Glendale, they just toppled over and they had a certain area roped off and the officers were around there. They were watching so that there wouldn't be looting. Some of the cops were crooked. They went into the closets and took some of the clothing. They took out suits; they removed the toilets and the sinks.

CLARENCE: Of course, here the water was going up to the top of the channel and it was plumb full. So now we know where the water will be in those river beds that are now concrete, but it isn't as beautiful. It isn't as relaxing. So we have both good and bad.

ELLEN: It's hard to know what to think any more. One thing, though, I think that knowing about farming and canning may come in handy again. They say there's always a possibility of famine. And one thing that I learned when I graduated as a nurse was that even though you have some food that appears to be spoiled, if you boiled it for ten minutes you might be able to save it. Add a little curry powder or something like that to reseason it, or add a little bone with soup or something like that and you can eat it. In case of emergency if you're real poor, or if you're in famine times, then you can save food. Without a refrigerator, you can dry it. You can dry it up just from the sun. You can put pears out and dry them. You can get that thin cheesecloth from the stores to keep the flies off. Even certain vegetables you can dry and recook them and have them for soup at least. And even in fishing; do you know how to save fish that you have extra? Well, you put them into the sink and wash them good and soak them overnight in real strong salt, and take them the next morning and you wipe that extra salt off, you see. And put them in the oven at two hundred degrees, watch it carefully, put it down real low and watch it carefully, and in about two hours it makes dried fish. And it tastes just like what you buy.

CLARENCE: I always liked fishing. Once I built a boat in our barn. I taught my ownself how.

ELLEN: He's very clever with his hands.

CLARENCE: I kept it down in Long Beach from 1926 to 1930. I used to go to Catalina with it, and almost drowned there once so I give that up.

ELLEN: It was a terrible storm and it almost took him a day to get back. It scared the wits out of him.

CLARENCE: Another fella and I were fishing and a storm came up and it looked pretty bad. We could go in at Long Beach, but there was no harbor there so we tried for San Pedro. But we couldn't make it so we went up to Isthmus and followed the current in, and it took us from 9 A.M. to 9 P.M. to cross and we were bailing water out. We didn't have any radio and no Coast Guard either. One of our friends was invited once to go fishing in a real nice boat, and he just disappeared. That channel can get awful rough and there were no airplane searches in those days. Last week was the first time I went back to Catalina since I was nineteen years old. It used to be very good fishing down there: swordfish, flying fish, you couldn't go fishing without the flying fish jumping, and sometimes they'd land in your own boat. But we didn't see a one on this last trip. And the dolphins used to follow the boats and jump right alongside the boat and we didn't see a one of them either. I guess the pollution's got them.

"We Mexicans are proud."

LUPE NIETO

Lupe Castro Nieto was born in Mexico on June 12, 1918. The Castro family fled the Mexican Revolution a year and a half later and settled just across the border in Santa Ana, California. When she was seventeen she met Frank Nieto, and within a month he proposed and they were married two years later in 1937.

In 1948, the Nietos moved to the San Joaquin Valley and settled in Firebaugh. The two youngest children were born here. Frank worked for seventeen years for the Miller Hotchkiss Estate, first as a gardener and then as cattle foreman. He later assumed the care of the grounds at the Firebaugh Public Schools and St. Joseph's School, and became head gardener at the V. C. Britton Ranch.

Mrs. Nieto proudly stated that all seven of her children have finished high school, while she only had a seventh-grade education. She said in her case it really wasn't necessary as she was married young and her husband was always a good provider. When her husband died, Mrs. Nieto had to give up most of her activities in order to earn a living. She took over part of her husband's work, and says she can make anything grow outside. She keeps up to date on gardening, studying the newest methods of pruning and the latest information on insecticides, reading articles and books on

*shrubs and flowers. The yearly planning of the gardens is left en-
tirely to her. She executes the plans and keeps the grounds beautiful. The other gardeners come to her for advice.*

—CLAUDIA M. CUNHA.
—JUANITA FOURCHY, ADVISER TO WESTSIDE RIF PROJECT,
FIREBAUGH, CALIFORNIA.

I WAS BORN in Mexico, but I was only a year and a half when we
came to this country. I didn't become an American citizen until 1958. We
were raised here in California.

For a long time I was very bitter; I felt bitter. A neighbor wouldn't let
her kids play with my kids because we were Mexicans, and she claimed that
my children had lice in their hair. Why, I may be Mexican but I'm not
dirty! And I didn't like that woman since then. That was the only woman
in Firebaugh that ever made me feel that way.

[We were looked down on in many ways. When we tried to rent an
apartment, we were told,] "Sorry, we don't rent to Mexicans." And in some
theaters they would not allow Mexicans. I'm the darkest in my family. I
have a brother and sister who have blue eyes and light brown hair. You
could swear they aren't Mexican. Yet they weren't allowed in a theater. A
couple of times we were not served in a restaurant. When somebody does
that to me—oh, I can be a demon! And the only reason I didn't say anything was because I didn't want to embarrass [my husband]. I would have
embarrassed him to tears. But I wanted to lash at them! We sat there and
sat there. People came and they served them, and they *never* served us and
they never asked us! So, what more of a hint do you want?

Another time was in San Diego. People came and they'd just ignore us.
So you walk out with your tail between your legs; what do you do instead
of creating a scene? That grew up with me for a long, long time. It wasn't
until just about ten years ago that it left me. But it does leave you with that
ugly feeling that you're inferior. Maybe that's why we've gotten into this
education. To me, you *have* to make *something* out of yourself. Especially a
Mexican. An education is an important thing really. That's where you learn
for your future. I did not have an education. Because I knew how to read
[is the reason] that I know what I know now. I mean, I go to the library
and I read and read and read; and, really, I educated myself. And that is
why, to me, reading is the most important thing.

The subject I really loved in school was arithmetic. That was my life. Oh,
that subject—I loved it. I had a teacher—he was rough. You have no idea

how scared I was of that man. It was in junior high. I was scared to death. You know, I had the problem, and I had it right, but just because he'd call me to go to the board, I was so scared of him that I thought I would have it wrong and he would chew me out. So I would say I didn't have it. That I had not worked on it. And, by golly, they'd give the answer and I'd have it right. And that was my main reason for quitting school, because that was the subject I liked best and that was the teacher I was scared to death of. I couldn't take it.

If I was a teacher I'd teach the child according to the child's ability and explain, make it to where the pupil *understands.* Don't just throw something at them and say, "Do that." You have to explain. If it's two or four or half a dozen times, if it's explained, the child will learn. I *know* the child will learn because I did. Sometimes it had to be explained to me over and over again. I was this kind of person. "Why? Why? But, how?" Well, heck, I wanted to know why and how and when, and I got the answer! It took a little time.

My father died when I was only nine. My mother had kind of a hard time, especially during the Depression raising eight of us. My thirteen-year-old brother was the one who supported us, really. Of course, at that time it didn't take much to feed a family; but still, you know, it was rough. And now, if a youngster doesn't earn a hundred dollars a week, why, he thinks he's not earning anything! I don't know—I just think that you should be satisfied with what you have, and make the best of what you have *with* what you have. You can't say, "I wish that I had this and I wish that I had that," and you're going to get it. You're *not* going to get it! You're going to work, and you're going to *earn* what you're going to earn and then you're going to live with what you have and make the best of it, that's all.

My life was changed again when my husband passed away. I have turned to hobbies to keep my life occupied. It does get very lonely, but they keep me going. Ceramics, macramé, knitting, crocheting, you name it, I can do it. Of course, God, above all, has helped me through this crisis. It was so sudden that, even now, I just don't believe it. So I keep myself occupied. I don't go out much. You go out and you're always a third wheel. I'm not anxious to go out. And I work eight hours a day.

Oh, I could go on welfare if I lied, but I have a car, and I have a little money in the bank. And I would not stoop that low as to go in there and ask for welfare. *That* is why I'm *working.* We Mexicans are a little proud, too. I will not accept charity, and I am one of them.

I am very thankful that, even though I'm not wealthy, I have my health. And that, to me, is most important because if I had money and poor health, money wouldn't do me any good. As long as God gives me my health and I can work, I'm gonna work. What I'm doing is yard work, and it's hard. Out

Lupe Nieto

in that 105° temperature. I get up at 6 A.M., go to work, and quit at 2 P.M. and I don't take no lunch break. I work right straight through. But I'd rather earn my own living. Now I know that if I didn't want to work, I wouldn't have to. My children would chip in and give me a certain amount. I will not accept anything from them, either. They have their families. Why should they give to me?

I am very proud of all my children, because out of the seven, only one does not have a college education. They have all made themselves what they want to be, and that is why they're successful.

Boy, today I didn't want to go to work [laughter]. Six o'clock comes along and I just can't make myself. I go plug my coffee in and then I get back into bed for another ten-fifteen minutes and then, of course, I *know* I have to get up! [More laughter] and I know I have to go to work! But after I get started I'm all right then. But getting started . . .

Somebody came in not long ago, and they were looking at all of the things I make and they said, "How come you're working out in a yard?"

I said, "Well, I have to make a living some way."

"Woman, with all the things you know how to make, you can sell them!"

I said, "But I don't want to sell them." It's a kind of sentimental thing. I'm the type of person who will *not* go sell anything. I feel embarrassed.

My children were real good. They came on [the anniversary of my husband's death]. They spent the weekend with me so I wouldn't spend it alone and so I wouldn't brood about it. Of course, God helped me too, because to

Lupe Nieto in her rock garden

me my religion is what has really saved me. But you can't change some things. How do you fight God? I mean, He brought him into this world and He was ready for him. And it was too bad for me. I just had to accept it. You know, sometimes I think that's the way God tests you. My faith and my religion, that's the thing my mother left me that I really, really appreciate. My mother was the one who went to Mass every day. She had calluses on her knees from kneeling. She was only thirty-eight when my father got killed in an automobile accident. She managed to raise eight of us during the Depression with some kind of government checks to help us out. Every time my mother would take a check to the grocery store, she died a million deaths. She told us, she said, "I've got this check. You have no idea how embarrassed I am to go and pay the grocery bill." She hated it. And, by golly, no sooner did the orange crop come in and my brother could work, then she was happy, because money was coming in that the government wasn't giving to her.

My children will help me when I need it, too, but now I don't tell my troubles to my children. They have families. They have their problems, too. Why should I bore them with my problems?

Raising my seven children—that's my proudest achievement, I believe.

[I think raising good families is a goal all of us can strive for. And being fair and just. I'd like to be remembered that way.] Justice is important. You should not take advantage of people. I can't stand anybody taking advantage of anybody else. I'm not a good person either! Don't think I'm a saint! [Laughter.] I'm just an average, Christian, American citizen [more laughter].

I think it's a pretty good world if we only knew how to really go about it and live it. What we haven't learned is to have peace amongst the nations. That's what we haven't learned. And, of course, between ourselves, too.

If we don't start acting more with love and brotherhood, believe me, something terrible is going to happen. Because it's happening already, and we just don't seem to see it. If we try to understand each other and live with one another, I think that's the only thing that can really save this world.

"Four o'clock in the morning you was on that floor."

CHARLIE HOUCHANT

Charlie Houchant, Jr., was born May 24, 1908, in Richmond, Virginia. He moved with his parents, Charlie and Lucy Houchant, four brothers and three sisters, to West Virginia in 1915.

When in the fifth grade, he quit school to work in farming. His work experience includes: waiter on the Chesapeake-Ohio Railroad; brickyard worker in North Haven, Connecticut; paper mill worker in Lomo, Virginia; and service in the U. S. Army from 1942–45, where he was discharged a corporal from Davis-Monthan Air Force Base in Tucson, Arizona.

He married Leona Clyde Houchant in 1944. This marriage ended in divorce. His present wife is Gertrude Jackson Houchant, whom he married in 1960.

Baptized in the Mount Pleasant Baptist Church in 1961, he presently serves as a deacon in the South Phoenix Baptist Church. His civic responsibilities include membership in the NAACP,

Masons, and a representative for Title I from Dunbar Elementary School, where the RIF classroom project is located, funded by the First Institutional Baptist Church.

His hobbies are fishing and hunting.

—CAROL BAXTER.
—MRS. NORMA NEDD AND MRS. JEFFREY ARCHER,
ADVISERS TO DUNBAR SCHOOL CLASSROOM PROJECT,
PHOENIX, ARIZONA.

I WAS RAISED in the country. We come up rough. I didn't know it was rough then, though. We had plenty to eat and clothes to wear, but I was doing man work when I was nine years old. Plowing in the field with two mules. Yeah, my dad had old scrubby land with lots of bushes on it, and he'd do the grubbing—taking up trees and roots and things—and I'd do the plowing.

My oldest brother, he was working by the day making a dollar so he could help my dad support the rest of us. The sisters, they'd be hoeing corn, tobacco, potatoes, things like that. This was in Virginia. That's where I'm from.

Our money crop was tobacco. From the time you put it in the ground till you put it on the market floor you were working doing something to it. Every day. We didn't have the opportunities to do what kids do now. I tell my little boy now, "When I was nine years old, I was doing man work." From sunup to sundown. And when we come out of the field, we had chores around the house to do. Feed the hogs, milk the cows, cut wood. And six o'clock in the morning didn't nobody catch nobody up in the bed. Four o'clock in the morning you was on that floor. By four-thirty you'd be in that barn milking those cows and feeding the horses. It was work, honey. But we put our minds to it. We made it.

I'm gonna tell you the truth: I don't care what it is and how well you can do something—if your mind is not on the thing you're doing, and you're thinking about something else, you're not gonna give justice to either one. There's no way for you to do it. If you're here teaching, and your mind is on taking a trip someplace, you may as well give up! My father taught me that. When you're going to do a certain thing, forget about the rest, for there's no way a man can do two things at the same time. You've got to quit one and go to the other one—you've got to make up your mind. If you want to be successful [at anything], put your mind on it. Just do *this*, and then when you get through with *this*, go to something else.

Charlie Houchant

Home training and care are so important. There was a lady back at my home—she had twenty kids, and her husband died before her kids was grown. And she raised those twenty kids. Had about thirteen-fourteen boys. But she had them trained so well and so much discipline in them I never heard talk of any of her boys going to jail or fighting or getting into no kind of trouble. A woman, now, raised that many kids. But we don't have that home training no more.

What makes me feel good and makes me feel wealthy—I have a comfortable living and Christ in my heart. That's what makes me rich. If someone was to give you a million dollars and the Devil got the whole bill of sale on you, and give *me* a hundred dollars, and I'm with Christ, I'm more happy, more wealthy, and more satisfied than you are with your million dollars.

[First I want my children to get an education. That can't be took from you.] Then if my children are to get money, I would want them to get it honestly—work for it. When you have enough to get by comfortably, you should be satisfied with that. A person shouldn't lust after money. I don't go for this big run of money. Just what we need—if we can get what we need and what we can get by with and be comfortable . . . . I believe in a person having a nice home, good clothing, and food, but a big pile of money, naw. [But if you're lucky enough to get more than you need, remember,] we are not going to carry nothing away from here. We didn't bring nothing here. And that money you got piled up, if you don't do something with it, if you didn't distribute it around 'mongst the little children that don't have no mothers or the old people who have so little to fall back on or whatever you can do . . . Look, we got to die. That's promised to us. So when we are into eternal life, we want to go in rest. So if a person spends his life on earth—a grasping life, stingy, and never satisfied with nothing—you know God ain't pleased with that. So I'm gonna give you advice: If you got more than you need and you don't divide it, you ain't done nothing.

I'm glad that the Lord has seen fit for colored people to now be on the level we're on. We ain't equal yet, but we got better jobs, better schools, better homes than the colored race ever had. We got a ways to go yet, but I'm glad the other has passed away. A lot of young people today have a better chance than I had when I was coming up.

"I hunt the alligator for two years."

AUGUSTE LANDRY

Auguste Landry was born on December 14, 1880, in Choupic, Louisiana, a small lumber and trapping community located eight miles from the nearest town, Thibodaux, the parish (county) seat of Lafourche Parish. As a child, Auguste worked in the fields taking care of tobacco plants his father grew.

When Auguste was nine years old, his father withdrew him from a school he had been attending because the teacher changed the curriculum from French to English. With only two English-speaking families in Choupic, it seemed a waste of time to study English.

After only eighteen months of formal education, Auguste went to work in the swamps beside his father cutting timber. At the age of fourteen he earned "twelve nickels a day." He worked from sunup to sundown, six and sometimes seven days a week cutting shingles, crossties, and cypress planks. Sometimes he supplemented his income by building dugout pirogues and hunting alligators. Auguste worked in the swamps until he retired, but he never got lost even in dense cypress growths because he had his own built-in compass. He could determine direction simply by noting shades of coloration of trees that resulted from varying amounts of sunlight.

At the age of eighteen he started to work for a man who spoke English. To learn the language, he bought a book and taught himself. Later he used this method to learn surveying. Sometimes he "carried" an English word around for months before he learned its French equivalent.

In 1902 Auguste married Aurelia Clement, who was also a native of Choupic. This, he says, has brought him the most happiness in his ninety-five years. His one wish is to be able to spend another seventy-three years with his wife.

Since retiring in 1962 at the age of 82 from his lifelong work in the cypress swamps, Auguste has kept busy. He traced the Landry family tree to his Acadian ancestors in Nova Scotia and his wife's family to France. Currently he is writing a chronicle of his early years. To speed up the process, he bought a typewriter and taught himself to type. Because of arthritis in some fingers, he developed a unique style of hunt and peck. Even in his nineties Auguste Landry refuses to assume that advanced age or lack of formal education can deter him from any task he sets his sights on.

—TOM BECNEL, JULIE MARTIN, AND SHEELA PLATER.
TRANSLATED FROM THE FRENCH BY TOM BECNEL
AND EARLINE LE BLANC. PHOTOGRAPHS BY
GEORGE DE GRAZIO AND JULIUS ADAMS.
—TOM BECNEL, ADVISER FOR LAFOURCHE HERITAGE '76.

I GOT NINETY-FIVE years old. I got a daughter that's got seventy-two years old, and there's one that got seventy. But I'm not too old. I'm still young.

My great-grandpa was Joseph Landry. Marie Madeline Bourque was my great-grandma. My great-grandma, she got seventeen years old and my great grandpa got nineteen years old [when they] crossed the sea from Canada to go to France. And when they went over there, he was put in jail for one year. After that he was sent to Spain. They stay about eight months in Spain, and Spain send them to Louisiana. That's where we from.

I can remember back to when I was three years and six months. I remember my room. One plank got sides—that's my bed. At that time we make that [mattress] with black moss and corn shucks. All the lumber—big tables —were sawed by hand. And the old people used to put a stand, you know. They call that [a] *chantier,* but I don't know. Nobody can't find me the name in English. But you put four posts about six feet high, and then [a frame] on top of that. [The log is put on top of the frame and the men take a long saw,] one man on top, one man under that. And they saw all the planks and everything to build the house. My house—seventy years come October that I own that house. I made that by myself.

For light, they make their candles themselves. They got some [device] could make two candles at one time. We used some grease from the deer, all kinds of things like that.

When I was six years old, I don't know how to pull on a [pair of] pants. We went to a big, big church, and the first pair of pants I put on I was seven years old. Before that we wear dress. The first pair of shoes, I was eight years old. When I start to walk, I fall with that doggone thing on my foot!

For food, when I was young, they raise some sweet potatoes and they raise some corn. If you don't work, you starve. You didn't have nothing to buy. You got to make your tobacco, you got to make your butter, you got to make your corn—white corn to make your flour, your grits—and every damn thing. And you got to raise your hog, you got your cattle and everything. When I was young, my daddy and my uncle worked together. And if you don't make nothing, you got nothing. You can't buy nothing. The first thing, you got to make your corn and raise your hogs, raise your cows and have your meat. You got to raise your rice, and after that, raise your chicken. You got to raise your tobacco and everything. The tobacco, we plant the seed, you know. And after that, we transplant that. And when it was [little plant], the snails and everything come to eat that. I was a little boy, and [my job], I killed the little snails all around and all the insects that come in there. And after it was grown, it comes yellow, you know; and when it was yellow, the people say it was ripe. We cull [the leaves] and we powdered it, and hang that in a great big building till that thing was dry. And after that, we roll it, you know. We call that in French, *torquette*. After that, we leave that about six months like that. After that, we break that and we put them all together in a sack and we tie that pretty high, then it come black. It comes some juice in there. Then you can put that in a pipe, and somebody make some cigar with that, you know—somebody who know how to make cigar at that time. And somebody chew that. They put some sugar sometimes in that; it makes it sweet to chew you know. That's the way we make the tobacco.

And the rice, you cut that [when it's ripe]. You cut the rice sometime toward the summer. And after that you put that in a pile, you know. And after that you gotta bring that to the house, and now you put some quilt about twelve feet long and you put all the rice there and you beat that to get the rice out. That's better rice because it's not polished like the rice you buy now.

Auguste Landry

And every farmer had some white corn to make you flour. We got a mill and we made flour and grits. That's what we did, thank the Lord. That's why we eat. The first piece of bread I see [like] the bread we eat now, I got twelve years old. I was raised with the corn bread and the grits and rice. And you can't buy no lard. You got to make your lard. You got to have your hog and everything. You can't buy no meat. Young people make the life so easy now. Push-button, you know.

For groceries, well, they got some carts passing. Old man Shulyer Breaux, he got a store and sell some groceries. And sometime nobody can't come with no groceries. The road is so bad, nobody can't come. I remember I had about ten year old. The only thing we had to eat for about three days [was] some sweet potatoes and peanuts. We can't have nothing else. Nothing in there. You can't go get it. We had no roads here. When I buy my first car, we didn't have no roads, no gravel and nothing like that. You know where I used to drive, I go to Cypremort trapping and everything, and I had a shovel in my car. I had a piece of plank about four feet long; when I stay stuck, I put my jack on that and I jack 'em up and put some dirt—some dry dirt or some piece of wood or something like that—put under there to come out. When you meet somebody, you can't give the way. I take my shovel, I make a way, I back and all that; and after they pass, I go back again.

One time at Bayou Boeuf they had a big rain on Good Friday, fourteen inches of rain that day. And the road come bad enough you can't go over there in a car. I went and leave the car on this side of Bayou Ron-pon-pon, what we call; and on the other side they got a place where you can park. And one day I say, "I'm gonna go to Bayou Boeuf in my car." I buy me two planks fourteen feet long, about one feet wide. Put that in my car and that's the way I go.

There was no mail. Nobody didn't write nothing at all. Nobody didn't have nothing. But everybody was satisfied. And now everybody got too much. Everybody got more than they need and nobody is satisfied. You know that yourself. Everybody wants more and more. Since a boy, I was married for seventy-three years and four months. I got ninety-five years old and it is changed. It is changed like a hundred. Five for one. Nowadays a man earn five, six dollars an hour—three hundred dollars a week—and us, we'd make thirteen dollars a month. Imagine what changes here in seventy-three years!

We had some school here. We were all French. The first lesson I had, I learned my lesson [spoken in French]: "Return from school to your house without stopping to talk modestly, that is to say without shouting and neither thinking of anyone on the side of the road." That's the first lesson I learned. I had seven years old and seven months. I start to school at seven years and six months. I was there one month when I got to read that.

Everybody was French. Then the Yankee come here and start to steal the French. Start to teach English and don't want to teach the French no more. When I left school, that's why I left school. I believe everybody ought to speak French and English. I think you gotta speak both language. But they don't want to teach in French. My daddy said, "If they don't want to teach you in French, you gonna leave school." So I had to leave and go to work. No education.

When my daddy made me leave school, he put my brother and me to cutting wood. We sold the wood for fifty cents a cord. I got nine years old. We felled the tree with a *pas-par-tout* [crosscut saw] and we threw it down and we would cut it sixteen inches long. We would split it all in small pieces, and then we would cord a cord about eight feet long and four feet high. Mr. Olezipe Chiasson, he had a mule and cart, and he would come there and get a cord of wood and he would go and sell it for $3.00 in Thibodaux. There was no electricity. We were heated with wood.

We went through all kinds of times. Once the crevasse broke [the Bayou Lafourche levee and the Mississippi River levee broke at the same time] and the water came in the house six inches over the floor. We moved to my grandfather in back of the L. T. Plantation. They had water over there, but there were some canal levees that weren't covered. And to have something to eat, they would have to put out some lines at night to catch some fish. [What we didn't need,] then, they would put them in a basket and put it on their shoulders and go to sell that for five or ten, fifteen cents for a catfish. That's how we lived for about eight weeks that we stayed there. After that, we returned here and my papa started floating some cypress that had fallen down. They would cut some wood from those trees.

We did all kinds of work. Work don't kill nobody I don't think. I hunt the alligator for two years. Hunt them everywhere—Donner Swamp, in Labadie—everywhere in the swamp. That was in dry weather, you know. All your swamps was dry except where they got a hole where the alligator make a hole. He keeps some water [that way] all the time. Sometimes he go ten feet underground. We have a hook where you hook him and you pull him up outside. Sometimes it takes two men to pull one. We killed one back at Donner that was fourteen feet long. Then we skin them. We sell that about a dollar and a quarter a skin. We make two-three dollars a day every time. I make more money at that time on the alligator than [when] I work for somebody else.

And I used to raise pigeons. And I buy some furs: mink, coon, possum, muskrat. Everybody make a living with that. We sell them in New Orleans. I used to buy for St. Louis. I work for different companies. We buy [the furs from the trappers] on five cents' commission—five cents on the dollar. If you spend a hundred dollar, you got five dollars [to keep]. In 1938 I buy

Auguste Landry and interviewers

for ninety thousand dollars of pelts. I handle a lot of money in my time; I didn't have any.

And then I made a lot of pirogues. I made some for sell and I make some for myself too. The first time I see to make a pirogue, I was five years old. My daddy and my uncle were gonna make a pirogue, and my brother was about fourteen years, but he was good chop. We want to take a tree around the Coulon Plantation. We pull that tree green and [hew the boat out while the wood was still green]. If the sap is still up when you [hew it out], it's gonna stay many many years without dry, you see. [You halve the log] and make two pirogue with the same log. You dig that inside out with a kinda thing like a hoe. It takes about five or six days to make a pirogue. There's a lot of work on that. Then sell it for about ten dollars. Nine dollars. My father-in-law have one he could put about six men on it. It got thirty-six inches wide and eighteen feet long, and it go six men on that. I don't have one no more. Nobody don't make no more like that. You buy some plywood, make it in plywood [now].

[But the main work I did was in timber.] I'll tell you, how many [things] you can saw in swamp, I make it. I make some pickets, some shingles, barrel staves, anything you can make; deadening tree so he will float out of swamp—you got to dead that tree before he float—make some crossties, float some timber, every kind you can imagine.

At seventeen years old, I can't speak a word in English. And I start to lose a little bit English now because for about eleven years I didn't talk English no more. My wife still don't talk English at all, so we talk French all the time. Talk English with the children sometimes, you know. [But] when I used to work with people, I got to talk [English] because I work with somebody that don't talk French at all. I work with Joseph Rathborne and Company until it was thirty-six years and six months, and those people didn't talk French at all. Old man Duet, I worked twelve years for him. When I start to work for him, I can read his writing. He write like a shorthand. Nobody can read his handwriting except me and the two Martinez. Sometimes he can't read his own writing. He write two letters to one word. I learned that, you know.

When I get married, I go make crossties in the swamp. We make about a dollar a day. Every other week we make a hundred ties. That's twenty dollars. You got to make that tie in the swamp, haul it twelve miles in the swamp, bring it to St. James at the Bayou Arpent back to the river, and pile that crosstie. We make 110 ties, and that ten extra ties we never get paid for that. That's a back tie [to replace any that are defective].

That's where I got my education. I would go in the swamp. I look at the tree—cypress to any kind of tree. She got five inches, ten inches, twelve inches—and as high as sixty feet—any kind of length, and I'm gonna tell you how many feet they got in that tree. I'm gonna figure out how much each tree. I learned that with my books. I buy my books and I figure. The other day I got five of my granddaughter—[they] had five, six years of college—and we all sit down together. I look at her. I say, "You got a good education." I say, "Poor Grandpa. I got a little figure for you all." I say, "I want you figure for me a hundred feet around, how many square feet it make." She start to look each other. I say, "Well," I say, "you're so smart. I want you tell me." I say, "I want you tell me. A hundred feet around, how many square feet it make?" [No answer.] "How many time twenty got on a hundred?"

"Five."

"Take off twenty. How much you left?"

"Eighty."

"Exactly eighty feet square." I learn that by myself. I had the book. All my grandchildren study but they don't learn that. College is no good no more. You know what? I find a man about three years back in the street. The man has five years of college. I give him the same problem. He take his pencil. I say, "That's something, eh?"

"Well," he say, "Mr. Landry, we never learn that."

"Well," I say, "the way you talk you know every damn thing."

And I never get lost. I go in the swamp, and I got a compass in the swamp. You know what it is? You can't imagine. Listen. The sun pass that way every day. This side, the southwest, never dry because the sun never dry it. All the trees dark on this side, and this other side clear. Now if you get in there, you [know how] to go north. And you know that's west, that's east. And the color of the trees, that's my compass. And I never got lost. Sometimes I would come out a half mile from where I entered, or a mile, but you will never lose me. [That's my education.]

[I do good work for that lumber company, too. I learn a lot there.] I went to work over there, the first job he put me over there was skin some logs. I skin some logs for about two months. After that, my brother-in-law told him, he say, "Mr. Landry can run that company."

"Oh, I don't believe," he says. He come see me one day and he said, "Mr. Landry, what can you do?"

I say, "I can run the mill."

He say, "I don't believe that."

"Well," I say, "I can show you." And I start to show him. And one day the rain start.

He said, "Let's go to the shed."

I said, "You can go. It didn't rain where I come from." I put my raincoat. When the rain stopped, I had all my work done.

He said, "I'll be doggone. I never see that before."

I say, "You never learn nothing." I say, "Me, I learn everything." I say, "When I was a kid, everything I learn for me I learn in the swamp." And after three months, he put me boss. I worked thirty-one years and six months for that company. Sometimes I had fifty men, sometimes seventy men, sometimes a hundred fifty men. On Friday night I got to make that payroll to go get the money on Saturday. I pass some night, plenty nights, sometimes four o'clock I didn't finish, by myself doing that.

When I was young, I fight. I don't give a damn about man. There's no man big enough to stop me. I fight with him. But after that, when I start to be supervise for the company, I have to learn more. Like if the man cross me or come insult me, I leave him tell me. After he finished, I say, "You finished? Well," I say, "not me. I'm not finished." I take my checkbook and I take his time and, "Here."

He say, "What's the matter?"

"Well," I say, "you don't like me. I don't like you." I say, "Go ahead, you son-of-a-gun. I don't need you no more." After two or four weeks, he come back again and I say, "*Non, non.* When I need you, I'm gonna call you. Sometimes if you have nothing to eat, I call you back." So he come see me [later] and I give him some work. I make a better man. I make some good man.

Man what was supervise all the company make a dog's life. Good people, you don't need to watch him; but the bad people you got to watch him all the time. The bad man come to you [to] tell you such-and-such man do this and that, don't believe that. That's the damn one you got to watch. That man [that] come report to you, watch that man. I catch that man like that often.

I know how to control myself. A man have a quick temper, he comes here, he ought to go back and think about that. If you're wrong, then you come back again and tell that people that you're wrong. If you're right, well, you tell him that you're right. Everything you tell somebody, somebody gone tell one another. Don't do that. If you knew something against me, come and see me—Mr. Landry. I'm gonna tell you what it is. After that, we gone get together and be friends. Don't get mad and kill somebody. If you want something you don't have, come see me. Maybe I can help you. That's the way I work every time.

When I start to think of all that I have passed through, it doesn't seem true. It looks like a dream. There's plenty people come here often and they tell me, "Mr. Landry, I can't believe that you've had only eighteen months of school and have done what you have done."

And I tell them, "Often," I said, "it's not the school that makes the head of the people. It's natural."

If you got education, try to learn something. Something, any kind of job.

A job you can stand on it. A doctor. A bookkeeper. Something good for your life. But if you didn't learn nothing, your graduation is no good.

We got trouble now. Too many lazy people. Nobody wants to work. *Too much education*, maybe. I don't know you. I can't say you bad because I don't know you. But I think you're a good man because I don't believe you come to see me if you *not* a good man. I didn't see no bad man come see me! Every other week I got somebody like you over here. [But listen.] The difference I find now is United States give 'em too much. You got a lot of people here, I know, who work three months a year. After that—relief. It takes seventy-two, seventy-three dollars a week. After that, they get a hundred dollars in stamps. He got everything. That's not right. You know one thing? That's the trouble with the country—giving too much. If you need something, it's okay. But if you got to work, you got to work. I work for all my life, for seventy-two years. Once I was sick. I went take the shot every week. But I still worked. Sometimes I'm weak; sometimes I got to sit down, but I work.

A lot of young people work eight hours a day, and he has a complaint. It's too long. And me, we start with a sunup to sundown for twelve nickels a day. I never did make no money in my life. But in my line, I believe I know just as any man go in college. I'm not smart, no, because everything I learned, I learned on myself. I learned to type. I got all my machines—the adding machine and everything. I was bookkeeper for the company for fourteen years. I'm the one keep all the books, get the money. I'm the one run his business. For sixty-three years I was supervisor and tell the people what to do.

But right now, if you give me two thousand dollars a month, I don't want to go and do that [same job] because you can't tell nothing to the young people no more. He know better than you. I don't care how old you are, but you never learn everything. I have ninety-five years and I still learn something.

The education's not right. They have a lot of girls go to the schools for twenty years, and when they come back, they don't know how to put the egg in the lard to cook it. And a man like you, go twenty, twenty-two years, he come back this way, he don't know how to handle the shovel and the hoe.

They ought to have a plantation—everything—to show a girl what to do; to show the boy what to do. [Then] if a depression come in, you know what to do. If it come in [now], it got three quarters of the people don't know how to do. Me, I had six years old I was in the field with the shovel, clean the drains. Don't see no children like that [now]. Neighbors we know get up at four o'clock in the morning. Holler for his children. Don't know where

Mr. and Mrs. Auguste Landry

they at. Four days they never see them. I didn't blame the children. I blame the parents.

Now for all day the children, like the hogs, run wild, run hog wild. The children get up before the mama and papa and go around all day and nobody don't even know where they at. That's the kind of children we got now. Everywhere you go you'll find that. It's not the mama and papa that's boss. It's the child what's boss. The papa and mama is no attention. How much attention you all get now? There's going to come one day when man won't know how to work, he is gonna suffer. He got to learn how to work. I was nine years old when I learned how to cut some wood in the swamp with my daddy. Start in the swamp and I retire eighty-five years old and I worked all my life in the swamp. Enjoyed my work.

Now, I tell you, in all ways too much liberty. When they stopped the punishment in school, that's where they made the trouble because the parents take up for the young people. That's where it comes. And that's the trouble with television right now. That's why the young generation don't learn anything. Television ought to be stopped some kind of way. You got some [programs] that people that got no respect on it. And the children learn that, you know. In my time, it was different.

They got a lot of trouble right now. Everybody is in trouble. The dope. Everybody is doped over here. I got some relations stay Kentucky come here and they tell me the same thing. Everybody was doped. I don't know. But I know if we no have no change, it's gonna be too bad.

I don't know. [My life is done now.] I done my share. I hope you live as long as me. I done the right thing all the time. If I owe something, I like to come see Mr. Landry and I'm gonna pay it. I don't believe I got no enemy. If somebody got something against me, I don't know. I told you, like I say, I treat everybody right, everybody treat me right. I made a good living.

When the God gonna be ready to take me, I'm ready to go.

"Raise chickens, sell eggs, raise hogs, sell that."

STELLA QUEEN

Stella Woods Queen was born December 27, 1892, on Acadia Plantation, deep in the sugar-cane country of Louisiana. Her father, Harrison Woods, had emigrated from Texas in the 1880s to Acadia, where he served as head teamster until the 1930s. Her mother, Varinda Walker, was a local girl.

As a child, Stella attended formal school only three years. At the age of twelve she stopped attending school and, like many young blacks, went to work planting sugar cane. She would continue working on Acadia, either in the fields or as a housekeeper, for most of her life.

Stella's first marriage was to Joseph Woods, a childhood sweetheart, who worked on Acadia. Unfortunately the marriage was short-lived, lasting only a little less than four years. Woods contracted a disease in 1911 that was unidentifiable at the time, and died September 11, 1911.

Mrs. Queen stayed on Acadia following the death of her husband, working and living with her sisters. In 1914, Tom Queen, a native of Houma (in Terrebonne Parish), while visiting relatives on Acadia, met Stella and settled down with her. Stella at the time still worked in the fields, cutting cane by hand with a cane knife, and also working in the boardinghouse on the plantation.

The Depression years changed things on Acadia, and for a while the Queens worked as sharecroppers. In 1939 new owners took over the plantation and restored it to its former prosperity. After World War II, the Queens were semiretired, working their own gardens.

By the 1960s the Queens were fully retired, living in the same house they had shared since 1913. Mr. Queen became ill in 1972 and died in 1975. During his illness, Mrs. Queen made one of her infrequent trips from her home to visit him in Baton Rouge.

Today at eighty-three Mrs. Queen is still extremely active. She lives by herself now, on Acadia, still doing all her own housework.

—RICK ESTEVENS, RANDALL DETRO, DAVID PLATER.

PHOTOGRAPHS BY MURPHY COLE.

—TOM BECNEL, ADVISER FOR LAFOURCHE HERITAGE '76.

MY DADDY HOME was from San Antonio, Texas. He was a young man—he said he was working as a cowboy, you know, with the cattle and things. And, he said he left home and came to Acadia. That's what he told us; he said he left home, he left all his people behind. I know we got plenty people out there, but we don't know them, you see. And he come out here, and he settled out here and he married my ma. They got some bad— they got good and bad, and I was born right here on this plantation. And I made my eighty-three years old. I'm the oldest one on the place. I was born right here in a one-room house.

My daddy was the head teamster. He used to ring the bell, right by the boss's window in the yard, and then he would go to the window and knock and the boss would get up and tell him what to do. And then he'd go around to every house and he'd wake up all of the people in the morning, now. And then they would get up and go catch the mules. They used to ring two bells in the morning. And the last bell, then the field hands would go to work. They used to get a dollar and forty cents a day hauling cane. They was the teamsters. They put it in the wagon and bring it to the carboxes. They had a hoist there. Would unload it off their wagon and put it in the carboxes, and the railroad dummy would come there and pull the carbox to the sugar factory. All of the men would run the factory. They've died, it's been so long. And most of them were colored men. And they used to make the sugar and everything, and [when we were children], we used to go in there every Sunday. They would let us go in there every Sunday and go all up on top the sugarhouse—all in the rooms. But we couldn't go in there in the week, you know, when they'd be working. They didn't want us to come in there in the week time; they'd be busy. And we used to go in there worrying them for the lumps of sugar what they used to make. Miss Nanny used to tell them, to leave us do it every Sunday. Miss Nanny and Mr. Andrew owned the plantation.

The white people that used to be here, they used to be friendly. They used to be friendly and they did like the colored people, you see. All the white people would be on the place, they would like the colored people. And any way they could help you, they'd help you. And never did have no fuss or nothing between the colored and the white. They all used to get along nice together on the place.

The people used to be kind and nice to you, and help you, you know when you'd need help. If you didn't have nothing, if you didn't have food, or clothes, or anything, they would give it to you, you see. They'd help you out. I like most every boss on this place.

Now, my cousin used to drive Mr. Andrew and Miss Nanny. Used to drive them in a big black carriage. I'll never forget that. And it had a top all the way 'round, and my cousin used to drive them every day. And when Mr. Andrew got paralyzed, he couldn't turn his head, you see; he'd have to keep his head straight when he got paralyzed. And my cousin had to drive him every day down here, and when we used to see him coming, we'd run out there to the road to meet them out there. And he'd sit up there laughing at us. That was a number one good man—Mr. Andrew Price. And when Mr. Andrew Price died, Miss Nanny had a train come in here to git his body.

But they treated us good then. We could go to the boss and get how much money that they'd need, they'd go ask the boss to lend it to them. And the boss would lend them just what they asked for. And when they would work and make a payday, they would take two or three dollars at a time till he paid that paying. Now if they needed any more, they could go get more, and if they get sick and needed a doctor, I don't care how many times you'd see the doctor, they gonna get the doctor for you. You see, the place would pay that doctor.

When they was too old to work, this place used to set them free. They would give them so much a day and they would give them the board. They had a big boardinghouse here, and they had women in there to cook, and all they had to do was to go there and get their three meals a day. They go there and if they want to eat it there, they eat it there, and if they didn't want to eat it there, they'd take a big bucket and go there and get it in a bucket.

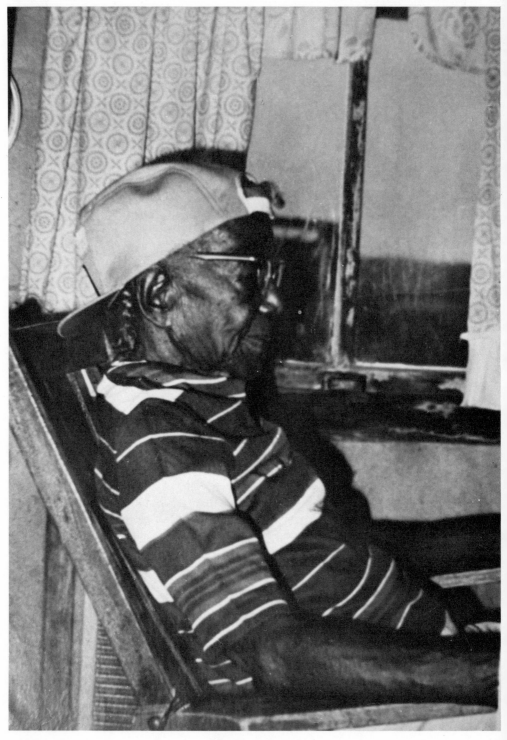

Stella Queen

Now, when my first husband was sick and dying, they never took nary a nickel from me for the payment of none of them doctor bills. They paid it themself.

The people didn't have to worry. You see, they didn't have to worry. They saw them free. And they'd give them so much a week, you see, to buy tobacco and cigarettes, and they didn't have to buy no clothes because they used to furnish them clothes. They used to furnish them clothes and they give them money to buy their cigarettes, their tobacco, and any of them other stuff they wanted like that. Every week they would give them money for to buy that.

They used to tell me I used to work so much. I started to working in the fields when I was twelve years old. The first work I done was plant cane. And I used to cut cane—I used to cut by the ton. I cut with the lead men in the field. I cut the row behind them, the lead men, and we had to keep right with the gang like the other people; they didn't see how I done it.

Then they paid us with Acadia tickets. They was white—almost the size of a dollar bill. How many days you made, they would have it punched on that card. Just like if you make thirty or forty dollars, it would be punched on that card. We was working by the day, and it would be punched every day on that card. But every month we could cash them in, and every store in Thibodaux took them. But some of them people, they never had none to cash because they used to spend them before they cashed them. But any store took them tickets. And if you go and buy with them, that what you had left out of it, they gonna give you the cash money—that's what they gonna give you. They give you your change in cash. They were good to us there, like I said.

Now the overseer that I was working for, Mr. Joe Smith, I was working for him when I got older, and he stayed in the boardinghouse. He never was married and he stayed in the big boardinghouse, and I worked for him all the time, and I had to take care of everything he had. And I had to go over there and work for him every morning—I'd go clean the room up, put his water and everything in there and fix everything, and take his dirty clothes and bring them to my house and wash and iron them in my house and take them back over there.

I used to work in the field and work for him, too. I used to get up at three o'clock in the morning and I go work for sixteen dollars a week, then I'd come back and I'd go in the field and work. Sometimes when I didn't have time in the day, we'd grind meal at night and Tom would help me. And Tom used to have to tend to Mr. Joe's chickens. Mr. Joe used to raise plenty of chickens, you see, and Mr. Joe used to have two cows there at the time. And Tom used to have to tend to his things, and tend to his horse. And when Mr. Joe got sick, Tom would have to go to Thibodaux every day and get his paper. When Mr. Joe didn't be sick, he'd go hisself. And I used to be scared for Tom to ride Mr. Joe's horse, because Mr. Joe's horse was wild, you see. He was a great big red horse, and he was wild. And I say, "Mr. Joe," I say, "Paul's gonna kill Tom."

He say, "No he ain't. He ain't gonna do him nothing." But I used to be scared. Every day Tom used to have to go get his paper when he be sorta sick, and laying in the bed.

And I had the three rooms to clean in the morning, and fix everything for him. And I had to wash his clothes, and I had to iron them. And I had to take it over there, and then his bed and things would all need clean things on them. I had to change them. He didn't have to tell me nothing. I had it in charge. And the morning he took sick, it was lucky they had a high wind that morning; I had the door unlatched, and the wind blowed it open, and he was over at the boardinghouse calling for Tom, and I went to shut the door and by me shutting the door, I heard him calling for Tom. So, I jumped down off the porch and I runned on over there, and I asked him what was the matter, and he told me. He did call me Stella; he never did call me "Coot." Mr. Joe used to call me by my right name. And he said, "Stella, I'm just as sick as I can be."

And I say, "What's the matter?"

And he said, "Go get Tom quick."

I said, "Tom's gone to set his traps." Tom was gone to set some traps over in the pasture. Tom would catch rabbits and coons in his traps right there.

So he said, "Git him right away."

So I got scared, you know, for to see him sick like that, because I did love him, you see, because he was so nice to me, you know, to me and Tom. So I went running. I liked to fell, and I hollered and hollered till I made Tom heared me back there. And Tom heared me and I told Tom, "Come here quick." And Tom got close to me and I say, "Come on," I say, "Mr. Joe's as sick as he can be."

So Tom come, and Tom made it there, and he told Tom, he say, "You run and git Tay Brown." And Tay Brown was in the field farming, making cane. He say, "You run and git Tay." So Tom made it out in the field and got him.

So when he got there, Mr. Joe said, "Take me to the hospital right away." So he went and he got his cart, and Mr. Joe called me when he got ready to go; he called me and he said, he say, "Stella, I gonna send back, and I'm gonna tell you what to send. But," he say, "now you know what you do." He say, "You do just like you've been doing in here." He say, "You come every-day, clean up, open the boardinghouse, let it air out." That's what he told me when he was leaving to go to the hospital. He say, "Do like you're doing all the time." He say, "I don't know how long I'm gonna be in the hospital, but," he say, "you just do just like you always do." He said, "Stella," he say,

"I'm going." He say, "I might be back and I might not." And them's the last words he told, and I started to cry when he told me because I didn't like for him to tell me that. He say, "I might be back and I might not."

And sure 'nuff, they took him along. I went in there and they put on a paper what for me to send him, you know. How many pair of 'jama suits and night suits for to send up there to the hospital. And I went on and I got them, and I sent them to him. He didn't live no more than about two weeks.

And Mr. Joe owed us for a month's work, but after he was in the hospital, we was waiting until he came out of the hospital to get us pay. So when he died, Dr. Gray and them had it in charge, and Dr. Gray come and he told us that he was going to pay us all. You see, he was going to the bank and he was gonna take some money out of the bank and pay us. And that's what he done. And got us money.

And the day Mr. Joe died, Mr. Joe had two big big pistols right on the chair by his bed. That's where he kept the pistols, you see, right on the side by his bed. And they had a big old box of bullets. He used to sleep in there by hisself, you see. And if anybody would come on him, all he had to do was reach over and get them.

One man he shot through the window. And it was lucky that Mr. Joe wasn't sitting by the window that night. Mr. Joe would sit by his window every night and read his paper. They say it was him done it; they couldn't prove it, though. And after that, Mr. Joe wouldn't take no chances. Mr. Joe kept his pistols right there on the side of him.

But Tom and me made a good life there. Everybody had two mules to work. Everybody, they would work two mules to the plow, and the cultivator, and the moline. They'd use two mules, and everybody what worked the mules, they make five days a week; and on the Saturday, they go and catch their mules to go work the land for theirself. Once a week, Tom would knock off, he would work for himself. And he would knock off once a week and take my things and go sell them, and that's the way we made us a living at this house. Make Irish potatoes, beans, cabbage, mustard, turnips, and we used to sell them by the cartloads. Raise chickens, sell eggs, raise hogs, sell that, and we all the time had money in those days. We cleaned all that land up back there, over that bridge. We used to make patches. We clean it with a cane knife and briar hooks and hoes; that's what we cleaned the land with.

Anywhere we wanted a piece of land we'd ask them for it. They tell us, "Go take it." And we go clean it up. They used to tell us, "If you want the land, go take it where you see they ain't using it." And then we go down there and clean the land up.

We'd plant Irish potatoes and sweet potatoes. And we used to make so much Irish potatoes we didn't have place to put them. We used to crawl under the house and put them all up under the house in the dirt, and we used to sell them in the summertime.

Then inside of the crib, they had a great big old partition. And inside the crib was where they kept all the corn for the mules, and if we want shucks, we used to get them there for the mattress. And moss. That's what we used to use. We used to go in the swamps and pick the moss. You take a stick and git it off the trees. We'd get it green. We would pile it up, just stack it all up in a big pile, and pour water on it everyday. And we used to turn it back, you see. We'd put that water on it and turn it back. And when it gets black, we'd just take it up and take tubs and wash it and hang it all out on the lines to dry. And after it was dry, we pick all the sticks out of it. We used to sell it. Sometimes I would sell about ten dollars' worth at the time. The carts used to come in here and get it from us.

I'd have one shuck mattress and one moss mattress to the bed. Then we'd take some of that moss and make pillows with it. And we'd wash them mattresses twice a year. We'd split them down on one side and we'd wash them mattresses and pick the moss. Finally I went to the store in 1958 and I bought one mattress and I paid on it on time. I paid sixty-eight dollars for that mattress. They had it sent to my house, but I still have moss pillows.

So we got along fine. One thing Tom had that he was proud of, he had a great big horse, and that horse would let you know if anybody was coming to your house. He could be in the yard; all you had to do was look and that horse was gonna let you know. That was some horse, and Tom used to drive that horse in Thibodaux, and I would be scared for Tom to go to Thibodaux with the vegetable cart and the horse because sometimes he would get scared of them cars, you see. I thought she would run off with him. When the horse died, Tom like to cried about that because that horse wasn't sick at all. And when your daddy come [speaking to David Plater, one of the interviewers], your daddy seen that horse running in the pasture. And he slipped. There was a little ditch running across there and he slipped and he fell. And when he fell I was looking at him. He didn't move after he fell. And I called and told Tom, he was back over there cleaning up some lamps. And I called Tom, and Tom answered me, and I say, "Come see." I say, "I believe this horse dead."

So when I told Tom that, Tom looked like he didn't want to come, and he looked at him and he say, "He sure is dead."

And a little while after he died your daddy come and he looked at him, and he told me, he say, "Coot," he say, "he must have had heart trouble." I didn't know no horse had heart trouble. That's what your daddy say, "He must have had heart trouble."

I say, "They have heart trouble?"

They say, "Yeah. That's what he had." That's what Mr. Plater told me.

But we had a cart, a small-size cart. The day before [going to town], we would gather a gang of vegetables and would be up till twelve o'clock at night bunching them—you know, putting them in packs. Tying them. And we, oh, we used to sell corn. Let it dry, and cull it, and then they'd allow us to go in the fields when they'd pull corn and scrap all the corn we wanted, and we would take all that and sell it in Thibodaux. I had a square of sweet corn, and the corn was getting ready to sell, and Mr. Plater's cow was broked out and got in it. Oh, did she ever get in it. And I cried. I cried. And so I told Tom. I say, "I'm gonna tell Mr. Plater about his cow when he pass by here." So, when I seed him coming, I run out there and I told him, and I say, "Mr. Plater," I say, "your cow has just done ate my corn up."

Rick Estevens

And Mr. Plater looked at me, and he say, "Well, I tell you what you do." He say, "You go back out here and see how much they ate," and he say, "When I come back you tell me." And he say, "I'm gonna pay you for it." And he paid me. He come back about two days after that and I was at the house, and somebody knocked at the door. And I come to the door and Mr. Plater was sitting on the bench, and he had this book. He say, "I want to pay you for your corn." He say, "I'm gonna pay you for your corn now." And I was so glad.

And we used to make pumpkins. I couldn't raise them pumpkins up. They was too big. And I had two big henhouses and I had chickens all in that henhouse, and every week I used to sell a cage of chickens. I used to sell a cage of chickens; and the eggs, me and Tom used to live off the eggs. Tom used to have wire fence for me to raise the younger chickens in. And I used to have two milk cows. They was slick black and they had white faces. I done forgot the name you call them. They had white faces, and they titters were about [six inches] long. Oh, great big old titters. And talk about milk. They used to make so much butter till I used to sell it to the people. I was milking two cows, and they used to give *some* milk. Tom used to get up and milk them in the morning before he go to work, and I'd milk them in the evening time.

I would sell the calves. Once I had a little calf what was three months old. And it was another man and he had another calf. My calf was four days older than his calf. And he told me, he said, "I'm gonna sell my calf." So he went and got the butcher to come and look at his calf.

So I told him, I say, "When the butcher come looking at your calf, tell him to come to my house and look at mine." So the butcher looked at his and the butcher came to my house and looked at mine. And he asked me how old my calf was. I said, "He's three months old."

And he asked me, he say, "Well, what you been feeding him with?"

I said, "I been feeding him with sweet feed." I used to get some sacks of sweet feed and feed him all, and then I used to leave him plenty milk.

And he said, "Well I do declare." And so the man bought my calf, and he didn't buy the man's what went and got him. He told him he'd buy his another time. Oh, mine was big, big, big, and this wide. He had a white face, and he was red, and oh, he was some big and pretty. And things was cheap. And the man paid me seventy dollars for it and it was three months old.

And we used to sell gumbo—we would make a big old pot of chicken gumbo and we would put oysters in that chicken; and we would make pies. I used to make pies all day Saturday. I was the one used to make the best pie. I would start working and I had a big old clothes basket—a great big brand new basket—I didn't use it for nothing but to put pies in it and it was about this high. I'd be baking pies all day Saturday till it was time for the fair that Saturday night. And we used to make money, too.

So we made some money and we put up food for ourselves for so we had plenty to eat. They'd plant, oh, the peas and things in the field. They'd allow us to go there and pick green peas, pick dried peas and put them up for the winter. Those cowpeas, we used to have them by the barrelful. We used to go twice a day. We used to go in the morning and pick green peas to have for us dinner, then we'd take a big old sack and we'd go after dinner for to pick dry peas to put up for the winter. And the people would have barrels of peas in their house for to cook for the children. Miss Nanny Price and them, they'd allow us to do that.

And we used to raise and eat beans, Irish potatoes, cabbage, mustard, all them different things. Snap beans.

We used to cook out in the yard. We used to take bricks and stack them around, you know, then we used to get us a piece of tin and lay it over them bricks and make fire under there and cook on there—put us pots on top of that tin and cook in the summertime when it was real hot. In the wintertime, you cooked in the house.

We used to cook us food and us white beans. We used to put them on to boil and let them boil until it starts to breaking up. When they start to breaking up, we'd get us onions and parsley and green onion tops, and we would cut them up and we'd put meat to fry. And when us meat fried, we'd put them onions and parsley and things in grease and let it fry brown and we'd put in beans, and we'd let them beans cook down, and we'd put salt and pepper in it. And I'm telling you it was something, too.

And we used to cook us snap beans. We'd put them on with the meat and the lard, and we'd let them cook; and we'd get Irish potatoes and we'd cut Irish potatoes up, and when the snap beans get most done, we'd put Irish potatoes in the snap beans whole and let them cook until they get out. That's the way we used to cook snap beans.

And cabbage, we used to put us cabbage on; we'd put the fat on to fry and then put the pot about half full of water and then we'd put cabbage in there and we'd cook us cabbage down. That's the way we used to cook us food.

And we used to shell us corn and me and Tom used to make all of us own meal. We used to grind it. We bought a big-size mill and we'd sit down and shell us corn, and then we would grind it in that big mill we used to have. We'd put it full of corn and we'd grind it. And when we'd grind it, sometimes we used to grind it three times to get it fine. We never did have to buy meal. Then we'd make corn bread.

I used to make that all through the week, and I still make it. I made some yesterday. You take your corn bread and you sift your meal in a pan. You put your salt in there first; then you make it up, and then you take your one egg or two egg, if you want, and you bust it in that corn bread, and you beat that. Then you put the baking powder in there, and you beat it. Then you put it in a pan and run it in the stove and bake it.

Then we used to make us own light bread. I can make good light bread. I never used to buy none till here lately. We used to bake enough bread to last us the whole week. We'd bake a big pile of bread like that on us wood stove. I just there lately sold one of my wood stoves what I had to a fellow at Larose.

And we used to pull candy. Every winter my daddy used to get a whole barrel of syrup from the sugarhouse. They would let us have a whole barrel for five dollars, and they let us have a whole hundred pound of sugar for five dollars. We never had to go to the store to buy that 'cause we'd get it from the sugarhouse.

Then in the springtime, we'd make all the candy we wanted because they had tanks in the sugarhouse. They used to have their soft sugar—brown sugar—in the sugarhouse, and they used to have syrup in there. And when we wanted to make candy, we'd just take us water buckets and we'd go there and get it. They'd allow us to take it. They'd leave one of the doors open where we could go through in there and get it.

That candy, you see, you cook it. You can tell when it gets ready to pull. You cook it till it gets ropy; then you get you a big pan and you pour it out in there. And time it commence to get a little cool, you takes some butter and you grease your hands all over with that butter. Then you get it out there and you start to pulling it. Then we could cut it, you know. We could cut it and make pieces.

Then another thing, the colored people had the pasture back in there, and they had the stable there, and that's where they kept the mules and things, in the stable. And that's where they raised the hogs in. They used to have hogs three feet tall. The place used to be full of hogs. And they'd kill a big one on a Saturday and sell it to us, and we'd get a great big piece of meat for two bits. We used to salt it, and sometimes Tom used to get gunpowder, and Tom would put it in the barrel and you'd put it all over that meat. And talk about good eating meat. Just let it stay in there and then eat it, like pickled meat. That gunpowder used to give it the taste. And we never did have to buy no lard no time, and no time never did have to buy no meat, me and Tom. We used to raise all that.

You know where I used to walk to catch fish? You know the Chacahoula? I used to walk to Chacahoula out there and fish. We'll get up early in the morning, rising about four o'clock, and we'd leave and we'd stop there at Schriever. And, we'd wait till the stores opened and we'd get us a lunch;

and before it'd get night that day, we'd be back and we used to have sacks of choupics upon us head. Tote them from Chacahoula; and we used to dry them and we'd smoke them; and when we smoked them, then we'd take them and put them in us icebox.

And we used to crawfish. We used to catch crawfish and things in Bayou Blue. It was a small bayou that started right in back of my house.

And they used to give big fairs. They used to allow us, if we wanted, to give a big fair and make us money. They'd tell us we could give us a fair. All we had to do was to tell Mr. Willie Price we want to give us a fair Saturday, and he'd say go ahead. And right out there, they had the open place. They didn't have no houses in it, and they had trees planted on in there and they had them little pens made around the trees. And they used to keep them whitewashed, and that's where we used to give us fairs. And we used to have the band to come and play. And the people would come from all around and we would be there all night selling. We used to do that, sometimes every month.

And we wouldn't have no trouble at all. All the different people used to come from all around and we used to have beer in them kegs, and we used to sell them five cents a glass. And the people used to come from all around when they'd hear it say somebody over here was giving a fair. And we'd get some wine and we would get some whiskey.

And we used to sell gumbo for the fair.

And now other Saturdays when we weren't having fairs, we go to the sugarhouse and get us hot water. We didn't have to heat no water. We take us tubs and go there and get us water and wash, and then we'd mop up the house on a Saturday night, and put all the clothes down in a tub. And on a Sunday morning, we'd get up and hang them up and then we'd go to church.

I was fourteen years old when I made up my mind to get religion. And after I got religion, they start to run a revival meeting to get some more to join the church. Well, they got eleven besides me. My sister got baptized with me, and my daddy got baptized with me. I was the first one in the house got religion; then they got religion, my sister and my daddy.

The religion don't teach you no mean, evil things, you see, to do to your neighbor. Your religion teaches you to treat your neighbor like you want them to do by you. That's what religion is. You got to treat the people right. Then you'd be feeling God. And when you do that, you're gonna have a blessing, and He's gonna always take care of you. If you lead a good life, He's gonna take care of the balance. That's what He's gonna do for you. He give me a long life. And look at my husband. He was ninety-three years old.

And God is not like man. Now, if you do a crime, God is not gonna jump

up and kill you because you done that crime. He'll make you suffer in a way for it, but he ain't gonna jump up and kill you. Your days is so, your bounds is so. And now you ain't gonna die till that time comes. If you was borned to get killed, or get drowned, or anything happen like that, that was set for you, you see. That was set for you. And, you ain't gone till that time comes.

And He don't sleep. His eyes is over the whole world. Now, some people wondering how that is, but God do not sleep. He sits on His throne and He watches the world. And He got His eyes on everything in the world. And He know the good from the bad, because He made us. If it wouldn't be for Him, there wouldn't be no world, and there wouldn't be nobody in it. Now the people don't know how that was done; and they ain't never really find out who made God. They ain't never really found out that. That's a wonderful thing, you see. Who made God. They ain't never find that. They done searched the Bible and everything, and they ain't never find out how God commence, but He's there.

And them that's died, they only sleeping. They gonna rise when that day come, when the trumpet gonna blow. They gonna wake them up. You see the flesh is gone, but the soul is living; and when that day comes, they gonna rise. And the kingdom is gonna be sitting right here on earth.

Tom believed that, like me. The Lord even called him to preach. Did I tell you how I met Tom? His home was in Houma. That was his home and this was my home. He had a sister living here. My husband had been dead one year and Tom's sister was living over the street in the front of us, and when I saw him step in there that evening, I had never saw him before. He come to see about his sister. He had on a Stetson hat, you know. Those Stetson hats were in style then. And he had on a black suit; I never saw a suit like that before. And he had on a pair of black patent leather low quarters, and he had a small-size feet; you see, his number was a six.

So I was on the porch—I had a chair out there—and I was leaning over the chair and looked at him when he come to his sister's house. He stayed there a couple of weeks. And she told him, she say, "You can get a wife." She say, "I know a good wife that you can get you." And she say, "She stay right over the street, over there." They say, "Her husband is dead."

And so, sure enough, he come over there and he made himself friendly. My mama's brother told me, he say, "You courting, huh?"

I say, "Courting, courting how?" And I laugh. And I laugh and I say, "I ain't courting nobody."

"Yeah," he say, he say, "Mr. Queen coming here to see you."

And I say, "Well, he ain't never say nothing to me." I say, "He must be coming to see my other sister."

My uncle say, "No, he's coming to see you." He had told my uncle that, you see. That's why my uncle told me that. My uncle told me, "You don't believe me, you ask him."

So, I did. When he come back to us place, I asked him, "Who are you coming there to see?"

And he said, "I'm coming to see you." That's what he said, "I'm coming to see you." And sure enough he did. And about three months after that he wanted to marry me. I was scared to marry him because I didn't know nothing about him. But ask me he did, and he made me a husband for sixty-three years. I lived with him for a year before I married him.

My husband used to make me happy. He never hit me a lick. Sixty-three years and he never hit me, nary a lick. We fussed sometimes, but that was all to it.

Now I know what he done for me. The doctors ordered me once to go in the hospital. I swole up about this big around, and I couldn't lay down. They couldn't put a spoon in my mouth. And the doctor ordered me to go to the hospital, and he weren't willing for me to go to the hospital, and neither was my mother. My mother told the doctor that day, she say, "No, we ain't willing." She say, "If she die," she say, "let her die here." That's what my mama told the doctor. She say, "We ain't willing for her to go."

So the doctor went on back that day, and he doubled right around and come back again and he told 'em, "Now if y'all don't send her to the hospital, don't let her lay down in the bed." That's what the doctor said, "Don't let her lay down in the bed. Make her sleep in a rocking chair"; and he say, "Prop the rocking chair with a stick," the doctor told them. And, "Let her sleep in there and put two pillows behind her." He said, "Don't let her lay down in a bed." And eighteen long nights I slept in that chair—eighteen nights. And Tom worked every day and stayed up with me *every* night.

I always try to treat my husband good, and I always done what's right by him. He never had no complaints about me doing him nothing of the kind. I always tried to take care of him. When he was in the hospital, the doctors wanted me to sign to put him in a home. He wanted to put him in a home, and I wouldn't stand for it. When we married we stood on the floor and we said we was going to stay together until death do us part. And I fall on my knees. When I got married, them was the words I said, "Until death separate us."

And that's what separate us.

"Go sit outside and say hi!"

BLANCHE GOLDEN AND ANNIE LARKINS

Blanche Golden was born October 21, 1913, at Horse Cave, Kentucky, which is about ten miles from Mammoth Cave. She married when she was sixteen and has helped to support her ill husband and her children since the Depression. To earn money, she has baby-sat, worked in a laundry, tended bar, worked in a dry cleaner's, managed the candy counter at Kresge's, and worked for the railroad. She worked in the roundhouse at the railyards, as a switchman on the "goat," a type of motorized cart. She also worked at Admiral, the appliance factory, for eleven years and then managed the Galesburg Salvation Army Store for eight years before her recent retirement. Presently, she keeps active by reading and plays bingo several nights a week. She manages to win often and the money always comes in handy. When I called to talk with her recently, she told me that she had been dreaming about playing a bingo game, and she thought she finally got the last winning number. She sat up in bed and called out, "I've got it!" She laughed when she told me the story. "I guess," she said, "that it just goes to show ya' that we people who are so involved in life can't even get away from it in our sleep."

Annie Larkins was born in Monmouth, Illinois, and went to public school there. She was part of a family of all girls and says they

were close then and have remained so. She worked in a local pot-
tery factory for over twenty years, leaving occasionally to have chil-
dren. Although most of her time there was spent in the greenware
division, she says she worked in about every area of the factory.
She says factory life can be a lot of fun because you can joke and
talk with the people working around you. Annie also worked as a
farmer for seven years. She's plowed fields, milked cows, and sat up
all night with sick hogs, and says she wouldn't want to farm again.
Later she worked in the Farm Bureau as a soil tester, where she
learned how to give advice about the chemicals needed to make
fertile soil. For the last few years Annie has worked at the Gales-
burg Salvation Army Store and loves the variety of people she
meets there.

—RENÉE BUTLER, SHERRY DYE, LYNN BALLARD, CINDY GUSTINE.
—SHERYL LEE HINMAN, ADVISER FOR LOMBARD JUNIOR HIGH
SCHOOL, GALESBURG, ILLINOIS.

BLANCHE: I was born in Horse Cave, Kentucky, October 21,
1913. It was a very small town. They named the town Horse Cave because
there was a horse that fell in the cave that was in the middle of the town
and when they put the railroad through and got a post office, they called
the place Horse Cave—it's about ten miles from Mammoth Cave.

My father was a sharecropper in Kentucky. He raised tobacco. Since I
was so small, four or five when we moved, I have very few memories of that
early life. Mostly it's made up of little silly things. Like I remember that a
kid called Jimmy D. said that if I would get him a can of worms and grasshoppers then Ma would make me a pie. I worked like a trooper, and was I
mad when I found out I'd been tricked! She wouldn't make me a pie. She
didn't know anything about the deal. I remember we had a horse and
buggy. Once my parents told me that we were going to meet friends. Then
I heard them say they'd have to go by a spring. Well, I didn't know what a
spring might be. I got so frightened that I hid all the way under the lap
robe.

We left for the north after my father got a letter from relatives who had
already moved up. They seemed to have settled in well, so the family
moved up too. You know there's a rumor about Southern people. They say
that they aren't friendly, that they're kind of closed. I think that's untrue.
I've always found them very warm. I was glad to have some Southern people with me when I first came up, because right then this area of Illinois

had a lot of foreign settlers. There were groups of Swedes and Lithuanian people in the town. We didn't mix much for quite a while. You know, I wish the kids of today would work to create a feeling of friendliness in America. It's hard. TV and air conditioners have drawn people off their porches. I want to say, "Go sit outside and say hi to people more."

There were lots of crazy things going on when I was a kid. They'd never get by with it now. They upended outhouses or pushed 'em back so people would go to step in the outhouse at night and they fall in the hole. Not just on Halloween either.

And I remember the first lady I saw smoking. It was in the evening, and we lived on Third Street in Kewanee. There was a flower shop across the street. She waited until she got a block and a half from town. And I thought that was really something to see her light a cigarette and go down the street smoking.

And when I was about these girl's age [thirteen] they had no taverns. They were "blind pigs," bootlegging joints. You'd knock on the door. Somebody'd look out, and you'd say, "Joe sent me." I can even show you one place in Galesburg that used to be one. Down by the Deluxe Cafe there was a stairway there, and there used to be hotel rooms up above. I went there with some people, and they knocked on the door, and they named who sent them. Then we were admitted, and that was fun. A lot of them were in people's homes and in their basements, and it had to be pretty quiet because the neighbors would complain. The only times I went it was mostly just drinking home brew, beer. Over on Park Street a man had a whole back yard like a cave underneath; he made Kewanee Red—whiskey. Geesh, how did we get on that topic sitting here in the Salvation Army!

I was married when I was sixteen. It was terrible getting married early. It was during the Depression. I lived in a twelve-by-eighteen-foot room with five children and a man who had epileptic seizures and wasn't able to work. So I'd work, and it was just hand to mouth, believe me. Because of that, to this day, it bugs me to see someone leave food on a plate. There were a lot of things I don't even like to think about because it was so sad. Course we were all in the same boat almost it seemed. I was fortunate to be where everyone was in the same condition I was in. We leaned on one another. I remember we used to get a relief order. They gave you an order for enough meat for your family one day a week. Well, we had friends. Our last name began with E. Theirs began with R. So they'd eat with us the first part of the week when we got our relief order with meat, and we ate with them at the last part. So we shared. The rest of the time we ate beans and lots of them. In summer you'd have a garden, but with a twelve-by-eighteen-foot room you didn't have much place to store anything.

I've baby-sat, worked in a laundry. I've tended bar, worked in dry clean-

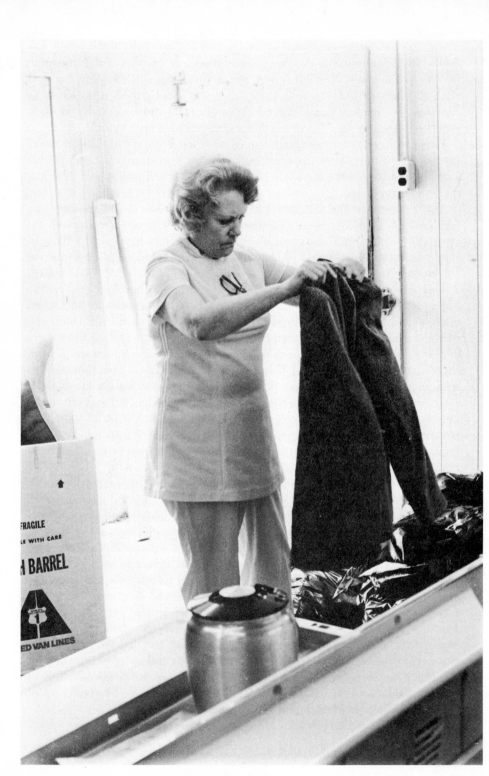

Annie Larkins

Blanche Golden

ing. I had the candy counter in Kresge's. I worked in the roundhouse at the railyards. That was a building at the railroad yard and it was round. It was a place to look over the trains. When they came back from a trip on the road, the engine was completely gone over. There were specialists for each part—the lights, the wheels, etc. If they brought a train in on a Monday, we could probably send it out sometime Wednesday. There was quite a crew that used to work there, and I still see a lot of them when I go to the bingo nights. The retired men and the wives all come down there. My first job down there, I sprayed that round front end. Then I got down and sprayed each firebox. I used a kind of silver spray. Then I got promoted to be the switchman. There were lots of jobs to do for the trains. Someone had to wash out the tanks that held the water. I bet there were ten to fifteen on a crew to clean up the engines. There were people who checked all the brakes—people who knocked all the fire out of the engines. Ashes and everything had to be cleaned out. They would paint or refinish any little nick that appeared. I don't know how they take care of the diesel engines, but I know we really were careful back then with steam engines.

Then I worked at the Admiral factory for eleven years and here for eight years.

ANNIE: I worked down at the Farm Bureau in the lab testing soil, before this. The farmers would bring in all the soil samples from the different fields. We'd grind it up until it was real fine. Then we'd make three tests on it—lime, phosphate, and potash. Then we had a lot of forms to fill out. We could tell the farmer what kind of fertilizer he should have.

And I worked in a pottery for years. It was over in Monmouth, Illinois. I was there twenty-some years altogether. Most of the time I was what they called a finisher. I got the green clay pots that came from the wheels, and then we would finish the pots by smoothing out the rough edges. Then we'd take it out to put on the drier floor. Later other girls would do the slipping [adding glaze]. It was fun, because we were in a room where there were a lot of us and we could always holler at each other and carry on with jokes and all. Right beside me there were about four of us. Now a lot of that is done by machines. It really cut out a lot of jobs. Factory work can be a lot of fun.

BLANCHE: Oh yeah, you never found a funnier place than a factory. You can carry on teasing and still work hard, too. They used to say out at Admiral Appliances where I worked that if you'd been there a half hour and didn't hear a rumor, start one!

ANNIE: When I was working at the pottery during the war, and that hasn't been so many years ago, they never hired colored people there. The bosses wanted to start hiring colored people because we were short of manpower. They came around and asked everybody that worked if we would mind working with a black person. Now isn't that something?

BLANCHE: I worked by a black man at Admiral and never met anyone nicer. That was 1952 to 1960. Things have changed for the better. Maybe we'll eventually get around to treating other people as we like to be treated.

Anyway, now me and Annie run this Salvation Army Store. I knew the Osburns, who were running the store, and they needed help three days a week. I took over in 1968. I used to be really frightened of some of the people who would come in and insist that I do a particular thing, but no more. You learn to think quick. Like when someone says to you, "Are you married or not?" I say, "Yes, she's married or not." You have to be flippant sometimes so things don't get too serious. I've been here over seven years, and I think I've had to call the police only three times, and I think that's real good.

ANNIE: It gets so that you can just pick out people that you are gonna have to be careful around. But one did fool us the other day. Just last week there was a kid outside walking up and down counting his steps. I figured he must be trying to measure the size of the building or something. When he came in I asked him what he was doing. He was a grown man. I thought maybe he was in construction or something.

BLANCHE: He said, "I'm waiting for my parents. May I sit down?" He just sat there in the chair and shook his foot. We could sense after a while that he was mentally retarded, but he didn't look that way.

We've had some weird ones. We had a lady come in very sincerely looking for a bra for her cat. When we were in the downtown location, we used to watch some of the local town characters having parties at the square. They'd hide the bottle in the burn barrel. Where the park benches are, there'd be five grown men sitting on one park bench. Course, the end ones would be hanging over, but they were all on one bench. And they'd take turns drinking. The police'd come over and shake 'em down, and they didn't have a thing on 'em. But one day the police hit the barrel. It had about four or five bottles of wine they took from there. I never saw such a sad-looking bunch of men in my life. Every once in a while they'd get mad, and they'd square off at each other, but they could hardly stand let alone give each other a fight.

ANNIE: We must tell them about the time when Old Jack came in for new clothes, and socks and all. We had to literally cut the socks off him. He'd been wearing them that long. We cut them off with a pair of scissors. We got him a decent set of clothes. It was sad. It really was sad. You meet all kinds.

BLANCHE: We've called the law a few times. We had one lady come running in the store and she said, "Call the police! Call the police! This man's chasing me down the street." This woman is morally a fine person, but she never meets a stranger. She talks to everyone. So I'm nosy. I go look out the door, and sure enough he's coming up through the parking lot. He's got a red cap on. So he went by the store and he sat in the park. Pretty soon he comes back. She's back in that store terrified. Terrified. He came in. I asked him to leave. He could see no reason why he should, so he sat and I went out the back door and went to the music store and called the police. They got him to go away. The next day was Annie's day off. It's along about three o'clock in the afternoon, and I'm talking on the telephone and somebody comes in the store, and I turned around, and there's that man looking at me. He told me he wanted an outfit of clothes, and I told him he'd have to go down to the church to get the order. I mean, if somebody comes in and wants something and needs it, we let 'em have it, but not in a situation like that. So I was kinda worried about that. I called the girls and told them he was coming. They were frightened of him, too, because he'd been in there the day before. So they locked the door, and I locked the store and

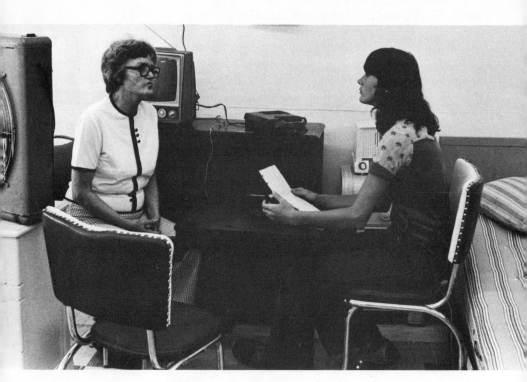

Blanche Golden and interviewer

went home. That guy was weird; there was something wrong with him. He's at the Mental Research Hospital now. The police finally had him put out there. The time the police took him from the store they got a clear bottle of liquor from him. They had to bodily pick him up and put him in the police car. He acted so limp, but he walked into this store under his own power.

We have one guy that comes in from the mental hospital. He wears women's shoes. He tries to get women's shoes all the time. I called security and asked them not to let him come in any more. We have one man that comes in and buys girdles and underpants. And then we have another one we call the Pocketbook Man. He goes through every one of the pocketbooks. If he came in now, he'd saunter all around and end up at the purses.

Most of the people are just down on their luck, and we try to welcome them and help them. A lot of the success of this store has come by word of mouth. We have a lot of people come in just to chew the fat. And yesterday a woman came in and dropped off some of her extra cucumbers from her garden. She said they were for anybody who came in and would like some of them. That's really neighborly and it shows that she feels comfortable enough doing things like that around this store. At the center, they call places like this the "country stores."

The things we sell are all donated, and people can write off the value of their donations on their taxes. Then we set the prices. I try to charge what I think I could pay if I were in their position or in my position as it is. And I will not put anything out, if I can help it, that one of my own family wouldn't wear. Now that's what I go by. Setting the price—sometimes that's hard, 'cause say a person brings in a suit and says, "This is all tailor-made and it was very expensive." That may be true but it was tailor-made for someone else. So values would change there. Value is in the eye of the beholder.

ANNIE: Like my son says, "It's a Salvation Army store, Mom, not a resale shop." That says a whole lot right there 'cause the Salvation Army stands for more than a resale shop. The money made in this store goes up to Davenport for rehabilitation. Sometimes they have seventy to eighty men up there. They're men that have lost their way—addicts, alcoholics. Sometimes they bail people out of jail and try to help them. The Salvation Army is a family thing. If a man is an officer, then his wife is too, and they hold the same rank. They are very religious and very strict. They have their own hospitals, doctors, insurance companies.

BLANCHE: The income from these stores goes to centers where the Salvation Army tries to rehabilitate people. And they get donations of things to sell from everywhere. Gosh, you couldn't begin to estimate it all. Everyday, all day long, people bring donations in to us. Think about that all over the nation and the world. The Salvation Army has got to be a billion-dollar corporation. The Salvation Army doesn't own the little buildings that have these Red Shield stores, but they do own the corps [church buildings] and the centers [rehabilitation areas]. The centers are the places where they rehabilitate all the men. And I think they do have places for women, too, but not in this vicinity. One day, though, some people called looking for Captain Briggs. They had a woman over in jail. The Salvation Army will bail poor women out of jail and help them that way. In Davenport the work programs are just all for men. They have an electrical shop, a shoe repair shop, a furniture repair shop. You can't imagine it all. They have one room just for all the dishes and odd novelties that come in.

If a man wants to get into the center, he has to be signed in first. The man would go to Captain Sullivan and be interviewed. Captain Sullivan is our boss. His main responsibility is the running of the stores. Lots of times it's men who are on parole, dope addicts, alcoholics; they're men in need of help. Up in Minnesota there are places where a lot of prisoners will come out for the day and work in a center then go back to prison that night. There's no set time period. A man could be there two weeks or six months. You never know. Some will stay a year and then head east, west, north, or south to another center. In fact, there's a little story about that I'd like to tell you. The night they had the going-away dinner for Brigadier and Mrs.

Aimic, she said, "There were a couple of ministers that died and went to
heaven. When they got there St. Peter said, 'I haven't got room for you
now, but if you'll wait a while, we'll let you in.' Pretty soon two other guys
came up and St. Peter let them right on in the door. Well, the ministers
were pretty curious about this so they went right over to the pearly gates
and asked St. Peter why those two got in, when they didn't. St. Peter just
looked at 'em and said, 'Oh, those two guys were Salvation Army truck
drivers, and you know them . . . they were just passing through.'"

And you couldn't ask for guys who treat us any better. Like the truck
drivers are usually real gentlemen to us.

ANNIE: You know the Salvation Army people have the greatest sense
of humor. I just delight in tormenting them. I went to the wedding of the
brigadier's daughter. He performed part of the ceremony, so when I went
through the line I teased him. I said, "Say, is it really legal if the father performs the ceremony?"

Salvation Army people have the image of being real serious. They can be
and they can be very business-like, but they are smart, well-trained people.
The women are strong. They don't believe in divorce, so the women know
they have a place. The women have a strong voice in deciding what's done.
You've never seen such workers in your life as you'll find in a Salvation
Army family. The kids and all. They just work like horses all the time. They
never want for much either. They make do with what they have. They're
good people to work with and for.

BLANCHE: And I think they make a difference! Right now I don't
think people are interested enough on a common sense level in other people's lives. I mean, not gossip. Just down to earth interest. Like a young
man came in the other day. He left. A few minutes later he came back. He
said, "Who should I call? There's a lady collapsed up here." He called an
ambulance. I asked if there was anybody out there with her. He said, "No."
I thought it would look a little better if another woman went out. I stood
till the ambulance came. It worried me about her. So I thought and
thought. I finally called the ambulance company later and they told me. She
had been on her way to Cottage Hospital to be admitted and collapsed. I
couldn't get it off my mind until I knew she was all right.

As for kids, I can't see a thing wrong with the kids today. There are a few
that have been troublemakers—but that was so even when I was a kid.
There's always good and there's always bad. Ninety per cent of the time
the stinkers grow up to be good citizens.

The one thing I can't stand is, if a kid does something bad they publicize
it. A lot of it could be kept out of the newspaper. I don't think it's fair. Why
not publish the good things that children are doing? That's human interest
as far as I'm concerned. I have twelve grandchildren and one great-grand-

daughter, and if I'm not gonna stand behind them, who's going to? I don't want kids labeled.

ANNIE: You know one of the best things to happen is not having any dress code any more. You're not labeled that way, either. You can be what you are—not what you got on. That's good. In my days you really had to wear nice clothes to be anybody. That wasn't fair, I didn't think.

BLANCHE: Another thing that makes me mad is groups that close other people out. Annie and I go to bingo at the Galesburg Moose Lodge. There's a group of women there that make me mad every time. They cluster together, save whole tables of seats for just their circle of friends, and stare at anyone who comes into their "territory." I can't do those things to people and I won't admire or associate myself with people who do. But I try not to be angry much. I'm too old for that. I'm sixty-two already. Maybe I should retire in three years, but I hope I don't have to. It means that you have time on your hands, and no goal. Unless you have a lot of money—then you can travel. I think it's cruel to make people retire.

ANNIE: You know, I think that's where a lot of the liberation movement came in, because women didn't really want to step down. They didn't want to go back home and keep house. They wanted to keep their jobs. Strong feelings about women and careers began right then. There's only one kind of work that I wouldn't care anything about going back to and that's farming. I just don't want to be a farmer again, and drive a tractor and all that. It's all too risky. You hurry up and get crops in and hurry to get them out.

BLANCHE: Right. And I'm slowing up every day. I could retire now. But I know if I retire I'll sit on my rear and get lazier and lazier. I have to be involved in life. Of course, if I could only find a rich man! Seriously, I've never wanted a lot of money. If I have enough to pay all the necessary bills and buy a few things, I'm perfectly happy. Those fabulously wealthy people don't look like they have much of a life of their own. If I had their money, I'd go down and make faces at the bank for the rest of the day.

ANNIE: They couldn't go out like us and play bingo. Maybe they ought to make us President and Vice-President. We could sure get in there and decorate the White House, couldn't we? We could bring in all our Salvation Army furniture.

BLANCHE: Sure, and set up a few bingo games there!

"I feel like they've broken our Great Spirit."

BAXTER YORK

Baxter York was born at Standing Pine, Leake County, Mississippi, in 1907. Born on a plantation, Baxter was able to start school in 1912, but soon found himself going to a government-operated school. In 1919 he transferred to a boarding school in Oklahoma and remained there until 1929. After high school he worked in an oil refinery in Ponca City, Oklahoma, but his interest in sports soon attracted him to Jim Thorpe's Oklahoma Indians' baseball team.

But because of his mother's failing health, the Choctaw Indian found himself returning to his native state, where he was immediately accepted as a new leader. His mother died shortly after his arrival in Mississippi, but Baxter was able to maintain her close relationship with other tribal members, and he soon was working with the tribal council as his mother had done. He was influential in proposing that the tribe formally organize, a vision that was realized in 1945.

After some twenty-seven years of service to his people, Baxter retired from public life, but not from helping his native people. Interested in all aspects of tribal affairs, Baxter enjoys working with the young Indian population and has a great popularity among them.

He devotes his time to the preservation of Choctaw cultural matters and is eager to share his knowledge with all.

—RICK BILLY. PHOTOGRAPHS BY JIMMY BEN.
—CHARLES PLAISANCE, ADVISER TO NANIH WAIYA,
PHILADELPHIA, MISSISSIPPI.

MOST OF OUR CULTURE and the language is, you might say, lost. And now we are in pollution, too. I feel that the people are multiplied so fast they are the ones that cause the pollution by not taking care of the waste that they have had in this country. Just like gasoline. We older people say that they are gonna run out. The people are using gasoline so fast, so many cars using gasoline they gonna drain this country. In the future they'll use up what we had in the ground so there won't be any gasoline. Pollution, if made by man, can be prevented. But they didn't realize that until lately. So there we are in deep pollution. [In the old days] we had virgin timber. There was no pollution because the virgin timber took care of what little pollution the Indians put out, and everything was clean. Water clean, everything was clean. As I say, the population was increasing fast when European people came in and begin to multiply. Indians begin to multiply, Negroes begin to multiply. Why, then, those are the things that cause the pollution.

We got to work on these problems. Someone got to teach how to preserve the cane, bow and arrow, the timber. And blowgun. They got to plant these seeds up in the swamp and keep this thing going, and the nature will take care of it for you. If you plant it, and fertilize it if it needs it, it will grow 'cause our land is not muck like. That's the only way I see that you can preserve and have the arts and crafts. Someone that knows how to teach it. They'll set a time and a date to do only things they know, and they'll learn to make ball sticks, balls, baskets, beadwork, anything we have as arts and crafts. Somebody that knows how will have to just teach our younger ones. So I think the student must be interested in learning how to make these things before he can catch on much quicker, but if you're not interested in making anything, why, then, you won't catch on much at all.

The dances have to be taught, too. Some of the social dances have been remodeled. Back in the old days the dances were education for our students. The young warriors will get out and go and find ducks on the water. Why, then, they'll kill those ducks and bring them in. Then when they bring the ducks in, the woman folk would cook the ducks and they'll have a big feast over this. When they get through with their feast, the big elderly, the old man, will ask the warriors, "How were you acting when you run upon them and killed them? Show us." Then the warriors began to tell how they were acting. Then they want them to go through the action because the little ones here are going to be warriors later, so they train them to become warriors. Go through the motions of how the ducks were acting. That's how it was; that's the reason why today they call it "duck dance." It wasn't a dance at that time. It was education. They were trying to train the little ones, but Anglo race people came to this country. They began to call that dancing. So they say "dance" now.

The quail—same thing. How the quail acted before you killed it. When they get through feasting, they will go through the motions what they called "quail dance."

Then the corn was introduced by the wild geese. They'll go over at the spring of the year and they'll come back at the fall of the year. The geese picked up the seeds in old Mexico or somewhere, and they fly through here and drop the seeds. And the land was rich back in the older times. When they introduced the seed, the corn would come up and grow and make corn. At first the Choctaw didn't know how to eat corn, but there were birds and wildlife that like this corn. They could see them eat the corn and they began to grow. The coon, crow, possum, birds—like redbirds, all kind of birds—began to gnaw on that corn. We eat the wildlife quite a bit. And they liked it so it must be good, so the Choctaws tried that corn and, sure enough, it was good, and ever since that corn has been the main thing for the Choctaw people.

And then we have the language to preserve, too. It was once often said by the old Choctaws [that] the Great Spirit has given you the language and the culture. You don't want to lose that 'cause the Great Spirit is the law and the Great Spirit's law shouldn't be broken. Nature is also given to us by the Great Spirit. The Choctaw Indians are the closest to nature than any other race 'cause they were the first native here. They preserved these medicines out of weeds, grass, leaves, and sometime timber, to use in medicine. So [Choctaws should] keep the language and culture that the Great Spirit gave you. Learn white man's law later. Now the only way I know to preserve Choctaw culture is to think about the Great Spirit that gave you the culture. You don't want to break His law, so keep your culture. But lots of time white teachers say, "Don't talk Choctaw. Talk English in school," and so on. Back ten, fifteen, twenty years ago, they punished the Choctaw students for talking Choctaw language. That wasn't too good an idea by the white teachers. I feel like they've broken our Great Spirit, so I wouldn't believe in that too much. Finally, Will Rogers' son from Los Angeles came over and made a talk by saying, "That's the Great Spirit. Don't break that law. Keep your language and the culture He gave you. That's the God's law.

Baxter York with Rick Billy

This isn't the man-made law. It's the Great Spirit's." So now the Choctaw students talk their own tongue and they carry on the work although they learn English because they gotta cope with both of them. So they carry on in that manner today.

They start off a bilingual program and you must learn how to read and write your own language in order to preserve your own culture. You got to do that. Then in the future the little ones got to learn the same way to keep the culture. And we got to learn English. We got to learn both together in order to get somewhere. We got to cope with both cultures in order to get along in life.

Now I'm going to talk about government. First the Choctaws back in the older days had their own government, which was democratic way of life. Most of the laws maintained by the Choctaws were translated to English. The United States Constitution holds some of the items that the Choctaws had in the democratic way of life, and it was practiced and carried on by the chiefs and the twelve men which were the jurors—the ones that usually take the case and weigh both sides. They decide whether this person is guilty or not guilty. Then they turn it over to the chief, and if the person is guilty, why then the chief usually decides what day he will be punished.

Now the Choctaw were the true people of the world. They were recognized as the true people. That's why they didn't need no jail or nothing, but they would come at a certain time when the chief tells them to come for his punishment. He'll show up at that time and day and he will begin to serve the sentence. If it's a major crime, why then the man was punished by death, and the chief will set the date for his death and he'll show up at that day. Then the speaker of the house will begin to speak to him to make him brave so he just can almost take anything. They already dug the grave, and they build the coffin and set that man in the coffin. They mark the heart red. Then the closest kin of the man that was killed will shoot him with bow and arrow. Immediately they would bury him.

That was the law that the Choctaws had, and today they've gone into the white man's world; white man's law and practice toward democratic way of life. But at the same time their languages are different. They don't understand [each other] so they think it's entirely different, but it's not different. They're both democratic way of life. And now Choctaw today begin to practice the modern law to gain experience at it. They'll become understanding about the county law, state law, and the federal law [and they adopt white customs]. Some of the Choctaws still carry on their native marriages—often called the common law marriage—but very few have carried that native marriage because they're getting used to this modern marriage. They learn the modern culture—what we call white man's law. They buy a license, get married by a preacher, justice of the peace, and that's where they are today.

Get along with the dominant white society is the first thing you got to know. Government—self-government—means that you practice your own government. It is self-determination, and Choctaws are beginning to practice that today. Now the self-government begin to be practiced in 1776 by the dominant group, which is the white people. We call them Anglo race people. All right, they wrote the Constitution and bylaws and begin to practice self-government in 1776, and a lot of amendments been done by resolution, and they practice it and they made great success [over] a period of time.

But they know how to produce. They went ahead and came out with a lot of production, and if the Choctaw Indian know his self-government, he'll practice the same thing as they did in 1776. We only start practicing back in 1918. I think it was 1934 when self-government was passed by Congress. If you know your self-government, why, then you get along with the self-government of the dominant group.

Tribal government is good if it's carried out by the leader like it ought to be. Now this organization we call Mississippi Band of Choctaw Indians; when they organized, the main thing they have to do is to build themselves up on economics. You got to have economy in order to have anything.

So the main thing is to build up your tribal treasury. You can build it up so high. You build it up so high you might be able to pass a proposal, resolution. You can build your treasure so high that you can do almost anything you want to do in this country, because the money—the capital—is the one that makes the ball roll in this country. If you're out here depending on government to help you; and if you depend on them entirely, it don't help yourself at all. Why then you won't get nowhere. That's how we stand today. We always hold our hands to the government instead of trying to help ourselves. We're deep in poverty. We lost our land. We lost everything we had.

Some Choctaw say we don't have enough land to operate on for agriculture, but there's always a way where you can get land to farm, raise your own food and feed. You could rent, you could lease some land from the white individual. Land you could lease it in cash. Those things can be done. There's always a way to do things, but we don't do it somehow or another; our leader can't reach far enough to see it, so that's how come we haven't done it. We should have been in cattle program long time ago. We should have two, three thousand head of cattle, but we ain't got nothing. Swine, same thing; chicken, same thing, anything on agriculture; we could do it because we're agricultural people. Our ancestors were agricultural people, but we ain't doing it somehow.

We Choctaw have a lot of work to do.

Baxter York

"I lived mostly on deer and elk for about twenty years."

JAMES HENRY YEAGER

Back in Pennsylvania's Allegheny Mountains in September of 1885, James Henry Yeager was born, the seventh child of his parents' thirteen. At an early age he was nicknamed "Sy." At age seven, he began school and continued until fourth grade, when he had to quit and work with his father, who owned a meat market and slaughterhouse. He also spent a lot of time farming the ranch. In 1911, he left the homestead to come West; he had heard it was good for your health and he liked to travel. On the way to Colorado, he stopped in Wisconsin and worked on a Chippewa reservation for two years in order to earn more money to continue his trip West. In 1914, he reached Colorado and ran cattle in the Hooshire Mountains. Then, in 1928, he bought a little ranch house in the outskirts of Carbondale (present population over 1,000) and settled there; he married and adopted a son.

He still lives there and cooks over the same potbelly stove. His adopted son was killed in the Navy at age seventeen, and soon after, his wife died from the shock. He has no brothers or sisters living.

But his days are still active; he gardens a lot and tries to keep a tidy house. He says, "I'm ninety years old, and that's not too old yet."

—GUY HELMS, KATE LESLIE, AND JILL RAVITCH.
—NITA GRACE BUNNELL, ADVISER TO THE COLORADO ROCKY
MOUNTAIN SCHOOL, CARBONDALE, COLORADO.

I COME TO COLORADO in 1915, and then I looked around and I kinda liked the place; but it was kinda wild then, you know. Everybody got off the horse and they didn't have time to take the chaps off, but went right on. I was a greenhorn when I came here and by golly, you know, they'd say, "Well, come on, Sy, let's go so-and-so"; pretty soon there'd be a fight, you know, and I'd be the one that started it! Ha! A lot of times you get a black eye. I was always getting pounded up a bit. Otherwise the people was good.

I had a little cabin of my own back in the Hooshire Mountains—way back in there. I'd go up in there and stay in the mountains two weeks, three weeks before I come out. I had to. Them cows, you know, I'd take them up there, and I'd have to just sleep up there and watch with my other dog.

Then I was married in '28 and I adopted a boy. His mother lives up here in Mount Sopris Tour Court. And he went to the Navy when he was seventeen. I tried to talk him out of it, but it did no good. He got killed. It was a shock for my wife, and she had four or five operations and cost me about twelve thousand dollars, but I don't care; money doesn't make any difference if I could-a saved her, but I couldn't. So then I lived by myself. I got used to it. Now I say, "Do what you want to do, what you think's best for you." That's the way I do. Yeah, I'm living a good life. I do just what I want to do, and when I get a little tired I sit down a while. If I get hungry for anything, it don't make a difference what it is, I go get it. Yeah, and if I want a drink of anything. I go get it. Well, that's all I got left in my life. So why not?

Now, a little place like this, you can't see much work on it unless you're used to it. You have to irrigate pretty near all the time, and there's always some fence to fix; you got to paint and get your wood and get your coal—all that, and feed your chickens. I keep busy pretty near all the time. And, well, I have to cook and wash the dishes and sometimes I sweep the floor when I get around to it. So you find something else to do pretty near all the time. You get just like I am and you got to do something; if you didn't, you wouldn't have no mind at all. You just lose ambition and everything. Pretty soon you wouldn't want to do nothing.

[Now I'm not the smartest person around.] I never had much school. Had to work all the time. Course, I can write my name, you know. I can write pretty good. I learned the ABCs in school, and I did learn a little bit about writing and a little bit about reading; and then afterwards, when I was about thirty years old, I got a bunch of books and started to study them, and that helped a little bit. Still, you know, people say, "Well, that's a dumb Dutchman," so I guess that's what I am, I don't know. But school's not altogether your whole life; there's a lot of things you can learn after you get on your own: ways of people, things to do, and how to do it, and all things like that.

And I always tried to take care of myself. You had to stay healthy or you couldn't make it. For a few years I was pretty wild, there's no question about that, but I never misused myself. No. I'd take a drink, but I wouldn't get so slogged up that somebody would have to carry me away, or lift me on a horse. I could always get on a horse myself. And I used to box and wrestle—make a little money that way. And I think for my age I'm a pretty good man yet; I do lots of work. I work every day. I'd rather have my health than a lot of money. I think a little work like I do is good for you. I've worked all my life, and I wouldn't know what to do if I wasn't. So I think that's a good idea, and I know it's good for me. So I raise a big garden. I raise all my own stuff that I eat as far as garden stuff, you know. I haven't bought a potato or onion for five, six years. I've got that root cellar down there.

I been working around stuff like that for a long time, you know, raising gardens. When you're on a ranch, you've got to do that in order to have it. Supposing you're way out, miles and miles away from a store! You'd have too long a ways to go to buy your provisions. You'd have to go, oh, miles and miles, you know, with a little old Ford pickup and you didn't know whether you were going to make it back or not. It was a gamble, too. Yeah. When I was back in the Hooshire Mountains, I'd get the pickup and go down and sometimes I got stuck in the mud in Spring Valley, and I'd be in there four or five hours and nobody come along, and I'd just cut brush, you know, and finally fill the hole, then away I'd go. Yeah. But it was always a gamble.

You didn't go out much. There was lots of game. You didn't have to buy any meat. And then, of course, if you wanted some beef, why there was plenty. You'd get out there and rope you one; you didn't look whose it was because it didn't make any difference, you know. You just kill, butcher it. And if it was one of yours, all right. If it was somebody else's, all right. If somebody else come in, they'd do the same. If you have a bunch of cattle,

J. H. Yeager

why, you'll hardly ever miss two or three or four. [That wasn't considered stealing by anyone. That was accepted. And there wasn't any robbing much like today.] No, it used to be, you know, somebody would rob you and the boys would find out, and if they'd ever get him, why, he'd never rob anybody else. That's the way it worked.

But I lived mostly on deer and elk for about twenty years. You have to go way back in to get elk. The best elk country is up in this rim back here on the Hooshire and Mount Sopris and on through Meeker and Craig. That's where the best elk hunting is. Now they're overstocked over there by Craig. They got more elk in there than they got feed, so I don't know. Up here, well, there's a few elk up here, but they're pretty near all gone. They just go somewhere where there's more food. You know, the feed gets short, and, of course, the Cattle Association runs all their cattle back over in here, too. And that takes a lot of feed away from the game. Used to be when I went out in the mountains, I'd go back up in this country way back between Hooshire and the Basalt Mountain and get on a little flat there where maybe there was a lot of grass and a few trees and I'd sit back in the brush on a horse—they don't pay much attention to a horse—and I'd see a row of elk come along, hell, like twenty-five or thirty, one right after the other. They was going somewhere. Well, you'd pick out just what you want.

And then that cabin I had down there had a door on the east side. There was a big spring down here and the deer would come down and that's where they'd drink. Well, if I needed meat, I'd just stand at the door when they were coming down and find this nice two-point buck and I'd just shoot that one. I don't believe anybody knew where that spring was except myself. It was back in the oaks. And I'd kill one, skin it, and hang it up in there. Sun never hit it, you know, kept it cool. Up higher than it is here, it gets cooler at night.

[That was a pretty good life, and I live a lot the same way now. I never have got used to the way it is outside now. And I don't mean things like long hair like some of you young people have.] If they like it like that, it's all right. When I was a kid, my hair was down to [my shoulders] before my mother cut it off, and I remember I bawled like hell! I don't mind it. I got a niece that comes down here and she got a boy about, oh, seventeen years old, and he's got the reddest hair I ever saw, and it's way down to [his shoulders]. And he's got it combed nice, and gosh, he's got a pretty head of hair. Yeah. I told him not to cut it. Leave it grow way down [to your waist] and then braid it; he thought about it, but he didn't know how long it would take him to grow it that far. No, I don't mind that. Sometimes my hair gets pretty long, too, before it gets cut.

What I mind is other things like all the people, and these crazy gadgets and things that I can't figure out. There wasn't as many people as there is now, and there was more freedom then. They come now, and they look at your place and they'll measure your house and they'll go inside and see how much furniture you got, and the first thing you know your taxes have jumped way up. Before, you paid poll taxes. And everybody was alike. Well, it ain't like that now. And things like that clock there. I got that clock and the electric goes off, and the darn thing, I don't know how to set it, so I don't know what time it is. And sometimes, when I don't have too much to do outside, I think I'll buy one of them little TVs. I think I could buy one for maybe a hundred or a hundred twenty-five dollars. And I'll put it here somewhere and then I'll watch it. I could sit there by the bake oven door and raise the curtain and turn my TV on in there, but I don't know. It flitters so much, you know. You watch it with the eyes and it makes your eyes kind of tired.

When they start to build up all around here, then I'll start to get out, go somewhere else. I'll go over there to Wyoming or western Colorado. I got a little cabin over there; I can live there. But it's way, way, way out. You never see anybody out there. I'd go there, maybe spend the night or something. But I would never go back there to live. No. When you get old, you want to get somewhere close where there's a doctor. You might need one.

But then again . . . Just like the old preacher when he was saying a little prayer because he was burying a man. And he said, "From ashes to ashes, dust to dust, if God Almighty don't take you the Devil must." When it's time to go . . . But I think when you go, well, you know. You take an animal. Out here we drink water, they drink water. Same as we do. They breathe the same air we do. And they die, they go underground. That's it. Well, a person's probably the same thing. I'm just here until my time comes and then I'm gone.

"I don't know how many people I've fed."

MARY TURNER

Mary's world is geographically small. Moving from Dixfield to the house which her mother bought in 1920, Mary's surroundings have always been the mountains—Hedgehog, Zircon, and a dozen others that rise and roll through the Peru, Canton, and Dixfield region. Yet, as with Thoreau's Concord retreat, Mary's world has been as full and eventful as that of any jet-age cosmopolitan.

Mary's value system is the product of her environment, both human and physical. Her friends and neighbors are "simple folk" (by her description). They live close to and dependent upon the land. They raise what they can, including a few chickens, a pig or two, maybe an old milker. They pick berries, apples, dandelion greens—anything that's free and edible. And, like them, Mary has developed an acute awareness of the "ways of nature." She has become as self-reliant and self-sufficient as any rugged pioneer, and yet, beneath her gnarled and ancient exterior, she has retained a compassion and sympathy for life, the innocent humanity of a Sunday school girl.

An example of Mary's sensitivity to others is illustrated in her explanation of "berrying." She speaks of the quantity of blueberries, the type of berry, its uses, and then, as an aside, she mentions that she always used to leave a trail of old rags on bushes and trees on the way up the mountain, so that anyone else who should climb up in search of berries would be able to find his way to her berry patch. In fact, Mary's concept of nature and the responsibilities of man are quite similar to the American Indian view. To her, no one owns what nature provides. Moreover, every person should bear the responsibility of caring for those who cannot care for themselves. That Mary adheres to this standard is obvious when one stops to count the stray dogs, cats, raccoons, squirrels, and other assorted animals that she maintains on her modest farm. Mary's "nursing back to health" has been the difference between life and death for countless animals and at least one eighty-eight-year-old woodsman, whom Mary refers to simply as "Gramps," the boarder.

Mary has been retired for ten years from her job, which she held for thirty-five years, at a local clothespin factory. Retired, however, is hardly the name to describe her active life style. She still mends her own fences, splits wood, cans meat, picks berries, and (for enjoyment and sustenance) hunts, traps, and fishes. In short, one of Mary's most obvious, but unspoken, values is her belief that life is a "full time job" with the wages set at a constant joy of living. As Mary says herself, "I live one day at a time." Life means more and lasts longer that way.

—MARY ANN SHROPSHIRE, MELODY RICHARDSON.
—FLORENCE AND ROBERT IRELAND, ADVISERS.

LIVING IN MAINE can be rough. It used to be even harder, though. Dirt roads piled with snow. And then in the spring of the year you just wallowed through the mud. If you had a horse and wagon you could go, but no automobiles. They'd stop every fifteen minutes.

When I worked, I had a hand sled [in winter] and I could get on and slide almost to get there. But I had to walk home after I got off from work. We had to work nine hours a day then.

That was at the clothespin factory. I worked for thirty-five years [at the local clothespin mill]. Used to have to walk. I had two boys. I had to hire somebody to take care of them for a while when they were small. I'd walk, then walk back at night, about a mile and a half. Then finally I got rich and got an automobile, and used t'go back and forth in that. But these cold mornings you never knew with these old clinkers whether they was gonna

Mary Turner

start or not. But I worked there a long time, and I retired when I was sixty-two, and I'm seventy-two now. I've never been back to the mill since I worked there. I figured I stayed in that damned hole long enough. No, I never went back to visit. I run a lathe and turned them clothespins out. Finally after a while they got rid of that. Then I worked on the automatic and all you had to do was sort your boards.

On top of work, everything at the farm had to be done. We didn't have refrigeration, for example. The way we used to get our ice—we had an icehouse out back and we'd cut the ice down here at the mineral springs. They'd saw that ice in big chunks, deep, y'know. They'd cut it up in squares and bring it up to the house with a horse. They had a big logging rigging they'd haul wood on, y'know. They'd have sawdust in the bottom, and they'd put the ice in there. My job was to pack snow all around that ice, all you could get. When they got all the ice they wanted they'd put the sawdust to it. They'd cover it all over with sawdust, and it kept all summer that way. We used it to keep our milk cool.

And we had a horse. Hauled the ice in on a wagon and a horse. Course the old barn down here fell down last winter. Stayed up a long time. I had this new one built. My son and four, five neighbors all come and chipped in. They started on a Wednesday afternoon and had my cows in the barn Saturday night. I had plywood, and it went up fast.

But I don't depend a lot on neighbors. I don't go many places. I ain't got the time. I don't go to Senior Citizens' meetings—I ain't got time. I have more fun staying home and looking after what I *have* got. Although Senior Citizens is nice for some people who ain't got what I got.

I get up about quarter past six. I drink my coffee, and I don't hurry. I say I'm my own boss. One morning I overslept and I got up at eight. Oh God, I stayed there and slept till eight o'clock. And I said, "Well, guess it's about time you got out of bed!"

So I get up in the morning and make myself a cup of coffee. This morning I built myself a fire—it was too cold! [Laughter.] And I'll sit here and drink that coffee. And about seven o'clock I'll take my milk pail. I'll take my stuff I feed my dog, get my stuff for the pigs, and I load it on my toboggan and I start for the barn. I have a toboggan because this knee here, it's lame. If I go with a cane, I'm all right. I can do a lot of work. But I take one of the red toboggans out here in the dooryard, and if I want to haul my pig swill and my grain, I load that thing right up with what I want. And I haul that thing right along and I ain't gotta come back for a second trip. It makes it easy for me. Course the cows are out in the pasture. Well, I go down and feed my pigs, and I got some rabbits down there. I usually have the feed all ready for 'em the night before. Then I throw it right in the pen. Then I come back into the barn and put the grain in the boxes, and I go out and get my cows.

If the cows ain't there all I have to do is holler all their names, and they'll come. When the cows are done I milk the goat. I feed her and milk her.

Then I got my geese—I let them out so they can squawk, and go at it. I had two geese five or six years ago and a coon got one. Well, the old fellow, he was left alone. But he mothered two or three flocks of ducks for me, go right with 'em, you know. Well, a year ago I bought four goslings. I paid five dollars apiece for 'em, just little babies. Raised them. Then somebody else come along the other day and gave me them white ones. I got two white ones. The new ones, they fight a little, but I don't bother with 'em at all.

Then I feed the cats and dogs, and the squirrels. Those squirrels, my grandson found 'em a year ago. They was just babies, didn't have their eyes open. I had four. I'd get up during the night with a medicine dropper and heat up some milk and feed them little fellows two or three times a night. I'd wake right up. I saved these two anyway.

Now in the spring, I make my own gardens. I have somebody to plow and harrow for me. I got some string beans now all cut. Got to can them—I guess today. In the garden I got corn, beans, peas, potatoes, onions, carrots, beets, turnips, pole beans, cucumbers. I got peppers down there now, too. Then I can. I didn't plant as many string beans this year. I still got a lot down cellar.

For meat, I like to hunt, but I can't walk so well now. I like to fish, too.

In the fall of the year when people was hunting—they don't so many come now as used to—they'd come up here to eat. I don't know how many people I've fed. They called it Mary's diner. I always had something for 'em to eat. I'd tell 'em, "You want some coffee? Come on in!" Then I'd get 'quainted with 'em; maybe wouldn't even ask 'em their names. I've done that many times.

But I get deer about every fall. Once in a while I'm not lucky, but I usually get one. Yes, and I raise my own meat. I had a beef I butchered last fall. And I butchered a hog last fall, and I butchered my roosters. I salt my own pork. I use it in baked beans and use it to fry stuff with. I give some of it away. I like to give things away. Somebody that has helped me, and they wouldn't take no money—you can't repay 'em—well they come and I give 'em some salt pork. Well, that's the way I pay 'em back. I make my own sausage. When I kill my pig I grind up the meat for sausage. Now if you've got some hamburg—depends on how much sausage meat you've got, you can put in some hamburg and that makes your sausage better. I make my own maple syrup. Many nights I've been out until twelve o'clock boiling my sap. You've got to watch it. It takes about thirty gallons of sap to make a gallon of syrup. The season starts—oh—in March. But that depends on the weather.

Melody Richardson and Mary Turner

Yeah, and I make my own mincemeat out of deer and rabbit. My son goes out and shoots a lot of rabbits. They make the best mincemeat. I use rabbit and apples, raisins, and sugar, a little molasses, and vinegar. You have to cook it slow, very slow. You got to grind all that, then you cook it down slow.

I learned these recipes myself, most of 'em.

Back when I was growing up we got by and lived on what we had. We didn't have what they got today. No televisions. I used to go over on this mountain here, Speckled Mountain. Picked blueberries. I'd start from here with two pails, and I'd walk up that mountain there and pick my two pails of blueberries and walk home. I used to go up there every year, but it's been quite a few years since I've been. I always went up and took white rags with me and tied fresh rags on every summer so other people could find their way up, you know. Lord, some of those rags are still hanging up there now.

At night I used to sew and make things. Keep the hands busy. Make rugs and quilts. I had chores to do, too. I made braided rugs. I ain't got none down now. They're all packed away.

I have cut my own wood a good many times. Saw it with a bucksaw and split it with an ax. I used to go in the woods with my old horse and get the wood, twitch it down. I'd have just a whiffletree and a harness on it. Had a chain on that whiffletree and wrap that chain around that wood and the old horse would bring it out.

And then I do help my cows calve if they need it. I don't bother them unless I think they need it. If the feet get out, and I think they're having a hard time, I pull as they strain.

And I trap some to get a little extra money. One year I trapped enough up here to pay my taxes! I got fox and coons . . . Course then, my taxes weren't too high. But I got enough to pay my taxes that year.

And sometimes I sell butter and veal calves. Now I get more out of veal calves. You gotta keep veal calves ten weeks before they're ready to go. I got one ready to go tomorrow morning. I'm selling calves now. All I've got's four cows now, and one cow's turned out to pasture. She's not milkin' at all.

But I stay around here and make it pretty well by myself. I don't know what exactly to tell you all. The future is pretty hard to tell. Looks kinda bad sometimes to me. I do think we'll have another war. I don't think I listen to the news enough to really make up my mind what's gonna happen. I guess we just have to live from day to day and just see what's gonna happen.

There's more deviltry going on. People stealing and crimes. I don't know that it wasn't radio and TV that started all this in the younger generation. Sometimes I wonder. The kids watch these pictures, and then they get hold

Mary Turner's yard

of a gun and want to do the same thing. I sometimes think they should cut some of that out on TV, though I like to watch it myself; but it's just these young kids that watch it and they get these darn things in their head.

When we was growing up, we had to work. And if we wanted to go somewhere, we walked. I think that makes you realize you got to work for what you got. I think the younger generation has had too much handed out to them. In fact, I know I've handed out to mine. I got two boys. Sometimes if you didn't give 'em quite so much and let 'em dig for what they wanted, it'd help 'em.

"I wish I could give my son a wild raccoon."

CHARLES SCHROEDER

Charles Schroeder was born in Emporia, Kansas, in 1927, and he remembers a childhood of miners and ghost towns, of dust storms and blizzards, and of bank robbers like Bonnie and Clyde.

Both his grandfather and his father were cabinetmakers and wood carvers, and his mother taught, from the age of sixteen, in a one-room country schoolhouse.

Before completing high school, Charles dropped out, joined the Navy, and served as a frogman and demolitions expert in World War II and the Korean War. After the latter, he earned a degree from Kansas State University, served as a fireman in Emporia, received a Master's in Fine Arts from California State at Long Beach, and then began teaching in California. He and his wife, who is from Playcenter, Kansas, and is also a teacher, have lived in California for the past twenty-five years. They have a son named Kevin. Charles now teaches art at the Suva Elementary School in Bell Gardens.

—DEBBIE EDENFIELD, KEVIN LEWIS, ROBERT STOUT, LINDA STOUT, SHERRY JONES, FELICIA PUSATERI, CASSANDRA BOINTY, SHAWN HARRIS, AND JULIE POMPA. —MICHAEL BROOKS, ADVISER, SUVA INTERMEDIATE SCHOOL.

I GREW UP in a one-room farmhouse in Emporia, Kansas, which was established in 1857. It's located in about the center of the state between two large rivers: the Cottonwood on the south and the Nenosho on the north. At the time that I remember best in the 1930s, this was a community of wheat farmers and people that worked on the Atcheson-Topeka-Santa Fe railroad—mainly quiet country people. It was really William Allen White's town. He edited the Emporia *Gazette* and is known best as the father of small town newspaper journalism. He lived in a large stone mansion on an elm-covered street, was a friend of several Presidents, and a conservative to the bitter end. He came to my junior high quite often to speak, and he would tell us stories about the movement of Indians across Kansas to the Indian reservations. It was a traumatic experience that apparently moved him a great deal. I could leave my home then and pick up Indian arrowheads in the fields. I enjoyed talking to him and listening to his stories. And his son, Bill White, was an important member of our community. You probably would remember him as the author of *They Were Expendable*.

I remember the town as being a very quiet place very much divided by railroad tracks. Those living on the south side of the tracks were poor people, people working as section laborers and day laborer type people; and those living on the north side of the tracks were the richer people. The main street, Commercial Street, ran all the way down to the Cottonwood River, and at that point it ended at a place known as Sodens Mill—an old dilapidated building right on the edge of the river with a large water wheel and millstones grinding flour from the late 1850s up until probably the early 1940s. It was there that the boys of the town would go skinny-dipping, and they'd ride up on the water wheel and dive off into the millstream; a place where you could go in the summertime and catch fish and go swimming and dream about building rafts to go down the river on. Of course there were droughts when the river would dry up, and also times of high excitement when the river would overflow, usually in the fall of the year. We used to go down along Patty's Mill, which was another mill grinding flour, and gather cottonwood trees that would float very well. Then we'd tie them together with rope or nails and put pieces of boxing board across them. We put shacks on them and maybe a sail, and then make long expeditions down the rivers. About every twenty miles there would be a small town where you could get supplies and sleep underneath bridges and smoke corn-cob pipes. I remember we smoked Indian tobacco which I found out later was some kind of wild marijuana. But it apparently wasn't too harmful because most of us survived. We took only the necessities on those expeditions: a frying pan, lard, some corn meal to wrap the fish. Wrapping a fish in mud and putting it in the ashes of the fire, you could bake it. And we gathered wild fruit. In those days the riverbanks were covered with very heavy forestation. Now it has all been chopped down. I remember one thing you can't find in that region any longer, and that's the pawpaws. That's a small tree similar to a rubber tree, and it has a fruit on it best described as a cross between a cucumber and a banana. Very delicious. They were our dessert.

Very seldom did a summer go by but a child or young person would drown in the river or the nearby lake. One of the jobs of the small town fire department that I worked on later was going out, diving, and dragging out the victims. It was quite an act to know where the body might be located because of the river current. Of course there was great concern about burying a person on dry land and not leaving them in the river.

Fishing was the greatest sport of river life. There were several ways of doing it, but I think the best was to seine large bullheads of the backwater. And we'd catch the larger catfish. Some weighed as much as forty to fifty pounds and could supply meat for a family for a long time.

We had lots of ways of entertaining ourselves. One of the things we did was to dare each other to do certain things like spend the night in the old mansion where someone was murdered. And also playing tricks on people who had given us a bad time during the year. For instance, I remember one man that we disliked intensely. He would scream at the kids to get away from his house, and so one Halloween we all got together and took apart his favorite Model T car and by use of ropes we took it up on top of his barn and put it back together again. Another thing we used to do was zizzing. Zizzing a house was an interesting thing. Most of the houses in those days had clapboard siding on them, and a lot of times it was loose and you could take a great long fish cord and hook it on to a large nail; then by prying up one of the siding boards, placing the nail underneath it, and stretching the line out behind a bush somewhere twenty to thirty feet away, you could draw it up taut and then run a stick up and down on the string. The noise would vibrate through the inner structure of the house, through the attic, through the walls, and it would give the effect of a moaning sound, or a whistling, or a dying cat or a mouse or something in the walls!

And those days you could buy a bottle of pop for five cents, a candy bar for two or three cents. A bottle of milk was three cents; a loaf of bread was a nickel. But in those days, of course, it was difficult to get money. I quite often would borrow the neighbor's milk bottles and cash them at the store and see a Tom Mix western for a nickel. In those days you could go see a movie and have a big box of popcorn and spend the whole day. You could go out to eat and get a hamburger for ten cents and a cup of coffee free.

It was a time we enjoyed, but in some ways it was a hard time. Gradually the Depression hit our home town and it affected people living there in various ways. It brought families closer together than what normally would happen. I remember my father, for instance, refused to take the WPA, the Works Administration dole, and instead did almost everything he possibly could. His salary ranged to approximately ten cents an hour and he would work ten long hours in a day. The children of the families all had various ways of making money. We picked up pieces of aluminum and scrap metal and sold it to the local junk yard. In the wintertime we would go out and take our baseball bats and kill rabbits, skin them, and clean them and wash them and soak them in salt water and hang them on the clothesline to freeze at night and then wrap them in red wax paper and take them around and peddle them from door to door for whatever we could get—usually about fifteen cents. Of course, a couple of rabbits would make a pretty good meal for a family of four or five for a couple of days. I remember when my father had a job digging ditches, and one time he came home telling me that one of the men had nothing to eat except potato peelings. His wife had peeled the potatoes in the morning to feed the children potato soup, and he was eating the peels for his noonday meal. I remember my mother sitting up all night long wondering what to spend her last twenty-four cents on—whether to buy flour or some other staple that could be used. By and large we ate a lot of mush. There was fried mush in the morning—a meal made out of a gruel or a messed-up thing with corn meal. Inside of that would be put fresh meats—sometimes sausage and things of that nature. Then it was fried in the morning and you put syrup on it if you had it, or possibly wild honey that could be gathered up in the woods nearby. Sometimes on Sundays, we would have mush with dates in it or walnuts or possibly raisins, and this was a rare treat. I think I was almost nineteen years old before I ate a steak. I didn't even realize there was such a thing. One time I was eating something that resembled hamburger and found out later on that it was my pet goat that my father had slaughtered and carved up outside in his workshop. Things were pretty bad. I don't remember anyone selling pencils on the corners or apples as you usually hear about the Depression, but there were a number of people going through the country robbing banks, and people standing in long lines for soup. And there were the Wobblies, which was sort of a Communist-inspired worker group who traveled through the country causing strikes and problems and things of that nature.

In the '30s in Kansas, Machine Gun Kelly and Bonnie and Clyde were very famous. Living in the geographical area that my town was in, we were sort of the crossroads of the United States. If any of these gangsters were afoot, usually people were asked to volunteer to set up road blocks, to get

Charles Schroeder

out their shotguns, and wait along the highway to stop them. Bonnie and Clyde were shot near where I lived and their car towed into town. A lot of bullet holes and real blood could be seen on it. Many people read accounts in the newspapers of these very colorful characters, and they considered them to at least be getting out and doing something about the Depression. They were getting out and trying their luck at something. I don't think anyone considered them altogether bad. I remember that there were several bank robberies in my home town. In one, Charles O'Brien, my favorite police officer, shot it out with a gang of bank robbers. He wounded one in the leg and later on, when the man had done ten or fifteen years in Kansas State Penitentiary in Lansing, O'Brien offered to personally get the guy a job and take care of him. I don't think the police actually hated any of these people, or really went out on a vendetta to kill like you see in the cops and robbers movies. I don't believe that feeling existed.

Then on top of the Depression came the dust bowl time. So many of the people in my area were poor. Then on top of that, their farms simply dried up and blew away. There was no way to continue growing anything. There were several years that they called "The Year of the Grasshopper." When I was a youngster traveling with my father, we passed a field that was full of corn, and by the time we passed back by in the evening the grasshoppers had completely eaten the field right down to the bedrock ground. There were stories of grasshoppers riding fish down the river, grasshoppers gnawing away parts of beds in peoples' houses, and all sorts of things. It was a very, very bad time. Many times you'd see cars in gas stations filling up and on top of the car was a mattress and on the side a washtub, cooking equipment, clothing, bedding, and maybe a small baby's toy. Inside were really sad-looking people. People were going to California thinking of palm trees, coconuts, fields of oranges that they could pick and eat, apples, free food, good jobs, bountiful farms. Apparently the stories of the bad things that happened, the hired guards at the borders of states turning people away, or beating people up—things you remember from *Grapes of Wrath*—apparently these things did not filter back to my home town because people continued to go to California.

The stories and letters they would write back would be glowing accounts of how they were doing. If they did come back to visit, they quite often were driving large cars and showing off their wealth. I remember as a child if you saw a car with a California license plate it was something of an exciting event. Something to talk about and tell someone.

Of course I went to school. It was a very traditional type school, an old brick building two or three stories high. Not very many frills. I remember a teacher there who was hard on kids. In those days you could discipline children in any way you felt was best to get them to learn. I also remember somebody throwing her out of the second-story window and how she ricocheted through the Lombardy poplar tree outside the window. Fortunately the old gal wasn't hurt, but it was one of the high spots in my memory of going to school.

Because of the Depression, it was necessary for my mother to make most of my clothes. I had shirts made out of flour sacks. Sometimes I had no shoes. I remember one time I attended school in the wintertime and it was quite a ways. There was a lot of snow on the ground and there was no way you could drive to school. At that time, I was out of shoes so I put on several pairs of heavy socks and wrapped my feet in rags and put on old buckle-up overshoes, and when I got to school, the teachers asked me to take off my galoshes and put them back in the cloak room. But I refused to do so because I was embarrassed with no shoes.

I don't remember whether it was a common practice to drop out of school at that time, but I know I was dissatisfied with school and became one of the first dropouts in our community. This was, of course, the war years, the later stages of World War II. Many of us felt that it might be our only chance to take part in what we thought was probably the biggest and the last war. Of course, if we had known that there would be several more wars, we might not have been so anxious to be part of that one. I remember dropping out and going to take my physical for the Navy, and my father's difficult decision the day I called him at the post office and asked him to sign the papers which would allow me to enlist. I remember him asking me if I didn't think an education was more important, and then coming to the conclusion that the bullheaded child that I was, I would probably run away anyway. He gave his consent and so I did join up and became a frogman at sixteen.

I served not only World War II, but I was recalled during the Korean War. In any war there are always gory stories and also stories of glory. I think, however, the ones that stand out in my mind are the funny ones. Once I was stationed during my tour of duty on the island of Saipan. We were deep into the boondocks of the jungle, and we were having trouble with infiltrating Japanese. They were beginning to realize the war was about over and they started to come close. Myself and my buddy had a small shack built there in an area where we were supposed to be doing some type of work very vitally important in the war effort. We had constructed a shower and every night the Japanese holdouts would infiltrate down and use our shower. We really didn't mind them using the water but the thing that upset us was they were using up our hard-to-get Lifebuoy deodorant soap. We decided finally that we would have to put a stop to this. So instead of killing them, which we were against, we decided we would take some of the dye marker from the life rafts. This dye was used by the Naval Air Corps to spot men that were down in the ocean. It's a clear material which, when placed in water, dissolves into a very brilliant purple dye. We put this material into several bars of Lifebuoy soap and placed them in the outdoor showers. The Japanese came down and used the showers, but stopped when their skin turned bright purple and they couldn't get it off. They thought they'd been diseased in some way. After I'd come home I ran into a newspaper account of men who were running a garbage dump in Saipan, and they ran into some Japanese who had held out a full year after the war was over. They were telling the men that they had sustained some type of injury and had turned purple. There were several doctors examining them to decide what sort of jungle disease they had.

Then I came back from the war and did a number of things. I was a fireman in Emporia for a while. Being a fireman in those days was not like it is today. You actually had to be a smoke eater. You had to go into the fire, and you had no inhalation or breathing apparatus. Sometimes these fires were quite dangerous. I remember one time we went into a building. The people had been heating their stove with kerosene from a drum of kerosene next to the stove, and as we went into the building, the drum exploded, blowing myself and a friend through a wall.

Another time, I had just finished a shift and I was taking a shower when the alarm went off. All of the fireman in the building had to attend, so I slipped on my rubber pants and raincoat and went outside and discovered that the temperature had dropped to about twenty-eight degrees below zero. I found myself going to a fire with no clothes on except the outer gar-

Shawn Harris, Robert Stout, and Felicia Pusateri

ments and covered with cold wet soap. So when I arrived at the fire I immediately grabbed the lead hose and went right into the inferno keeping myself very close to the fire mainly because I was cold. I got a citation for extreme bravery in adverse conditions, and an accommodation by the chief of the fire department. He thought I was a hero, but actually I was just cold.

Later I went to college and got my degree and became a teacher, which is a profession I still enjoy today. I think being a teacher is one of the most important things that you can do. It is totally creative. It's the type of thing where every single day is different. You're not only teaching others the things that you know and the things that you hold dear and important; you're also learning new things yourself. You're finding out that this change that's going on is a never-ending thing. I came to teach in the Bell Gardens area when it was in a vast period of change. It was essentially an area of people like I told you about earlier that left the Midwest and came out to California and did finally find their resting place. It was middle-class America. I enjoyed it a great deal. It's undergone tremendous change.

I think if I were going to leave my son something about my past, it would be to make him realize that all of us are really a part of history and each of us lives in a different era, a different time zone, so to speak, and that each one of us has an exciting part to play in that particular time, and there's no way to stop this sort of thing or to keep it from changing. I can think of one good example. The first time I visited the ghost town of Calico, I walked across the desert through the little cut leading into town. At the time I walked in there most of the adobe buildings were still standing. The ones still standing were the apothecary shops, the saloon, livery stable, several more. And of course the huge mine complex was very interesting to go through. I think I spent two or three days just wandering through the tunnels, going from one end of the place to the other. And of course, at that time there were things lying all over the ground which lately have become very important to collectors and people who like to purchase memorabilia of the mining era. Picks, shovels, whiskey bottles, things of that nature were lying around. I think it's important to remember that the jeep was not prevalent on the American scene then; no dune buggies, no motorcycles, things that could get people into the desert, so when you found a place like Vanderbilt, Providence Town, or some of the other mining camps of this region, you quite often found the accouterments of the period still sitting on the tables: cooking equipment, old clothing, long underwear that had been hanging on the clothesline for twenty years. People would simply just look at these and pass on, and not bother them. It is only the last ten or fifteen years that we see the people who collect bottles, the destroyers, people who enjoy tearing things up that have come to destroy these mining camps. It's too bad that they couldn't protect them, as some of them were quite interesting. It's really a shame.

I think it would be a good idea to realize that you are part of history. For instance, so often we say that history is something in a book or a hidden away place in a library, but actually it cuts very close to all of us. It touches each of us and becomes a part of us. I think, for instance, of the time my grandmother was telling me about when she was a little girl and taking care of some children in a tollhouse somewhere in Missouri, and how Jesse and Frank James and their gang came to hold up the tollhouse, and how there was no money there and how they enjoyed taking her fresh-baked blackberry pies and eating them and throwing them. The fact that my grandmother knew Frank and Jesse James seems to have brought history a little closer to me.

My parents' home on West Street in Emporia, Kansas, was built in the late 1850s by a couple of maiden ladies who owned a broom factory there. My parents still live in the old house. Just living in a house like that puts you in touch with history. History is not a dead thing, but it is actually a living thing. So I think if I could pass on something to my son, it would be that he realize that the things he's doing are important right now today, and that the past is something he can be close to and think about and be part of.

I think the future of America will always be great. I don't think there is any doubt about this. We make mistakes, we do strange things for our particular time, we pass judgment on ourselves, and we think about our early times. These interviews are good. To think that an ordinary person like myself may have some part to play in the entire picture of American history, that I actually am a part of it, that things that I did as a youngster may be very important. If I could pass on how to make a frog gig and how to catch catfish in the river when it's beginning to rain, and how to make stink bait out of the lining of a cow's stomach, some of those things. They are things I'd like to pass along. I wish I could pass on the sight of a group of desert bighorn sheep coming to graze near where I was camping a few years ago; the view of the desert fox, things that have since disappeared. I wish I could give my son a wild raccoon to teach him the joys of learning about animals. I'd like to give him that Christmas when I had only ninety-seven pennies to spend, and I bought my father a box of smoking tobacco and my mother a plaque of the Lord's Last Supper and I bought my sister some cheap perfume from the ten-cent store. I wish I could pass on to him a belief that what he's doing is important. An idea that the part of America that *he* grew up in will be just as important as the one I'm telling you about today. I wish I could pass all of that on to him, and to you.

"We would look through thick catalogues and wish for this and that."

BIRDIE LEE MAY

Mrs. Birdie Lee May was born in 1904 in Menifee, Arkansas, and now lives in Clarksville, Arkansas. Her father was a sharecropper, and they lived in a succession of homes—one log cabin, and one that had a kitchen with a dirt floor. Often they were up and working by four in the morning.

Despite a childhood that demanded that she do her share of work at home, she managed to finish high school, and in 1922 married Emery Howard May, a porter for the Missouri Pacific Railroad. They had a son and a daughter.

To bring in extra money, she has taught in a nursery school and has been a domestic. Her deepest satisfaction comes from watching the steady progress of her race. Kay Bagsby, one of her granddaughters, has won numerous talent contests, for example. Another, Ann Gilkey, graduated from the College of the Ozarks, was in-

cluded in Who's Who of American Students, *and was the first of her race to receive a Master's degree in the field of teaching the deaf.*

—CATHY ANGELL.
—REV. CHARLES E. ANGELL, ADVISER, RIF PROGRAM ASSOCIATED
WITH HUMAN RELATIONS COUNCIL, CLARKSVILLE, ARKANSAS.

MY MOTHER WAS BORN in Mississippi. She couldn't remember too much about her mother and father living together because her father wanted to come to Arkansas, but her mother's home was in Mississippi and she didn't want to come to Arkansas and they separated then. Her father came to Arkansas and her mother and her mother's sister stayed in Mississippi until she was grown—sixteen or seventeen. I remember her saying that a cousin of hers kept her until she was a big girl and hired her out when she was small. She had to stand on a box and wash dishes—that's how small! Appears she didn't know about farm life until she came to Arkansas. Her mother died and they came to Arkansas and got together with their father because he sent for them.

My mother married and I was born in Menifee in Conway County, Arkansas, December 6, 1904. I don't remember the house but I remember the little community. We didn't live there very long. It was a community back in the hills and we moved over near the railroad. Father was a sharecropper. I stayed home there and took care of the next children. I wanted to go to the fields because I thought it would be more fun than staying in the log cabin all day. They grew cotton, corn, sorghum—you know what that is, sticky like molasses. I more or less kept the children clean and out of things they shouldn't do. There were three or four under me and that was enough! I had to have the meals fixed for when my parents came home. I did this until I was eleven or twelve. One year we moved so many times it was sort of pitiful. Lived in a little log cabin for a while, and then we'd see another house that was better and move to it. It was pathetic. When I think of it now, the houses we have lived in. I have known some not to have a kitchen floor. Just ground. Didn't live there too long. Father built a little house after that. At the time I thought it was wonderful, but no one now would appreciate it. Mother was happy about it.

I have known times when Mother and Father were living together on a farm and got up at four in the morning to go to the field. Sometimes I could go with them and sometimes we had to walk five or six miles—or it seemed

Birdie Lee May

that long! In that fall it was awful chilly. Mother would carry vegetables to the field to cook and we'd eat it there. Eat by a shade tree by the road.

I liked to keep up with my brother. We would climb trees even though it wasn't too ladylike. We never had a radio while I was a child. We would sit around and look through thick catalogues, like Montgomery Ward's, and look at pictures and wish for this and that.

In the summer our well would dry up and we'd have to tote water two miles or farther. In the country we didn't have no nice roads like today. It was muddy or sandy and dirty.

In 1922, when I was eighteen, I married. My husband was almost five years older than me. He was a trainman. Worked all our young lives. He worked in the express office and it was a fine job but got Negro pay. But it was better than no job at all because so many others didn't have any job. Then he was a train porter and got nice money for those times. So when he retired he got a pension. After he died I received some of his pension. And I'm glad of that.

I think it's good to have some money for survival and comfort. I never had and never will have a lot of money. I don't worry about it. I like to have some if there is a need and if any of my children need anything. I like to have it for them. If you don't have money, don't let it worry you. Those who worry about paying bills don't need to, because God takes care of them.

If you ever need money, I would help. Once an old lady lived near us a long time ago, and she wanted steak and we did not get much money for our work. Well, I bought hamburger at twenty cents a pound for my family and bought steak for the old lady. I did that a lot of times. At church we pay dues and sometimes I would pay for someone else and pay my own later on. I didn't bless myself for it. I just feel like that God had blessed me just an inch or two above her. My husband always had a job and for a while his jobs didn't pay a lot, but a lot of people didn't have jobs. Some white people came in need of money and clothes and I have given to them, and didn't think nothing about it. Other people have helped me. It's not goodness on my part, just the grace of God makes me want to do the right thing.

Cathy Angell and Birdie Lee May

Now I work in private homes. Domestic work, cleaning. I belong to the Republican Women's Club; I was treasurer for a while. I'm on the Human Relations Committee and was vice-president one year. Now I'm Grand Matron of the Order of the Eastern Star of Arkansas. I'm vice-president of the district laymans of the African Methodist Church.

I can see things changing for the better. I was told when I was growing up, "You'll be thankful for this and that," but I thought, "I'll never be thankful for this kind of stuff!" I have it much easier now. Negroes, they have all my life felt inferior. Now the tide is changing and the other races don't mind this feeling too much and we have a few more advantages today. In the past I couldn't go to either restaurant in town. Negroes had a little nasty place. But I'm free now to go to any restaurant if I have the money to pay for it. Even to the best motels I can go to. Quite a few differences. There's a difference in schools. They used to say, "Equal but separate." That wasn't too long ago. Changing the schools helped.

I had just two children, Norma Jean, and a son who died. His daughter, Ann, went to school when there was just one room for Negroes. She attended College of the Ozarks but it was cheaper for her to live at home. But she got work through the Lytles with the Mission Outreach and worked her way through. After she finished and got married—Dr. Lytle married her in the chapel—she went to Little Rock and took special training and is making nice, teaching the deaf. She's been teaching seven years now. She was the first Negro woman to get a Master's degree in that area.

In time it will improve more. Some people are going far and some never will get out of the ditch. They don't care. People have to have a will to do besides an opportunity. So many of our people stay down so long some will never do much better than they used to. We have to do something about it ourselves. Can't sit around. I don't think too much of physical fighting, but we need to fight in some way. Some say I'm too antique, but I think we should set an example for other people, a good example. We should strive to make the best out of life. I don't mean all the time to strive to be rich or gain fame; always do the best you can in whatever you undertake. [That's one way we can fight.] I would hate to lose the high regard and respect of a lot of friends. I have quite a few white friends and I value them very much. I used to work for people and they used to speak to me when I was working and outside they wouldn't say one word. They didn't want to be called names. Some people think I'm old and "fuddy-duddy." But for years and years I have just trusted people because I trust God and I feel like He is not going to put things on me that's not right, and when things happen to me with somebody I trusted, I just feel like that's just one of my burdens to bear.

God has been everything to me. I think that if it's His will for me to have things better, I'll get it, and if it's not His will and I don't get it, I don't worry about it. Some people feel just because someone else has it they should have it, but I just don't see it like that. If you ask God for a blessing and He thinks it's right, He will give it to you.

I know I'm gonna die, someday. The Bible says we have so many days, borrowed time; well, see, I lived my day. I'm not willing to die, but I'm ready.

I want people to say, "She done what she could and lived as a good Christian."

*"If one instrument doesn't
care about the other ones,
they won't make music.
Just noise."*

FRANK GARCIA

*Uncle Frank was born in 1888 in the town of Juárez, Coahuila,
Mexico, "So we start it from there." He helped his father farm along
with his nine younger brothers and three sisters. School? He formally learned through the first grade. His family moved to the coal
mines in Rosita when he was fourteen in 1902. Here he learned to
be a blacksmith, to "form the iron and heat it myself and make
parts for the machines." In three years he became the foreman of
the shop. At about age seventeen, he began to read books and
study by himself. Because of the revolution in 1912, transportation
to the mines was blocked and the work stagnated. Uncle Frank decided "to see what I could do by myself" and came to the United
States alone.*

*In Medina Lake, Texas, at the age of twenty-four he worked as a
mechanic, pipe fitter, and home foundation rebuilder. A year later
he brought his brothers, sisters, and future wife to this country
where they stayed and raised their families. He was given charge of*

the private waterworks of an estate and in the same year married
Paulita Villarreal. The next year his only child, Enrique, was born.
In 1925, Uncle Frank moved into San Antonio and opened his own
machine shop in a shed he built himself behind his home. Here he
designed a dump truck body which he sold to Chevrolet, one a
week. He did not make much money on this project. "But it was
good, it was enough."

The Depression came and "times were pretty bad," but Uncle
Frank invented a pecan cracker better than the one already used
and had the plans for a machine that separated the nut from the
shell. He built this equipment himself and in 1935 moved his shop
to the Southern Pecan Shelling Company and worked exclusively
for them. In 1948 the company was sold, so they released him from
work. He then became a citizen of this country.

Uncle Frank next invented a plastic knot for men's ties, "But we
didn't do well and we lost everything." Uncle Frank laughed while
recounting his losses. His only son died from a heart attack in the
shower in 1950. The following year Uncle Frank began work at
Kelly Air Force Base as a journeyman machinist and stayed there
for nine years. His wife died in 1953.

Now Uncle Frank likes to sit out on his porch and sleep and
wants "just to take care of my people here—try to get them together."

—JOHN SANTOS, RHONDA NARRO, MYSSIE LIGHT.
PHOTOGRAPHS BY SCOTT HARRISON.
—NAOMI SHIHAB, ADVISER, TEXAS
COMMISSION ON ARTS AND HUMANITIES.

IT WAS A LITTLE TROUBLE coming into the United States, but
at that time it wasn't too strict. After I got married in 1918, I was six years
already on this side. My wife was from Mexico and we met there. Her family came with my family to the States and we got married here. Soon I had
no more ties to Mexico. My family was here, my wife, my son, and no one
wanted to return. So what was left? We didn't even think about it. Why
should we? So I started studying for citizenship. In 1948 it was granted. My
life was here.

I'll tell you this, the transition to the United States is not the same for all.
Many people aren't able to do nothing but labor work and it's hard for
them. But for those who have other lines of work it's not so hard. Of course

I can say that by experience. I had no trouble. I'm completely satisfied. It always was easy for me to make my living. It is hard for those who aren't able to do things.

I liked it here. For one thing, there was no work to be found over there. And I was a man who always believed in work my whole life. I liked all my jobs. I liked to be able to do a little of everything. I even worked on cars. My brothers and I had natural mechanical abilities. The first car I bought was a one-cylinder car. I had a time with that. It was a little truck. Instead of doors, it had two little chains on the sides. Then I traded it for a car they called the Star, Estrella. It was a new one and I didn't have trouble with it. Then I traded it for a six-cylinder car. So it helped me to be an automobile mechanic.

When I started working on cars I designed a dump body, a dump truck. You could dump that body from the seat without getting out. It was good then. It was very easy to operate. I made very little money on that, but it was good, it was enough.

We have to admit we like things to be easier than they were before. We don't have to say that the new ways we do things are wrong. If you were cutting a tree sometime ago, you did it with an ax and you worked hard till you put that tree down. Now you can put the saw right around the tree and cut it right down. That can't be bad. We can't be against those who make machines to help us. There will always be something for everyone to do. I can't see anything wrong in getting machines to do what we did by hand before. Not too long ago we had to put in a line of sewers and we had to use the pick and shovel and you would have to get many men to work very hard every day and they didn't pay much, just a little; and now you get a machine that just puts a line and the ditch is made perfectly. There's one man on the machine and the others are doing something else. It's done in a very short time. We have to admit that is good.

Progress is very natural; it comes from science and it provides for all. It's the natural way of being. If one man has more ideas than the other, then he'll put them into practice and help everyone. It is natural for everyone to be different. We each have our different faculties. God gave all of us abilities. Say I have an idea. If someone shows me a book explaining that idea, this idea can go farther. I have added my part and the writer has added his.

When I went to work at Kelly Air Force Base, I realized that many of my fellow employees had been through high school and were trained mechanics and they could consult a book when they were in trouble. They knew how to read this book full of pictures and diagrams. I was working from experience and I could help them but I could not help them through the books. I wasn't a technician. Many times I showed them how to repair the cars. But I didn't even know how to look for the book! I could under-

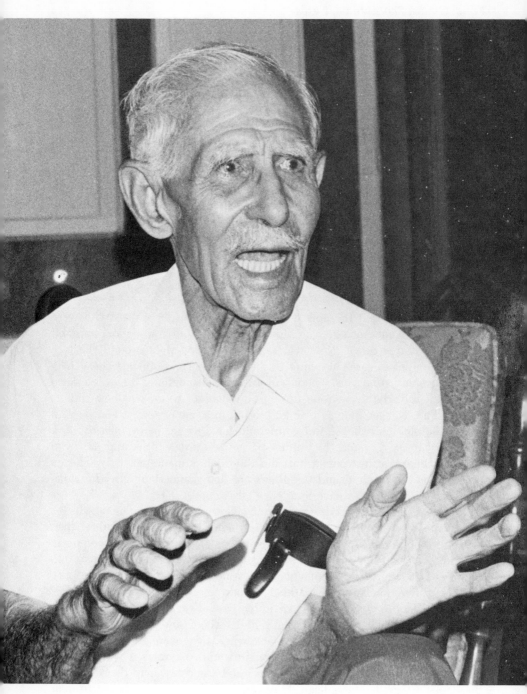

Frank Garcia

stand the pictures. I just couldn't read the English so I did without it. But books are of great value. If you have experience *and* get a book, the value is twice as high. Which is more valuable? Both are the same. It is a combination. He is the wise one who can gather experience *and* consult the book. You must know your faculty. One man may go to college and his knowledge is more than another, but this other one may be bright in something else that is equal.

I've always been religious. We're Catholic. This is the way we were raised. It's just natural; my mother, my father, my grandfather, his father . . . We never tried to get people to believe like we do, and if somebody else would try to get us to believe like they did, we just put them off or didn't listen. It is because of religion and faith that a family sticks together. That's the way it is—why our family is so close. If there is harmony there is faith. And love. Always try to be in agreement. It's the same as music, when those instruments play. If one doesn't care about the other ones, they won't make music. Just noise. There's no reason to argue about religion. There's no one in the world who knows what the truth really is. If you believe with your heart in God with the faith that you have, then you're all right. Really that's the way I think. It's the truth of faith. For me it's very simple to believe and live well. God is for all. We are for Him. This is the same thing. And we are all the same. There are no poor, no blacks, we are completely the same.

If minority groups don't get along all right, I can blame them themselves more than anything else. Let me show you: a good many people do not like us because we are Mexicans, but if they don't have a reason to push us away they won't do it. It's just the same with the blacks. You can't pity them, because they don't present themselves the way they should. It's very simple. If I don't respect you people and I just try to act the way I want to act, well, you're just gonna say, "That old man's crazy." We can live with everybody.

A good many of our people have been born on this side. They're a little different from the ones on the other side. It's not the same. No matter how poor the people in Mexico are, they're always willing to help you. They share with you. They seem to think they're obliged to help the others. It's the natural way. The people on this side are not like that. It is because the fathers raised the kids here differently and many of the ways I can say aren't right. Respect for elders? When we were on the other side they taught us to respect the older ones. This is past. For example, if an old man would be walking down the street, they would give him the sidewalk. Especially the woman. Respect, that is important. Here I don't feel the respect. They laugh at us. It happened to me already. I met three or four boys, like your age, walking on the sidewalk and they said things and laughed at me. They don't respect the old people. Why? It is because they are not raised correctly. When you raise your children, you have to teach them how to conduct themselves. I have a great-grandson and we already teach him these things. The right way is to respect the others. And be against nobody.

The way is very simple. Do the good to other people and it will be returned to you. Don't do to the others what you don't want for yourself. You won't have to worry if you do this. For example, if you go and help your neighbor you're going to feel satisfied, but if you throw a rock to him you

Frank Garcia and John Santos

won't feel happy. No matter what you do to help the others, that will help you. The conscience will tell you if you're right or wrong. You don't have to wait for somebody else to tell you. You yourself know. That is your conscience. As soon as I do something out of line I feel it myself. Listen and trust your conscience.

I am very satisfied with my life. If you were talking to someone, I would be the one to say that this country is very good. I never needed anything because I worked myself. I never had much money. I should have, but I didn't. And I've seen other people do better than myself. But now the Social Security money I receive from the Government gives me enough to live. When you have money is better than when you don't, but I have enough. I'm happy with my life. That is the fact. I like it. I used to read but I'm not able to read now. I know that I can't get into a machine shop again because I can't see well. I can't go to school because I'm not able to retain what I hear. So what I do, I go into my chair on the porch and go to sleep. Then I get up and do something in the yard or go out and get some groceries or what I need and try to pass the time. I just try to keep the place going. If everyone lived like me we would all be content, no worries!

My hope is that every house will know harmony. I consider now—I'm the elder in the family—and I know that they feel satisfied to have me around. And if I have some advice for them, I will be glad to do it, willing to do it. I always want there to be no friction between them. When you are as old as I am, it is natural for anyone to feel consideration for the old man; but something we have to keep in mind is that we have to conduct ourselves as best we can so they don't put us away.

In life today there are a good many things I don't like, but you can go by them, go around them if they are against you. For example, the way the big power, the men with big money, do whatever they want. They don't care about the people. Or maybe they care but they want to get what they want first. The poor are everywhere. But here in the United States, at least they can work to better themselves.

There will always be pain.

"I see beauty
in all these old timbers."

ELIJAH GOOD

The Mennonite culture is very different from the culture of main-stream America. It has, by choice, retained the simple ways of doing things rather than adopt the so-called "modern" way of life. The plain people still use horse and buggy for their transportation, and use horse-drawn equipment for much of their farmwork. Although electricity is now used for light and certain necessities, electric appliances, stereos, radios, and many of the objects we take for granted are forbidden by the Mennonite religion. The retention of the old patterns is just one way these people maintain a unique and separate culture. Another way is by focusing on the community rather than on the accomplishments of an individual. This places more value on an individual acting on behalf of the community rather than for personal gratification. Because of this, the old order Mennonite we interviewed has chosen not to reveal his identity. Instead, we shall call him "Elijah Good."

While talking with Elijah, we were struck by the fact that he often belittled his ideas and feelings. He explained to us that many of his people feel inferior to modern Americans. This is one reason why plain people are sometimes distant to "outsiders." Our view of him was quite different. Elijah is a well-spoken and knowledgeable man who expressed his feelings and beliefs with great sensitivity.

Elijah has lived his whole life in Lancaster County, Pennsylvania, where he was born in 1927. His parents were old order people, and were, like the generations before them, family farmers. Although his formal schooling ended after the eighth grade, Elijah has acquired a great wealth of knowledge through practical experience. Most of his education was acquired from his father, who schooled him in the art of family farming. Elijah believes in learning by doing, not just by studying in a classroom. His own education began in this way when he was a young child. Elijah does have one interest not shared by others in his community, and this is his interest in history. Ever since he's learned to read, he's been fascinated by the history of his own people, and of other people as well. He has acquired a large book collection over the years and is quite involved in learning as much as he can.

The family is also an integral part of the Mennonite culture. Having a wife and several children is necessary to the family farmer, as many hands are needed to run the farm. Elijah was married when he was twenty-one to a local Mennonite girl who was just twenty. At first they rented a few rooms in town while Elijah did carpentry work. They managed to save enough money to buy a small farm the following year. It was there that their first child was born. After continually working for many years, and with more children to help, they were able to manage a larger farm, which they bought in 1960. This farm, originally forty-five acres in size, is still their home, although it has grown in the past few years. Elijah purchased a dairy farm a few years ago, increasing his property to a total of seventy-five acres. He and his wife, along with their nine children, still live the farming life style of past generations, scorning modern conveniences for the simplicity of an earlier time.

Elijah has done many different things in his life, but all of them are related to his life as a family farmer. As a child, he helped with the many chores on his father's farm. When he was fourteen he was given a task all of his own. He grew broom corn, and hand-made several thousand brooms in the next year. Elijah now actively performs the many assorted tasks needed to keep a farm operating. To supplement his income, he paints houses and barns for nearby neighbors. All his energies are directed toward maintaining his independence and simple way of life. He is happy and content with his life style and sees it as far superior to the complicated and technologically dependent life of modern America.

—JOSHUA BEADLE, RICHARD DACOSTA, DAVID ENKE,
NICK MANDLEKERN, STEVEN OAKLANDER, CARL SWEENEY,
ANDREW WALLACE, DEBRA FARBER, HOLLY EVERHART,
LISA FIDLER, DEBRA JACOBY, NANCY JENSEN,
MARGIE KLAVER, LINDA MICHALOVSKY, NANCY OYER,
JEFF RITTER, NANCY ROBERTS, LISA SHULOCK, JANE UTIGER.
PHOTOGRAPHS BY JEFF RITTER AND LISA SHULOCK.
—DIANA COHEN, ADVISER, TRAILSIDE COUNTRY SCHOOL,
KILLINGTON, VERMONT.

Elijah, you said the other day that sometimes you're frowned upon by other people in the community because you talk to us and let us in, and I was wondering if you think that takes a certain amount of bravery or courage to be able to do that when you know that other people may not approve.

IT WAS QUITE the issue the first time it happened, but the reason for my being bold is just merely because of the amount of interest there is. Now if you were like some of the tourists—just here for the antiquity or just for the recreation or just for some amusement—then I wouldn't feel there's much need for doing so, but there is a sincere interest by people like you coming in here so I think it's a worthwhile thing to do. [But there is a lot of the wrong kind of interest, too.] I'll give an illustration. One of our meetinghouses is right along the road, and this area seems to be a weekend tourist area from New York or Philadelphia. That means that when they happen to go by on a Sunday morning when there's 250 buggies and horses tied to the railing at the meetinghouse, this strikes them to the extent that they just can't resist making a stop and taking photographs—especially when the services are over and people are standing around the meetinghouse just to visit and talk. It's just irresistible to people that actually want to be tourists and don't want to be offending. The sensible tourists drive by with a sharp look-see and the snap of a camera and don't just stand there and stop their cars, get out of their cars, stand there for a half an hour studying the thing. And this latter happens to the extent that during the summer the township has now appointed a policeman to clear out those tourists every Sunday. Every time a car stops, a policeman comes up and says, "No parking here." So what they'll do, the tourists that still want to outwit the cop, they still go and park a half mile down the road or half mile up the road and maybe walk down to the church on the neighboring fields and still observe on a Sunday morning. Or another thing they do quite a bit is, now, after the services most of the teams will either go west or east, so they'll know that by parking a quarter mile or half mile away from the church, they'll still see the horses and wagons go by and take movie camera pictures of this thing. Our people get the feeling that we're really being the monkeys and everybody wants to see the monkeys.

[And then another reason for our reserve is that] if this life style wants to continue, we can't be too open and we can't be too close to other people coming in here. The more modern Mennonites have to some extent, and they've changed. See, the more modern Mennonites started being missionary-minded and wanted to convert Jewish people or any other religion, so they went out and left this life style to actually get some education and try and visit other countries. But this is true of only a percentage of the Lancaster Conference people. Those that do that go for education and have no use for the separation any more. They'll drop all traditional thinking and become modern. That's happening at an increased speed. It has happened in so many cases that too much contact with the modern world has influenced quite a number of whole families to break away and make a switch into the English world. They are being influenced by looking across the fence and seeing that life might be easier, or they would like to be part of the world of entertainment, for example; or look into the world of ease, like driving a car that you can get around in, and expand yourself so that you can be part of the modern world. But most of us are going on strongly and keeping separate because it says in the New Testament that the strict followers will be separate people, so that it actually foretells that it's going to happen.

[The reason I talk to you goes back to when,] as a sixteen-year-old when I went to public school, I used to not play so much baseball. On recess I would read books—history books, religious books—and I was reading our German with an interest to the extent that even my public school teacher at that time would come up and comment on the fact that I was reading High German from books that I was able to buy at sales for the few pennies I was able to save from working. I guess it reaches down to almost the depths of what you're doing. I like to read about other people, especially people years ago. I was an odd person with these interests, I guess. As time went on, my interests also expanded into people beyond our own community, and my best connection with people beyond our own community was some of these antique collectors coming from the cities. They were more than happy just to talk with someone that would even say a few words to them, so they would converse. So I got to talking with those people, answering their questions about the plain people. When my wife and I invested in a small farm, we had contacts with these young people coming to the town. I guess I got into it like that. Last year I probably wouldn't have done this, but I think it will work out. I think what I'm doing will be useful so that it can spread out to others that can get a chance to read this.

[To begin, I should say that all of us have certain things in common—things we will not compromise.] We lead our own lives. We are not here to judge other people and religions. Our ancestors four hundred years ago decided that they'd try and go through the straight gate and walk on the narrow path as much as possible. That means live the religious life according to the teachings of the New Testament rather than to just live for yourself in a world of comfort and entertainment. Sometimes young people will go wild, as we say, and then want to come back. They're accepted, only they'll have to come under this life style, these religious regulations, and not own cars and all these other things.

But we're not here to judge what will happen at the end of *your* lives. We're not going to even think about it. But we're hoping that everybody like you will be consistent to what you were taught and strongly live your religious lives as you see fit. The first leaders in this country were of the same mind. They wanted to have all kinds of religious liberty here, urging each religion to live their lives and be part of a supporting community all over the United States—at least have religious lives so that there would be law and order within the United States. It says in the New Testament that we should not go out so much; we should at least live the kind of life that is being taught in the New Testament so that those people that steal might see that they are doing wrong; so that other people who do things wrong like killing or stealing or being dishonest—they can then see that they're doing wrong and that it's possible to live a life that's closer to the New Testament than those that are doing things that are against the law.

We read the New Testament and encourage our children to read the New Testament because there you can take the lessons out, the religious teaching which is the base of our culture. But we also refer to the Bible and relate that to what happens today. Really, if you read the Bible it refers to so many things that are closer to us as farmers than it would be to city people. What you read out of the Bible applies to almost daily life on the farm or family happenings.

It is always very important, for example, to be neighbors in the community. That has a priority, a top necessity. If you live in a community or move into a community, you're part of the community to the extent that if there's a need you leave what you have to do and help. If your neighbor's need is greater than yours, why you just leave what you're doing and help your neighbor. I guess friendship goes before yourself.

Let me tell you what my great-grandfather did that is uppermost in my mind. The thing I mostly appreciate about him is the fact that he was selfless. As a young farmer in 1840 before he had much of a family of his own, yellow fever became almost like an epidemic. It was a simple thing, almost an ordinary thing for him to do at that time, yet it was still a brave thing for him to do. Children were dying and there weren't enough doctors around so he went to work. He would visit these people with herbs and medicines to control the yellow fever. Some of these people were weak; whole families couldn't help themselves. But my great-grandfather was very knowledgeable in herb usages so he thought his obligation was to, without pay, go and help all those people that he could as fast as possible. He was taking away from his rest, morning till night, distributing medicinal herbs to those that were afflicted. There was the danger that he'd acquire the disease himself, but to avoid getting the disease, whenever he came home in the evening he would take his clothing that he wore off and hang it in the smokehouse and smoke it during the night. That was the best thing for sanitation they knew to do at that time. Then he took a bath and retired, and the next morning he would take these clothes that were smoked and go out to more people to treat. I have respect for him or anybody else who did the same thing in those needful times. That was very strong community thinking.

It has always been this way. It is part of our religious life and teaching from the New Testament about loving the neighbor. Simple things like that. Simple teachings. There are two school-age boys in the Ephrata hospital right now who are my son's age. One of them is the son of a family who can't pay the hospital bills. The community will be paying that hospital. That's another thing that has been handed down from years ago. [We learn about these troubles] by word of mouth, you see, like at auctions. The first things they'll talk about when they get together are, "Did you hear about this sickness or this death; some person's having difficulties." It's the main thing that's spoken about even after church or before church services when people get together. Count that as important news to relate to others who they think would like to know.

Now in a few instances you might have a neighbor in the community where he would rather not have your help. And, if that happens, you just wait to be the last one to come and help and let others come and help who might be better accepted in his life style. There's all kinds of religious people in the community, and in some cases, some neighbors in a community might feel that they would, first of all, look upon their own religious faith or their own kind of people to come. If they are modern farmers, why they would first look upon their modern farming neighbors to come and help or do business with them, or to work together in harvesting.

But we all have a strong religious foundation rooted in the New Testament, and a community commitment. Beyond that there are differences.

Some of us are more conservative. Let me give you some of my group's customs, still held today: old order insists on carrying on the simple ways of doing things. Now, officially, we are called now either "plain people" or "old order people." Then there's other newer orders. It seems that the newer orders are just a gradual switch-over to modern life. But once you start changing to more education, dressing less plainly, and allowing more modern living and thinking, why, this little change will not stop at a little change—it will keep on changing to where people will make a complete change-over. So the religious thinking back of it calls for a no-change thing. So what I'll talk about is the old order, the old way.

Just about all our people use the old-fashioned [wood] cookstove.

We don't have cars at all. We don't own them. That's a religious regulation that sort of came from the very beginning of making a strict line to follow. At that time it was easy for the young people to follow that, and we feel it's still easy for them to follow the nonuse of cars. There's a limitation to the tractors, too, which is a religious regulation. The tractor use is allowed with the stipulation that you have older tractors on steel wheels. Now the Amish, who are even stricter and plainer, they still are holding onto the strict rule of allowing tractors with steel wheels but not doing fieldwork with them. So they still do all their plowing and fieldwork with horses, pulling balers and combines and maybe two-bottom plows with six mules or so, and they can do very efficiently with it—especially in the line of the energy crisis that has come up. We can farm quite competitively with the modern, big operator. Therefore, this is why I say the old order or plain life style is also economically correct.

Voting is getting less now by all our people. We're depending more on prayerful thinking. It just doesn't help to vote. Practically no voting is done in national elections. Some voting is done in local elections. I was a registered voter, but now I'm lost out. I missed two elections. I'm not registered any more, so I can't even vote this fall. But that doesn't bother me. I think the officials are getting so far removed from the public they're supposed to represent that voting doesn't help. And we refuse military service. This military service thing is carried on strong as ever. We're lucky to live in a country where this is recognized.

Taxes are paid, but we are exempt from Social Security payment. It's part of our religious thinking that we don't get anything that we didn't work for, so all our people refuse to take any aid from the Government for free. Nobody has yet petitioned anything from the Government like lime or payments of property loss by floods; it doesn't happen, we don't take anything for free.

The women do the work in and around the house and in the chicken house, perhaps, and around the cow stable; but in the fields, no. Around the

Elijah Good

house includes in the garden, but in the fields they do not have a role, though they may help out.

The men have their role to do the fields and to stay out of the house [laughter], but they can help there if they're needed. The men's role is to do the heavy work. That's what you're promised when you do go into marriage.

Dating is still old-fashioned. It's only a Sunday night thing, from seven until twelve. It's the same practice as when I was young and when even my parents and grandparents were young, and that consists of seeing the girl friend in the farmhouse parlor at the girl's house. Usually the boys hitch their horses and buggies and go out to be there exactly at seven, especially on their first date. It's a rare occasion for the boyfriend to take his girl friend out, so they'll stay in the parlor for five hours, from seven till twelve. They start [dating] roughly around sixteen, sixteen and a half. The dates are not chaperoned. When they are over sixteen, they keep in line pretty well. When their get-togethers were in this farmhouse here, why, the rest of the family went into other rooms and the downstairs of the house was left to the young people for their good times. The older people stay away and let them have their good time.

Marriage age comes close to twenty-one for girls, twenty-two for boys. Usually they court about two or three years. They'll date around at sixteen or seventeen, maybe dates with three, five, seven different girls, and then finally settle down and go with that particular girl for two or three years; then get married.

The marriage is usually in the wintertime as everyone is too busy in spring. There's no divorce, not within the old order, the plain people. In our religious teaching, divorce is not allowed. The courtship is done so carefully that after agreeing to get married, there's no thought of separation.

Family living is a strong thing. Widows and widowers usually get married again.

There is no birth control—it's just whatever amount of children is given [laughter]. You can limit your family, but no [modern] birth control methods are used. Birth control is a foreign language. It's just that tradition tells them to continue having the ordinary size family, and on the farm you can *use* the ordinary size family [more laughter].

For as long as there are no children, the wives continue working, say, at a factory to earn extra money. Their aim is to work hard, to get as much income as they can so they can be property owners of their own.

They won't join a union. Religious reasons is number one. They wouldn't join a union even if they couldn't get work. They would rather do with less pay. The union principle is opposite or works against plain principles. All along, union and plain thinking are opposites. We are strongly against the union because it hurts the nation. The union has created and is going to continue to create increased amounts of problems for this nation. The unions are the main cause of inflation.

Our young people do not ask for increased amounts of money because it bothers their conscience to be demanding. Like the union worker who would rather not work, and so strikes—that is impossible thinking in our way of living. See, ours is opposite—we'd work for nothing rather than not work.

Birthdays are just mentioned and that's it. Holidays are also not celebrated except religious holidays are held like Sundays, where you don't work. Thanksgiving is our fall holiday. On that day, no one will work, but no festival thing, no. There might be a special dinner with turkey, but that's about all.

Music? There's quite a bit of singing but no instruments but one; that's the old-fashioned harmonica. It's still used by the young people when they have these Saturday night get-togethers. See, they don't date on Saturday nights, but they have these get-togethers where they do sing quite a bit— religious songs.

There isn't a strict ruling against electric, but the misuse of electric is what the ruling is against. The misuse of electric means to plug in modern appliances. That's the misuse of electric, that's strictly forbidden. TV just doesn't fit into this life style. Even modern appliances just don't fit in. It's economically incorrect and religiously incorrect. Movies are definitely prohibited. Actually movies are serious to the extent that a person who makes it a habit to attend movies will be excommunicated. Council is even against going to town where they would show movies or slides of farm equipment. And Council is against going to public schools where slides are shown. [That's one of the reasons for the] decision that our children will not go to public school.

Our children are encouraged to stay within this life style because it's a very beautiful one, we feel: successful financially and morally.

My daughter goes to a community school run by the neighbors. It's mostly used by people who don't want to send their children to public school for various reasons. The teaching is very near the same as it was when I went to school. The classes are in one room for first to eighth grade. The teacher himself or herself is really an uneducated person because it's mostly taught by younger people who are unmarried. So the teaching itself from the *State* viewpoint would be considered unqualified teaching, but yet they get taught the main things which are reading, writing, and arithmetic, and they end up reading very nicely with anyone who went through public school. So it amounts to a very good education—the type of education our young people need for their livelihood. All the State requires is that the attendance is there and that English is taught in the schools. Otherwise they feel that the one-room schools are very successful. We go along day by day. We have had some conflicts but it's worked out nicely. The Government allows that when the children are through eighth grade, they need not go to high school. So as long as the laws are going to continue the way they are now, we are more than happy to really feel that things are fine in that way.

We've never been against education completely. Even before the Government made you go to school, the Mennonite children would just attend classes for a short time during the winter for the boys to learn to write; women didn't write. The women at that time didn't learn to write their names but the men wrote their names and were taught some arithmetic. Women learned to read but not quite as much as boys learned to read. In many cases there were women that couldn't even read the Bible, but that was in the 1700s. In the 1800s it was a more common thing to do to get the girls to learn to read, but it was thought foolish to teach a girl to write. But the girls were taught to do simple arithmetic like addition so that they could do some business like selling some things. The education didn't amount to much because, like I said, school was attended only during the winter. As soon as the boys could do some arithmetic and reading and writing, it was sufficient. Now they go to public schools through the eighth grade.

Going to high school is not encouraged by us. There's a greater chance for them to leave the culture. It's proved out so often. Higher education like high school does something to them. It does one thing which I think you can realize. That is, after going at that age through two or three more years of school, it's harder for you to use the manure fork to clean out the cow stable. And common sense can't be acquired in school. The common sense things are a gift. School adds to reading, writing, and arithmetic, but to actually exercise your brain, school doesn't help you much in that.

Elijah, do you consider as education the things that your parents taught you about farming and things you teach your children?

Yes, learning to do things by hand, and learning to do things while *doing* them, is by far the most practical education. Common sense is when you have a practical answer quickly to certain needs.

To be a farmer you learn by just being around the crops. It's proven out in so many cases that the young people who went through high school just to be farmers ended up financial failures and had to sell out because of bankruptcy. It happens so often. What they learned out of the books was to do things in a big way; and to go into it in a big way, they had to go into debt and they didn't make it. What they did is to think that to farm, you sit at a desk and write things out from morning to night. That just doesn't make a profit in farming.

Others weren't quite this strict, however. They split off and formed a more progressive group. I'm sort of a split personality to a degree, because it happened that my father was the only one of his family that did not join the progressive group, the Black Bumper group. All the others in my father's family were Black Bumpers. My grandfather was involved, being one of the most influential preachers in the old order church. When my grandfather saw this thing shaping up where it couldn't be settled except that the young people were choosing to use cars, he decided to allow cars and hold onto the majority of the church. He and the bishop agreed that under the situation, the best thing to do is to become less strict and allow the use of cars, although they must be painted black—the bumpers and everything—black all over. So under this stipulation in 1927, my grandfather, the bishop, a few of the other ministers, and deacons continued having church. But there were others who decided that his change would not be old order, because if you start allowing changes to come in, why then there will be more changes. So the church actually divided in 1927. The young people would follow my grandfather's decision and permit the use of cars and other changes, while the conservatives on my mother's side were strictly maintaining their original regulations that you continue horse and wagons like the Amish. So my father had to make a decision and it was his own decision. He decided that he would support the original thinking of my mother's side. This was sort of unusual because it did tear right through families. These changes the conservatives feared are now proving out, for now, forty-nine years since that time, the Black Bumpers have discontinued the use of German, have changed some in their dress, and do not drive black cars any more.

There's been other changes. There's English people moving in and German people moving out. There are people coming from the city and buying places to build new homes on. That happens increasingly more so. This might be interesting to you. In all these years living in this country, people did not work on Sundays, no matter what religion you represented. You wouldn't do your washing on Sunday, you wouldn't mow your lawn on Sunday.

The hay spoiling or the crops spoiling on a Sunday doesn't bother us a bit. That's the definite day of rest. Not one thing is done on Sundays [that concerns] harvesting. Now on Sunday morning the *chores* definitely have to be done. In a family like ours, each in the family has their particular chore to do daily and on Sundays. Takes only like an hour or an hour and a half before breakfast, so that everybody does his part and the rest of the day is figured strongly Sunday; then the same thing for the evening, too.

Now eggs are not collected Sunday mornings. They are collected Sunday afternoons. So all these hatcheries allow that on Sundays there will be more eggs broken 'cause there'll be only one or two collections on Sundays. That's the only thing against having an egg operation—the Sunday work bothers a lot of people. If there wouldn't be that problem there would be a lot more chicken houses built by the plain people. They'll avoid that and would even rather choose to farm tobacco instead just because you don't do a thing with tobacco on Sundays, where with chickens or with cows you have to do all this work. Of course, some of my brothers just fatten cattle and that's another way of avoiding Sunday work. Now the Amish farmer made it a religious thing not to allow their milk to be sold on Sundays; not even allow the milk truck to come in on Sundays to pick up the milk, so they have to store Sunday's milk to Monday morning, and then the milk truck has to make two routes Monday morning.

But just go over to neighboring counties and now they are starting to work on Sunday. You might hear a hammer, someone repairing his roof, building a garage on Sunday, and doing his lawn with a power mower on Sunday. Such things were unheard of here, but these people that come from the city are introducing work on Sunday, which is very offending.

We all believe in hard work, but working all the time, including Sundays, comes under the category of greed. There's a verse in the New Testament teaching us our life style where it says in a few words, "With the sweat of thy brow shalt thou eat thy bread." Can you take the lesson out of this verse? That part of scriptures is also strongly taught that if there's more than you need to eat, why you save that for others or give to the poor.

This harvesttime of the year, the afternoon let up or rest is also practical and is commonly done by the old life style. You can get just as much accomplished because you start early and you'll be working late to take in the noon rest. You'll be getting about the same amount of work done as if you rushed the whole day. Actually even our tough bodies will wear out if they are overworked. You can't just go on and on. That's one thing where tobacco farming is frowned upon. During the tobacco harvest, most of the farmers won't even allow for a rest period during that rush to the extent that they work their bodies to where they lose pounds and get thin. We see overworking [to the detriment of health] as being greedy.

Also a very offending thing is the new style of dress or undress. To the old plain men and women, this wearing of men's clothing by women is also very offending. We try to maintain a consistency. Each one is dressed the same so that they are all alike, and there's no instances of where some will look down upon others who dress poorly as opposed to ones who have fancy dresses. When some women dress in such a way to show off, and are proud of their dress, that's looked down upon by the majority of the plain people. So, definitely all those things of show are looked down upon as objects of pride which are definitely taught against from the Bible viewpoint.

But I don't want to give the impression that I'm against *all* change. When we have sick people in the neighborhood or family, we don't hesitate to use the best thing available. That's what they did at that time, only they didn't have such good things available to them.

The key, I think, is whether or not the change is *useful* and not *detrimental*.

My great-grandfather on my mother's side was a small time farmer, but he had a shop that was run by water power. He would rather work with tools than do farming. We can still point out to people where his shop stood. He was considered quite a genius for his time. We shouldn't do this —talk about someone who accomplished so many things, and feel proud of it—because actually he didn't feel proud of these accomplishments himself. It just occurred to him that some of these things could be done better. And his family was one of the most conservative ones. Yet, he was the man that did quite a number of things. He made an improvement on the treadle sewing machines. And he made the cradles for the farmers in the community. I have one of these cradles that he had made that was made to order for a neighbor farmer. Then he also did a lot of surveying, and he did another important thing. He was born in 1820, and by 1840 the making and building of railroads was really important to the modern American at that time. When they had to uncouple railroad cars, they just had to pull the pin; but he thought there would be a much safer way to do it, so he invented the coupler that they use today. But he didn't get the patent on it. He didn't want honor or even want money. He just wanted to be helpful and that's all. He wanted to show people that there would be a better way. The railroad company then got that patent. His attitude about honor was because of the teaching of humility in the New Testament. Our ancestors never wanted to have much honor to their name. Christianity taught our ancestors to avoid selfishness very much. Actually seek selflessness. That is similar to the whole concept of avoiding modern comforts.

In farming, there are leaders who try new things for all of us. These are ones that are looked up to as leaders. They are mostly the ones in the farming community who have the better crops, the large yields, the cows that give the most milk, for example, or the most profit in pigs so that they should be and are looked up to as leaders who others can follow. Others in the community will come over and visit with this successful farmer and try and follow his practices so that they can also be successful. This has been done for hundreds of years, and that's why the community leaders are sometimes the ones that introduce improved methods. Just to illustrate, there was a conflict when I was still going to school at about age fifteen.

Elijah Good and interviewers

There was a conflict to decide among the farmers themselves in a community whether it was better to use the hybrid corn as opposed to the old corn, open pollinated corn. Years ago my dad and other farmers would collect the seed from their field. They would go out into the best part of the field and pick out the biggest ears of corn, and then one winter evening they would take this bushel of select corn and have the whole family get together and just select the best kernels of each ear of corn, meaning that at the end of the cob you would discard that corn and feed that to the animals, but in the certain center part of each ear of corn you would save those uniform seeds for next year's crop. That was open pollinated corn; it was fertile corn and would grow and germinate after planting. But now the seed company comes along and says we have a hybrid corn which is better and the conflict is there. We can't always trust the salesmen. So the leader of the community will venture out and give part of his field the trial on whether the hybrid seed corn is better. He just tests it out year after year and comes to a conclusion by results. And he's not only doing this for himself but other neighbors are watching him. And he talks to them about how he does this, comes up with figures of yields, until the whole community sees the whole picture of what's happening. That's just an illustration of one way a leader in a community can be a leader in crops and livestock.

I hear real old people who are now ninety, for example, say that the last fifty years made a much bigger change than the last 150 years according to their guess or estimation. Just to illustrate, let's go back to around 1825, when farming was still done like it was in Bible time, cutting grass with a scythe and harvesting grain with a sickle, and the sheaves were made and tied up just as was done thousands of years ago. Then vast changes came in. The greatest changes are the more recent ones, and the pace of changing is faster today than it was a hundred years ago. The pace of change is increasing. [But we don't necessarily want to go back.] Let's say it this way: in today's religious life, you take each day as it comes and make the best of it, not wishing for things that might have been better years ago; and, hopefully, there will be no worse days ahead. Just take each day as it comes.

I think I'm trying hard to be content the same way as I see others who are content who have things differently than what I have. I am comparing my contentedness with others. I think I'm just about as content as the average person is. I would be more content, just a little more happy, if I had been able to acquire a farm in the limestone area. See these people like myself, who live in the nonlimestone areas, are looked down upon to a small degree. You see, we live in the back here. When we first moved back here, people started looking down on us and all those others who lived in the back here.

No, it doesn't matter to me, but I have a personal feeling, it's sensible thinking, that it would be easier to farm the limestone soils instead of having sloping ground, rocky soil, erosion problems, and less fertile soils. The limestone soils are more expensive and more in demand. A person like me had to leave the area because of not acquiring the ability to purchase a farm in the limestone area. This farm was a cheaper one and that classed you as one who did not have quite the ability that others had. But again I was content and happy for the amount of health we had and having this much. If I would have worked almost day and night trying to maybe increase our property, we probably wouldn't even be as able to do as well as we do now. You see, being content means to be satisfied with what comes your way. Being content seems to be more important than financial gain. You can choose your own attitudes. The attitude of the farmers is that farming is a hobby to them where you work at your hobby all year round and the hobby can be and is profitable. Now if you don't have that attitude toward farming, why, it's a little harder, and it's mostly your own fault if you don't have that attitude of freedom. On these family farms you can actually live like a king, work as many hours as you want, or you can start your hours early or late and you're not tied down like you would be working under a boss in a factory.

But I would recommend, and most of our people would even recommend, that in the remaining hours that are in your life, own some ground and do some things with the ground-producing crops and have some animals to take care of. That would be good for yourselves, for your health and your thinking, and for everybody in America if we could be occupied in this way. They'd be doing something useful to America and to themselves. Every young person your age in America should think in terms of saving like our young people do for the purchase of ground that's productive. Americans have gone way overboard in buying very expensive furnishings, and instead they should have saved that money to buy land. I don't see beauty in expensive goods. I see beauty in woodwork. Woodworking to me is building barns and putting up anything in the old-fashioned way. I hate to see modern buildings. They aren't beautiful to me. Beauty to me in buildings is farm buildings built in the old-fashioned way. Why, I see beauty in all these old timbers, all these old boards; I see beauty in the slope of the roof, I see beauty in each part of the barn here. I see beauty in the hay crop here and I even see beauty in the way the bales are stacked. I even see beauty in old things like how hay was stacked years ago. I still regret some of the beauties you don't see any more, like the sheaves of wheat and the straw stacked in front of the barn, thrashing the old-fashioned way—those were real beauties to me. We heard the steam engine whistle today over there where Frank and I had went to get some things. The steam engine itself is almost a bygone thing which we won't be able to see the beauty of any more. Every hour of the day, there's beauty to think about being close to nature on the family farm. If you leave the farm and go into the city, it just blots out to ugliness.

The macadam roads as opposed to back roads. Highways are not beautiful to us, or anyplace where clouds of black smoke are coming from; and where there's crowds of people in a rush, unsettled. Places covered with buildings and industrial plants are vacuum spaces in our minds. They don't really exist. We don't have no business there. We just drive around those places and stay clear of them. Industry coming in, taking away farmland, means to us that that space actually is a vacuum to our minds as if it isn't there.

And we can enjoy those beautiful things while we're working, while we're traveling to town and back, or going to auctions; even the soil itself can be enjoyed when it's moist after a rain or seeing the earthworms; the overturned earth while you're plowing is appreciated. There's a lot of satisfaction seeing the fertile earth being worked, being made ready to plant. We see beauty in any kind of field, in any stage of crops being planted.

We never even wondered [whether or not there was a God]. No, I never wondered. You're testing my thinking. I think I can say accurately that every day we see there must be more than just nature. We're humans, and we're born on this world and it will be only a short space until we die and then there's an everlasting existence after that. Actually life here compared to infinite time is only a short space, which means that it's too important to waste with entertainment or for your own comfort or satisfaction just for yourself. That's why selflessness is taught in the Bible so much. You people might be thinking that much of this work is going on because each one is trying to get more farms. No. It's just that rather than wasting time and money on entertainment, we would rather just keep busy on the farm and keep out of mischief by working.

Death is inevitable. You know that it's happening all around you, and it comes so quick you don't know whether you're going to be here the next day or the next year, so you do try and live like I said before—every day individually and be prepared for that end that's coming so that you don't need to be afraid. We can also look back on our ancestors who had to give up a lot more than we did this day. See, when they became Christians and followed Bible teaching, many of them were persecuted because they wouldn't do military work and got in conflict with other religions that persecuted them. They lost their lives easily after believing what they read in the Bible. They were actually willing and happy to give up their lives.

They had to give up a lot more than what we have to today.

"Put your two cents in."

MARGE ORLOSKY

Marge Orlosky is the oldest resident of Marble, Colorado. She has been living there since 1928, when she married Charles Orlosky, a trapper. When Charles died, she remained in Marble and lives there alone, though her son Jack, a photographer, artist, and potter, lives close by.

She lives a life without frills ("I never did expect to have what my next door neighbor had, and I don't want it."), a life that remains much as it was when she was trapping coyote with Charles. After the interview, for example, we helped make sauerkraut and harvest potatoes. We grated about thirty heads of cabbage, salted the grated layers, and packed the sauerkraut in a large ceramic container. The harvesting was simply forking the potatoes from under the ground.

By the time the day was finished, we all got a taste of the living past, and a good feeling. Mrs. Orlosky is one of the finest people we have ever met.

—KAREN SPEVAK, KATHY WILSON, KENT BULLARD, MARK SINK. PHOTOGRAPHS BY CAROLYN PULEO. —NITA BUNNELL, ADVISER, COLORADO ROCKY MOUNTAIN SCHOOL.

I'M A CITY GIRL, you know. I was raised in Pueblo. I married Charlie Orlosky when we was over in Pueblo. We come up here in 1928. He was born in Coal Basin. It's right behind Redstone. It's where Mid-Continent gets their coal from. When he first come up here, he was only nine years old. That was in 1909. The town, Marble, was running well, not full blast, but it was running. His dad was a diamond saw man, he cut the marble with a diamond saw; but Charlie was always a trapper. He loved to trap. So the year after we came up here, I learned how to trap, so then we both had trap lines.

Charlie had a black horse called Jim that he raised from a colt, and the horse was interested in the traps and things. Charlie rented another horse that fall and took me up with him and showed me where the trap line was. Then I'd go up in the middle of the week with Jim, and if I didn't remember where a trap was, why that horse would go look. This was up around a little mountain near here called Arkansas. It's quite a trip around there. Only being up there once before with Charlie, it was kinda hard to remember the whole country and where the traps might be. But the horse knew. But if Charlie happened to set a fox trap or a coyote trap *behind* the horse, well then the horse didn't know where it was on the trail. So then I'd have to go by descriptions. He'd tell me where it was. Anyhow, I couldn't set a big trap, yet—I wasn't strong enough. So I always reset the small traps and took out the animals, and he'd go back on weekends [to get the big ones]. We trapped martin, weasel, fox, and coyote. I doubt if there are very few trappers left any more that are skilled enough to trap a coyote, because he's nobody's dumb fool; he knows what he's doing. I know. I feed them over here in the wintertime and I've watched them; I go buy a bone or something over there; you ought to see them, the way they monkey around before they even think about getting that bone. And then they finally get it all dug out around it, you know. And then one of them will grab it and throw it. They're waiting for a trap or something.

Trapping was the only way we supported ourselves for a while. Charlie went to work for the Government as a predator trapper in '39. He trapped ten years for them. He was a "co-operative trapper," as they called him. In the wintertime the sheepmen paid him for every hide he got. They'd give him so much money, say four dollars or something, and he got to keep the hide and sell the hide. In the summertime when the furs were no good, then the Government paid him and he'd save the scalps and ship them in.

When that 10-80 poison came out, though, he quit the Government. That 10-80 poison—there's no antidote for it. It will kill time and time again.

There's no way to destroy it. It doesn't take any amount of it at all to kill. As long as I've known the sheepman, he says he's losing sheep by coyotes *all the time,* which he don't, which is a big story. But he wants them all killed out. First, lathalium came out. It was so cruel that the Government only used it for just a very few years—two years, or three. It was made up in Denver and was very painful, took a long time to kill them. So then they came out with 10-80, and I think it was discovered in Denver, too. And there's no way to destroy it; that's what's so bad about it. Nixon outlawed it for about two years, I think, and then Ford just let them have it again. They're only supposed to have one 100-pound bait for every township. A township is thirty-six square miles. They always would put the poison in the forest where they're not supposed to put it.

Mr. Love, that used to own that ranch up on Sopris, was losing lots of lambs. Well, the trapper before wouldn't look at his traps often enough and his coyotes would twist out. So Charlie went down and caught the coyotes, so that helped. The group was well satisfied with him, but they wanted the poison, too. But Charlie just wouldn't use it, that's all. He took a leave of absence, and we came up here one winter and the man who took his place didn't bury his poison bait good and they were losing dogs and everything else.

So he just wouldn't work for them, that's all; just wouldn't do it. They weren't losing any sheep anyhow because he got the coyotes down till they were not really killing at all. [The ones that were left] were crippled. When he first moved up on Sopris, there for a whole year, he hardly ever caught a coyote with all four feet—whole feet. One of them didn't have but one foot left; the rest of them were gone.

Now they're killing all our bears off because the laws are not specific enough in saying that they must have killed sheep before *they* can be killed. I was up at a town meeting here this summer and they said that they could kill the bear if he was in the vicinity of the sheep herd. But, my Lord, they'd be in the vicinity all over the mountains—that's where the sheep are. The average bear is not a killer.

And when the sheepmen found out about cyanide gas guns they brought them by the thousands. They strung them all out over the hills and left them. And they were killing off the foxes and everything else. Cows will even suck on the things. I don't know why, but it seems a sheepman gets so radical on coyotes and predators it is just absolutely ridiculous. He doesn't want one of them left on earth.

At one place up here, these cattlemen were surrounded by sheepmen. And this was when the 10-80 first came out, so the sheepmen started putting the 10-80 all around the cattlemen. Well, the first thing you know the cattlemen was having to feed their cows hay in the summertime, because

Marge Orlosky

their pastures were absolutely dug up by the pocket gophers. There was no control. A coyote hunts like a cat and he bounces. He goes along in a field and when he hears something, why, he'll bounce down on it and catch. They're the best rodent-control things we have, is a coyote; he's just wonderful. But the sheepmen still wanted everything killed off—he still does. And it's not right.

Up in the high country a few pocket gophers is wonderful because in the wintertime they dig their burrows way deep, and then the snow melts and it holds the water way under the ground, which is fine. But when it's dug up too much then it's no good at all. [They need the coyotes to control the population.] The answer is to make the sheepman quit having so dern much power. He's got too big a lobby. Things used to always balance out. People say that foxes are pheasant hunters—they get all the pheasant eggs and all that. Well, if we had enough ground cover up here, things like pheasants and grouse would be protected. But the sheep are overgrazing and their hoofs cut up the ground. We don't have the vegetation on the ground to protect wildlife or hold back the snow because of the overgrazing of the sheep. This Arkansas Mountain up here was named "Arkansas" because it was so green. Now it's becoming a gray mountain. They're overgrazing it terrible. It's just awful. And like I told them up there that night; it's not going to only hurt us—it's hurting everybody. This *was* a good watershed. They're supposed to move these herds to a new bedding ground every night, but nobody's watching them.

During the Depression, Charlie worked for nine days in three years' time, but we got along just fine with trapping. We got the most for the fur that we've gotten since then. Furs were real good. Evidently they were shipped out to other countries. And we always had a garden so we had potatoes and other things, and then we had the wild meat like deer and elk. Of course, with no refrigeration, we hung them outside, and then when spring came, I made corned beef from it. Take salt, saltpeter, and make a brine. Soak it. They call it corned beef, but there is no corn in it. And we made all our own soap and such during the Depression. The train still ran and it wasn't that bad. We've had lots worse times. One year I had two operations. The same year a hay barn burnt down with a lot of our stuff in it. Charlie's panyards and this and that was all gone. Then we came up here and had a big flood and the little cabin got all flooded. I had a time that summer. We finally moved into Charlie's mother's house that was across the road. And we no more got settled in there than the man who owned it came up to tear it down. We loaded up everything I had there on a flat-bedded truck and took it on over to a house that didn't have any windows or doors in it and set everything in the middle of the floor and I just felt like settin' down and bawling. I'm telling you, you're weak after operations, and I had had two of them that year. I think I even forgot a lot of things that I once had till maybe I would think of it years and years later, you know.

When the flood was coming, Charlie was working on some government report and I said, "You better come and listen." I had gone through the flood in Pueblo in 1921 and I knew what this roaring was. I said, "You better come to the door and listen to this."

He did, and he said, "Oh boy, you better put on your boots and let's get out of here!" Well, I didn't want to put on my boots 'cause I thought I would get bogged down. But I did, and Charlie grabbed his typewriter and his guns and his pair of binoculars. And his reports. I grabbed our son's picture, a loaf of bread, a pocketbook, and a tomcat. I got up to our little '36 Chevy—had it parked up there—then I turned the horses loose and they came running out of the flood area. Charlie was waiting for me up there and I said, "Where's the dog?"

And he said, "I don't know, don't you got it?" And said, "Run back to the house!" And I opened up the door too fast and she got scared and run under the bed and I had go crawling under after her [laughs]. Then I kept running back into the flood and I'd roll up a bedroll and I'd take it, and got Charlie's pack; and he came back for his saddle, and I grabbed up some of his panyards which were loaded to go the next day.

Then he hollered, "You better get out of there. The flood's broke out over there!" So I dropped it and started to run; and we had raised minks at one time, and there was fence around the back of the house. So I run out the gate and all that water and stuff came and pinned my leg against the fence post. There I was. I never get hysterical or too excited until after things are over with. Then I have the shakes. But I kept hanging onto the top of the gatepost and trying to get my leg out of there. Once I thought I was going to break it. All that water and mud was just building up around me, but finally I just pulled my leg out of there. It had taken a lot of the skin stuff off it along with my dress off of the lower part of me; and I started through the mud and stuff. It was clear up past my knees. I couldn't make very good time and I got over there to where we had shallow ditches to kind of drain off water and it was kind of swampy and I went in one of those and about fell down.

Well, anyhow, I got over there and I was all right. I saw myself running from that flood so many times that night. I'd wake up and I was always all right. I just barely got out of there before the whole flood broke loose and covered where I was. So that's what we saved. A loaf of bread. A few things. Why the bread I have no idea. I thought we were going to be hungry, I guess.

But there's always been something protects me. Terrible things, really awful things, and I've always come out of it. It's not luck. I've always

thought that I was well protected; maybe that's why I don't get into hysterics. I'm not a hysterical person.

And then I don't carry my troubles to bed with me. If I've got lots of things to figure out sometimes, I'll wake up early in the morning when I'm part awake and I can figure it out then. But go to bed with troubles, I never do.

And I've always been a person who never liked bad habits like smoking or drinking.

But I do like to watch what's going on in the world. With the women getting an education like they do now, it's not good for them to have to stay home all the time. She feels that she's bound to that house all the time, and that's no good.

Now I think a lot of people don't have children because they know they're better off without them. That's good. Because I think all children take a lot of loving, and they should know even when you punish them that you're just punishing them for their own good. Who likes a brat? I think so many people are doing so much better with their children. I don't know why. I think people are learners. They love their children and are more natural with them than they were for a long time. But if you can't take care of them, don't have them.

I don't have an education myself. I only went to seventh grade. I've had a life education, but not a formal one. Wisdom doesn't always come from age, because I think so many times age is too set in their ways. They don't stop to see the other guy's point of view. And they don't go along with the times. You've got to *grow*. You've got to keep growing along to change your own way of looking at things. I think you learn through life to learn to go along with the times you're in. Now Charlie was very well set in his ways and he didn't like to see things change at all. But I believe you've just got to go along with the way things are and learn there are some things you can't fight. You can put up a protest about it but, if you lose, you can't let it get you down. I think you go along generally with the way things go and do the best you can; and get into everything you can that you think is wrong. Like fight the Placeda Dam. Fight the ski area up here.

I love how people live nowadays. They build a home. It's all glass. They have great big homes and great rooms they can't possible use. It's just, what would you call it, a status symbol. And all it does is waste our electricity and fuel. Look at how people waste their water. People won't realize their wastes until another depression. Whatever keeps going up has to come down.

I say if you don't put your two cents in and things don't turn out the way you want them, it's a lot your fault for not helping. If you fight and things don't turn out exactly the way you want, well, you can always feel, "I did the best I could."

"Change my life? No. I might do worse."

CHARLIE GRACE

Charlie Grace was born February 1, 1884, in Gentry County, Missouri, into a large family of brothers and sisters. Though he has seven children, twenty-one grandchildren, and seventeen great-grandchildren, he now lives alone in the farm home where he and his wife raised their family.

"Come in. Let's go back to the kitchen where the light's better and sit around the table," Charlie Grace always greeted us. "My eyesight's never been good and we can see out here." In spite of his eyesight and his difficulty hearing, it is hard to believe he is ninety-one years old. Always dressed in overalls and a plaid shirt, he looks the lifelong farmer he is. His son takes care of the farm now and has for the last five years or so, but Charlie still knows every bump and rock on his 160 acres.

He likes to get out and spends as much time as he can in his garden. "My children don't like me to come out here much." As he was hoeing his beans, he warned us, "Be sure and let me know if I'm hitting the plant instead of the weed!"

Charlie was a little shy at first and somewhat overwhelmed by the five of us eagerly listening and taping every word and taking roll after roll of pictures, but he always was disappointed when we

had to leave. Once, after we visited him, he was sick for several days. We hoped it wasn't from our visit. "Oh no," he hastened to assure us. "I think I just ate something. But, if it makes you come back to visit me, it'll be worth getting sick again."
[*Charlie Grace died April 15, 1976.*]

—JENNY KELSO, DOUG SHARP, SUZANNE CARR.
PHOTOGRAPHS BY STEPHEN LUDWIG.
—ELLEN MASSEY, ADVISER, Bittersweet.

I BELONG TO A CHURCH but I don't belong to a church organization down here. I've had a little different views on religion than a lot of people. I went to church here, and there was a lot of times the preachers here urged me to join, and I said, "I think whenever you become a child of God, you belong to Christ's church already, and I don't see any reason of joining anywhere else." And I never did. I joined the Baptist Church when I was eleven and was baptized in Muddy Creek, and they had to cut the ice so that wasn't very nice either. But I didn't catch a cold.

I don't know how you believe, but I believe Christ is the only gateway to heaven. If you believe in Christ, you are already doomed for heaven; that's it!

A preacher on TV the other day was going to tell us what belief means. Now what does he know about belief any more than we do? You know whether you believe something or not, just as well as he does. Christ said, "If you believe on me, you shall not perish but have everlasting life." And I'd rather take Christ's word for it than that preacher. I have always been that way regardless who the preacher is and where he is.

I never could believe very much in public prayer. They go to the TV and every sermon you listen to them pray to God, but they go to the microphone to pray to God. Well, they are praying to people, aren't they? If they are not a-praying to people, why do they use the microphones? The Bible plainly tells them that the Pharisees liked to get up and pray to be heard, but He told them not to do that, didn't He, but to go into their closets and pray in secret and he would answer them. The people that preach today don't believe that—at least they don't practice it. I don't excuse any of them or any I have heard on TV. I think it would be all right to talk and tell what they want the church to do and so on, but this preacher prays before they even take up the collection, and he prays again for that. It may help because they get the biggest collection there of any church I know.

I had a cousin that used to live in Kansas City and he said they hire singers to sing—that a church had to be carried on that way. I said they ought to hire their listeners, too. They deserve pay just as well as the others! I don't call it worshiping God if you got to be paid to do it. But there is going to come a day when all this is not going to amount to much to any of us, anyway.

My family is far more important to me than any of this stuff anyway. My wife and I, we lived about, oh, ten, twelve miles apart back before we were married. She would be up in our neighborhood a-visiting once in a while and it just happened on one Sunday that she came home from church with a cousin of mine. And it happened that when we went back to church that night, we went back together, and I don't know, I guess from then on I kept going with her. I expect it was over a year before we married. We were both twenty. She was about four or five months older than me.

When I got married in 1904, I had seventy-five dollars and I thought I was awful lucky to have that. Oh, I also had my team and a few little farm tools—plow and wagon. I was up in the northwest part of this state where we had bought a farm, but I didn't have anything to pay on it. I bought it on time. It was just a forty-acre farm, and we only lived on it one year. Then we went and rented bigger places.

My folks give me a dozen chickens and a cow. That helped out, of course, a little, but there we were. We had to live for a year before our crops were ready to gather. I don't see myself how people got along, but we always lived. Always had something on the table.

I've been a farmer all my life. Times were hard back them times, too. In 1905 our oldest son was born and in the fall of 1906 we rented a farm—paid cash rent—and it just took all the crop that I raised to pay the rent. I said, "I'll go to work outside." I sold off all the stuff I had and I went and for thirty-five dollars a month I worked outside for a year. That didn't suit me very good, either. So we come back and rented a place for two years and then we bought it, sold it at a little profit, and bought another one. I kept the last one six years, then the price come up and I doubled my money. Then I came down here to south Missouri in 1920 and bought this farm, the same size place for just the profit I had made on the other one. That's how I come to come to this country, just to get out of debt. But I always liked it here and I always stayed. When I bought this farm I paid for it, and therefore it was home. And my wife said, "We'll keep it." And we did.

I sometimes feel I accomplished very little in my life. But, well, I have a family. We have had eight children, seven of them are still living. They are all healthy and got good homes of their own. Therefore, I feel very thankful for all that. I have tried to be a help to them.

There isn't a great burden in raising eight children. You are always broke, but you have to spend your money on something anyway. It is a good deal

what my old uncle used to say—he lived here right by us. "It don't make any difference how much you make, if you spend just a little less than what you make, you will get along. But I don't care how much you make, if you spend more than you make, you are going to go broke." And I think that's kind of like it is in life.

I don't think I ever did try to influence any of my children in what to do, except Mary, and she didn't do it anyway. But I do think it's important for a parent to help get their child started. My father had eleven children and if I couldn't have got his name on the paper, I couldn't never have bought my first farm at all. I guess it would be all right for children to do it on their own if they had a way to do it, but there isn't but very seldom anyone who could buy a farm without their parents.

I need other people to help me. I found it out very young when I needed friends. I ran away when I was fifteen years old. There was eleven of us children. I didn't have any grudges with my father or mother nor with the children, but I thought I could do better alone. I found out afterwards that I'd made a big mistake. But I met a man that I went to working with. He was about ten years older than me. He was a married man and he just kind of took me under his arm and just kept me and protected me. But I always thought now, a fellow like that was surely a true friend. We'd be into tough joints where they was tough people and all that. He always told them that they were not to bother me. And his word always seemed to go. A fellow like that you couldn't say had any reason for it. Later on, oh, I guess six or seven years after that, after I was married, I moved out where he was working and got a job. We were just about a mile apart again. He never did forget me. And I always trusted him.

When I moved to this country from north Missouri, I hadn't been here but a little bit till I bought some sheep. I was just new to the country and didn't know anyone and this fellow wanted to sell me these sheep. I didn't have enough money to pay for them right then.

"Well," he said, "you go ahead and buy these sheep." He priced them to me cheap enough. "And you can just pay me for them when you get ready."

I said, "No, I wouldn't want to do that."

He said, "All I'd ask is that I just take your note for it." Well, he just talked around and he finally talked me into it.

I brought the sheep right on home and the next day I met him up here in town and I supposed he'd want me to go in and sign a bank note, but he said, "Now right in here they have paper." He went into one of them restaurants there and picked out the tablet and just wrote on it that I promised to pay and had me sign my name to it. He said, "That's as good as any other note to me," and stuck it in his pocket. I've often thought of him after that. Ain't very many people'd put a trust in a stranger that had just got to the country and he didn't know nothing about me. He said, "I just thought that I had pretty good judgment of people." So he was willing to trust me. I've always believed that most people are basically good and want to help you, don't you?

I never went much to school. When I was about twelve or thirteen I had —well, we called it granulated lids—and I've had them ever since. I just about lost one eye and I never did see good after that. I never did go to school any more. But the time I went to school I attended Lone Star. I've always felt education was a good thing. Of course, back in them days there were not very many country people that ever got farther than the eighth grade because they wasn't very many of the country folks that was able, or thought they were able, to send their kids on to high school. And there were lots of the people that didn't want to send them on. They didn't think it made any difference. They thought because *they* made it without an education it'd always be that way. I think it's always been valuable, and now, not only is it valuable, I think it's absolutely necessary if you aim to make a living.

There have been a lot of changes in school since I last attended. I went to school where we had eighty students and one teacher. The highest paid teachers would get up to forty, fifty dollars a month. When I was a school-boy they hired the teacher and the teacher done the janitor work. Teachers was plentiful and jobs was scarce and they'd say, "We'll take it." The first money I ever made was a nickel a day for sweeping the floor at school. The teacher would hire me and when wintertime came I built the fires.

I've heard that now methods have changed and reasons have changed. I've got a grandchild. He's a teacher and he's also been working in colleges. I said, "They don't teach measurements like they used to or anything like that."

And he said, "You don't need it."

And I said, "Well, I don't see why you wouldn't need it. I am still old-fashioned enough to think that if I go out there and buy a piece of land, I want to know how many feet it takes to make a rod, and how many rods it takes to make an acre and all that stuff."

He said, "They don't teach that."

I've seen a lot of other changes in my lifetime. Grover Cleveland was the first President that I can remember. There is not a lot of difference between all the Presidents which I remember. The biggest differences is only when they are running.

I think there's a lot of things need changing about our government, but I really don't think there'll be any change—only as things get beyond their control and they *have* to make changes. Our government has failed to be by the people and for the people. That's what it said in the Constitution. But

Jenny Kelso, Doug Sharp, and Charlie Grace

it's by the politicians and for the politician now and not for the people. You take your government today and they talk about giving to poor nations, but they don't give to the poor in the poor nations. They give to the leaders over there and the poor gets very little of it, if any.

I don't know that we're very much better off now than the Communists already. They got pretty near as much control of us here as they have there. The rich people over there gets along pretty good and that's the same way it is over here. It just looks to me like our government has got our country in such a shape, that it looks to me like we are liable to go most anyway.

Of course, I can't really look back and say that it was the good old days back in our time. One of the harder times for me was the Depression. I remember it was pretty bad. I guess it was in 1931 or '32 when the Depression was the worst. I don't know how my family overcame it. Well, course we was just like everybody else. We loaded our stuff and sold. And then in 1934 to add on to this Depression, we had the worst drought this country's ever known. There was no feed raised here. I had forty acres in corn and didn't even have a roasting ear that year. We cut our corn and in the year of 1934 it had just grown up about waist high; that's as high as it ever did get. We cut that corn and it didn't fill the hayloft half full. But we did have a patch of cane that we had sowed. It lived, and after the fall rains came it commenced to growing up. And we just lived.

One thing hurts in a depression so bad is when things went to booming, there was so many people that wanted to get rich. They took mortgages on the land they already had to buy more. And for years after that here you couldn't of sold that and got half what you give for it.

Our first depression was just after World War I, when things began to boom. I can remember well. I was raised in the same neighborhood where I lived then and I knew them farmers. Nearly all the older farmers owned their farms. But when things began to boom, there was any amount of them that bought new farms, either just to enlarge or bought for their children. And there was nine out of ten of them that lost their land. I had one brother that kept on buying all this high-priced stuff. He said, "It can't never go back again. Can't now, no. You will never see these cheap times again." But he seen them and he seen them pretty quick. And it just about cleaned him out, too.

Even though the Depression was rough on me, in a way I'd have to admit I've been successful in getting by this far anyway, and I got everything, I guess, that I dreamed of, so I think that would be success. I ain't been no big success if it means getting out and making wealth. I don't believe money can make a person happy, but it can come in pretty handy a lot of times. What would make me more happy than to have a lot of money would be able to get along with everybody in the neighborhood and be friendly and see things going right. That'd make me a lot happier than it would just making another dollar and putting it in the bank.

This McIntire that used to live down at Brush Creek here said his father and mother—back before Roosevelt's day when he guaranteed the banks— just saved and saved until they had about seven or eight hundred dollars in the bank, and the bank went busted. He said they'd been laying this money up—they didn't make much—just saving a little at a time until they got a few hundred dollars ahead there. When the bank went busted they only got paid back about five cents on the dollar. And oh, he said, they was just worried to death over it. He told them, "Now there's not a bit of use for you to take on about it. You still got them papers and that's all the good it ever done you anyway, so just leave them there and go ahead adding on to them." That wasn't very good logic, but it was about the truth as far as people is concerned. The money you lay away might give you a little pleasure to know that in case of emergency that you'd have it to keep you going, and I think it is a smart thing to do, but on the other hand, as long as you don't use it, it'll not do you any good.

I'd think a person would be a success if he was industrious. Even though he can't make a lot of money, if he can make a living and amount to some-

thing in the neighborhood, I believe he is successful. When I was married I didn't have anything and that held on for several years that I just had a hard time just keeping even, but I never met a time but what we *did* keep even. When we didn't make much, we didn't use much. But we got along, I guess, and had just as much happiness then as we did after we made some money. I guess my life is about like everybody else's. There's been ups and downs, but I can't think of any period of life that was much better. Of course the last . . . after my wife lost her health has been the worst period in my life. We were tied down and she was too. My grandchildren remind me of her. Our seventieth anniversary was in March before she died in August. That's a long time together, but it seems like it has been pretty near that long since.

I don't think people have changed much in my lifetime. Oh, they change in ways now, but you live together and work together and play together, and you go in some other neighborhood everything might be a little different in a way, but they all look on life about the same.

I never did believe that everybody's bad. I know I've seen some people that think everybody that had anything to do with you, they had a motive —they were trying to get you or something. I hear people talk thataway now. Well, just look over the country, they'd have to be good. If they wasn't there'd be more meanness than what there is. And I'm afraid that these boys that does get off and doing bad—these teen-agers that get caught for housebreaking and stealing and everything of the kind—a lot of that is caused, I believe, by neglect of their parents. They just haven't been looked after and been brought up. They see life—and there's others that see it— that the world owes them a living, and they don't care whether they get it off of you or somebody else, just so they get it.

I think a person should just be honest and true to convictions and always try to be a help to others, and I don't know what better advice I could give anybody to lead a good life than that. Because I think you get more enjoyment out of helping others than you could out of any other part of life.

I don't think I've lived my life to the fullest. Do you believe anybody has? You may say that about lots of people. They may write them up that they think they've lived life to the fullest, but I don't believe anybody has. I believe we've all done things we wished we hadn't done. I don't believe you'd call that living your life to the fullest. I'm just like other people. I go on day by day.

I expect there is a lot of things in my life that need a-changing. But really I don't know if I would change any of it. I might do worse.

I've had a long life and figure that death is something that comes to all of us. I expect I feel a little different about it than what younger folks do because I figure that I've already lived my time. I don't mind dying. I believe in a hereafter. I happen to believe the Bible.

"Nature makes people the same all over."

KYRIAKOS RAISSI

In 1903, when he was twenty-eight, Kyriakos (meaning "Sunday" in Greek) Raissi came to the United States with his mother and siblings to escape persecution from the Greek-Turkish conflict. From a small island north of Crete he arrived in New York, where he lived and worked. Mr. Raissi moved to Thompsonville, Connecticut, when the carpet mill (Bigelow Sanford) in which he worked moved there. In Thompsonville he ran a confectionery store and had a family of six children (five girls and one boy). Mr. Raissi is self-taught. At ninety he speaks with dignity, choosing his words carefully.

—JANET LANE, VALARIE BUTENAS, TRACEY LOVELL, JOYCE MORIN.
—DENNIS CORSO, ADVISER, ENFIELD HIGH SCHOOL.

I REMEMBER WHEN I came to New York, they brought us out past a garden. They brought us some candy, some dates, and the people were hungry. I ate a lot.

I was happy then and I'm still happy. This country is the best country in the world. It's got anything and everything in big quantity so the people can live better. They need that. This country is only a couple hundred years old, all foreigners. No matter if you came yesterday or ten days ago or ten years ago, you're all foreigners just the same. There are no Americans. We're all the same. No one better. Nature makes people the same all over.

I'm proud of this country. I like my old country, too, but if I go there, there's nothing. I came from a little island about eight or ten thousand. On the island we ain't got nothing there. No electricity, no water, no lights.

This country is the richest in the world. Used to be and is yet. The whole world has changed [for the] better, but here is the best change. Here you can always better yourself. Knowledge is what helps a person. If you can't get it, too bad for you. 1909 or '10 I had an ice-cream parlor. I used to make

Interviewers from Enfield High School

ice cream. Well, that was the best thing I could do. Didn't have no knowledge. I never went to school. I learned English on my own. I read books, read the encyclopedia, everything. Then I have children—five girls and one boy—and they learn English. Learn Greek, too. It's important to them. In the house me and my wife talk Greek so they learn. I taught them myself.

Now they grow up. I brought them this far, and I'm the cause of them being here, so I'm proud of them. I don't tell them what to do later [in life]. What my children do is up to my children, but I expect them to have a mind of their own and raise up with knowledge. That they have knowledge that's all right for *them*, then for me. Mind. Knowledge, that's the best thing. You ain't got knowledge, money's no good. So everything is mind. If he's got brains, you know, he make a difference. If he ain't, it's no good then. All is mind. If you got good mind you're all right. Some people they don't got mind enough, they don't go the straight way; but if he's got mind, he goes right. Develop your mind. Don't need no other help.

And I don't care if they have religion or no religion. Religion is the cause of everything. It is the cause of bad. Wars, catastrophes, rivalry. It's religion's work.

We can make the world better ourselves. We got to trust each other. If I don't trust you, you don't trust me either. If you want to live good, you have to trust them and give them right, not wrong.

And to have better place we got to give experience to the women. For millions of years, a man was a protector of the family and that kept until today. That's wrong; no justice there. If this world doesn't give to the woman what belongs to her, they never have a better world.

"I have preached
at least five thousand sermons."

HIRAM DRY

*Born and raised in East Texas, Hiram Dry served in the Navy
during World War I and in the Marine Corps afterward. After leaving the military, he became a farmer in his native area until 1933,
when he began preaching as a Baptist minister. Since that time he
has served as pastor for twenty churches in Texas and Kansas, and
is presently the pastor of the Bethel Church in Clayton, Texas.*

—PEGGY DOWNING.
—LINCOLN KING, ADVISER FOR LOBLOLLY.

FIRST OF ALL, I'd like to give an account of the date of my birth
and place. I was born over here at Deadwood, Texas, across the Sabine
River from Gary on January 16, 1900. I moved from there when I was a lad
of only two years as we moved to Center, Texas. I lived there until I was
seventeen years old, when I joined the Navy to serve in World War I, and
served until March 1919. I received an honorable discharge out of the
Navy. I joined the Marine Corps in December of the same year and served

Hiram Dry

until December 1921, at which time I came to Gary. I stayed here until the late spring of 1922 when I went back into the Marine Corps for active service. I served six years with the Texas National Guard with units in Nacogdoches and Beaumont. I was first sergeant with the former unit and senior line sergeant with the latter.

Of course, my military background has been a great asset to me. I served four years and three months in Europe, Asia, and Africa. And I toured with the seagoing Marines on board a flagship of the naval forces in Europe. And, during that time, I acquired a great deal of firsthand knowledge of people in foreign lands. As a matter of fact, there's some I wish I'd never acquired, but I did anyway.

I was married on June 19, 1926, to Miss Lema Ball here at Gary. We moved to Baytown, where I was employed with the Humble Oil Refinery Company. I worked there for a while and moved over to Beaumont and worked in a steel-fabricating plant at the shipbuilding yards. Then my wife's mother's health got bad and they insisted we come back to Gary and look after them. And that we did in February of 1927. Then in 1927, in August, I was saved for the Lord at the First Baptist Church in Gary.

Then, from that I went on lingering along. I knew in my own mind down deep that the Lord had called me to preach. But I wouldn't admit it; I wouldn't concede to it. And I drug along until August 1933, at which time we had a devotional service at Brother Claude Eaton's house up here. And there was a large bunch of men there and we were having the revival meeting. Brother John Waller was pastor of the church and he was holding the meeting. They called on me to deliver the devotional.

I never shall forget it being from the twelfth chapter of Romans. And I must have preached them a sermon because that night Brother Hope Hull got up and made a motion to license me to preach. I had never said anything to anybody about preaching. But, anyway, the church voted to license me to preach at that time.

Then, in September 1933, Brother Ottie Reed came over from Murvaul over here. Old J. H. Williams was pastor over there. He's dead and gone now. And he came over and asked me if I'd come over and help them in a revival meeting. Well, I'd never preached, and I told him I'm not much in that. I said I didn't know anything about preaching in the first place. He said that they just wanted me to come over. I went over there and started in with them on September 6, 1933. I preached my first sermon and I recall there were thirteen people came into the altar for prayer that night. That was a highlight of my life. And so I preached that revival. I think we had three converts, and Brother Williams baptized them.

That first meeting I held was over here at Murvaul and I preached a week there. They took a collection of $1.98. They gave me 270 jars of fruit and vegetables they'd canned. They gave me what they had and I never became impatient with them. I managed to get along with the many jobs I had. Most of the time churches paid me $150 a year. I pastored a church at Garret Springs and they paid me $16 for the whole year. One old boy made $2,000 in the tomato business one year. And they went to him and asked him to help the preacher a little bit. And he said, "I'll give a quarter, I don't want to make the preacher rich."

Our family is very small. I have only one son and he is a preacher. He has been preaching now since the summer of 1947. He has pastored churches all over Texas and we think he is one of the best preachers in the world. Of course, you would expect us to think that. He is now pastoring the New Salem Church south of Cleveland and doing a good job of it. And we're proud of him. My father was also a minister. He had been in the ministry for almost fifty years when he died. So we have three generations of preachers in the family.

As Owen, my son, was being ordained to the ministry yonder in Park Street in Mineral Wells, I told him, "Son, some of the brightest hours that ever rolled over a man's head will roll over yours. And some of the darkest will also come; but, don't let it overcome you. Remember the bright side;

remember when people come to the altar and say, 'Lord, save me, I'm a lost sinner,' that compensates for it all—all the sorrows, heartaches, and disappointments."

Back during the Depression days in 1933 to 1940, I was a man of many occupations. I never did have to get in the soup lines. And I never did have to go on WPA; but I did everything but that. I night-watched Gary here for five years, sometimes for as little as five dollars a week. I farmed and I sold Watkins products in the meantime. I took subscriptions to the Dallas *Morning News* part of the time. I would night-watch all night and come home and sleep until noon. Then I'd work all afternoon, pick up my lunch kit and go night-watch the town again. I did that for five years. That may be the reason why I'm no stronger than I am today.

I'd have those of you who have not been in the world quite as long as I have remember that back in 1933 to 1940, we didn't have much of any paved roads in Panola County. And the most of the roads that I traveled over was red clay. When it was cold I went, and when it was hot I went. It didn't make any difference what the weather was, I went. But I'll tell you one thing right now. I've pried autos out of bogholes with poles and I've done everything in the world to try to get along in this ministry.

I just started driving a little 1928 Model A Ford. And, of course, if I'd had a big heavy car I probably couldn't have made it at all. But I had some rough going around this place. I pastored eight churches at one time. I pastored Saturday at 11:00 A.M. and at 7:00 P.M., and on Sunday at the same times. I'd go in the afternoon at 3:00 P.M. and preach to a mission point on the same Sunday. I did this for nearly four years. And the total the whole group of them paid me was less than a thousand dollars a year.

I recall one time having had a group of people to baptize in Harrison Stocky's pond. When we walked up to the edge of the water, the moccasin snake heads were sticking up all over the middle of the pond. There was a willow log lying there with the bark loose on it, and I picked that thing up and walked back and threw it down. When I did, three big moccasin snakes ran out of it, and I picked up a willow limb and killed all three of 'em before they got in the water. I think none of us was really afraid to go in the water. I know I wasn't the least bit. I just didn't feel like the Lord would allow anything to happen to us and, sure enough, He didn't. Those snakes were in there in great abundance, but we went ahead and baptized anyway.

We went one time up here to Raglor Pricer's pond and in the edge of the water was a big wasp nest. I didn't discover it at first but I did later. I ran up against wasps and snakes and I ran up against most anything you can think of along the way. But it has been a great joy in spite of all this. I think I got stung twenty-eight times by that bunch of wasps but I went ahead and baptized anyway.

I regret that I did not keep a record of all the converts, marriages, funerals, and such things. One of the outstanding years was in 1936. I baptized 146 people from fourteen different churches here in East Texas. I have preached at least five thousand sermons during these past forty-two years.

If there's anything wrong with the young people today I lay the blame at the feet of the parents. I say they have let the gap down. They have thrown the responsibility off their shoulders, and the most of them seemingly don't care where it fell. Now that's the truth. And if there's anything wrong with the young people, I say they're not to blame. I've said that many, many times. I don't blame the young people for the things that are happening this day and time among them. Go back and trace their background and find out for yourself, and you'll see that this old preacher is right about that. The trouble begins around the family fireside. They lose respect for their parents because their parents don't command any respect. Then, when they leave there, they lose respect for the police force on the street because the police force doesn't command any respect. And, then, when they lose respect for the police force, they go from there and lose respect for themselves, and for the nation, and for everything in general.

I would say that the only advice that I could give young people is this: Jesus Christ is the answer. That's the only answer I have. And I'll say this while I'm on it, this modern child psychology is the rottenest stuff. And it's every bit hatched out from under the mud seal of Hell. It's the devil's work. They say: don't restrain the child, don't tell it no, don't do this or don't do that, don't ever lash it for things that it does wrong. That's all of the devil. The Lord gives you exactly the opposite of that kind of instruction. Bring up the child in the way it should go and, when it is old, it will not depart from it.

There are three things I'd like to say that I know. The things that I don't know would make a much larger book than the things I do know. But I say, first of all, that I know God for Christ's sake saved my soul one day. And there's not enough devils in hell or this earth or on this universe to convince me to the contrary. Then, I know that God called me to preach because I fought it for five long years as hard as a man ever did in this world. And my wife didn't even know He had called me to preach. And then, when I leave this old world, I know Whom I have believed and I know that He is able to keep that which I have committed unto Him against that day. And when the final roll is run, and I have stacked arms around the tree of life, I know that I'm going to go home to be with the Lord.

It has been a wonderful experience through these years. If I had my life to live over I would not want to live it any different from that which I have lived it during these past forty-two years. I would have made a lot of improvements. I wouldn't make near as many mistakes the next forty-two years as I have in the past. I'm sure of that. My wife has played a very vital role as she has been at my side all the way. And what little I have accomplished I credit a great deal of it to her. She is a good Bible scholar, a willing worker, and a consecrated Christian. She loves the church, she loves her husband, and she loves everybody.

I've had a very active work. I've been on the go constantly since 1933. I'm proud of a plaque from the church at Clayton for forty-two years active pastoral service.

"If you don't work, you have liquid hands."

ALICE GARCIA

Alice Garcia, a Navajo woman approximately sixty-five years of age, is a member of the Ramah Navajo Community, a group of nearly 1600 Navajo people. They live on the high plateaus of northwestern New Mexico, approximately seventy-five miles southeast of the main Navajo Reservation. Alice lives alone in a cement-block house built for her by the chapter house, the local Navajo governing body. The house is one room, about nine by fifteen feet in area. She has no telephone, electricity, or running water. An outhouse, forty feet in back of the house, serves her year round, though winter often brings several feet of snow and temperatures that have dropped as low as fifty degrees below zero. Her home is ten miles from the chapter house and thirty miles from Ramah, the nearest town. The dirt roads make her home almost inaccessible by automobile during the summer rainy season and winter, a total of almost nine months of the year. During this time, horse and foot travel are the main means of transportation. This interview is translated from the Navajo.

—LAPITA SKEET, DARLENE MARIA, GENEVIEVE PINO.
—BILL RADA, ADVISER TO TSA' ASZI'.

I WAS BORN down in the canyon [pointing south]. My mother told me I was born there when we used to live with my grandmother. I belong to the Tsenahbilnii Clan [Rock Ready to Fall]. My father was Spanish. I didn't go to school. My sister, who's with Pete Beaver, and my brother are the only ones that went to school. I didn't go because my parents used to chase me into the woods when some people would come to take me to school. They used to say, "Stay home and take care of your brothers and sisters." When my brother would be going to school, I would try to go with him. My parents would say, "What are you going to do there? It's better to stay. You have a lot of work to do at home." That's why I didn't go to school. I wish I had gone to school. I would have known English. It's bad when you don't go to school.

I was taught at home. We used to live in a shade shelter [made from saplings and brush]. We would get up early in the morning and have a little lecture for the day on how to live a better life. My parents would say, "Make food. Learn how. We won't be making food for you all your life. When you have kids, they and your husband won't starve. Then teach your kids how. Clean the house. Never leave trash around. Shake and hang up your sheep pelt [for sleeping] every morning. Brush your hair before you make food. Wash your kids." That's what I was told in my younger days.

In those days we wore buckskins. Antelope skins were used for clothing. The skin was sometimes dyed red just to give it decoration on the sides. They said not to make shoes out of antelope hide. But we would make bags out of it. We used them to carry our clothing on long journeys. We also used goatskins for water bags. They were stored in a cool place under a tree until ready to drink. Later we had baskets which we would paste with tree sap on the inside. Water wouldn't run through the sap if it was kept cool.

When I got older I was told to learn how to weave a rug, to spin and to card wool. Then when I got older I could weave a rug. I used to herd sheep with my aunt who lives by the radio tower [about eight miles away]. I was told, and knew, that herding sheep was our only valuable thing. I believed it so I took good care of them. We used to get all our needs from the sheep—milk, wool, mutton, and clothing from the pelts.

When I was little I hunted prairie dogs by filling their holes with water. After they put their heads out I'd grab them by their necks and wring them. I'd usually bring home three or four of them. I didn't do this just to play around. I brought them home to fry.

We used to make moonshine, too. Those men and women used to get drunk on it, but they never fought like they do today.

I was proud of my grandma and respected her. She told me all the things I needed to know about our people and taught me to respect the old ways. She gave me some sheep and told me to take care of them. She also gave me a horse. I took the sheep out every morning before the sun rose. My sister and I used to sit on one horse and bring the sheep back at noon. In the wintertime the sheep stayed out all day. We would bring them back when it was night.

Sometimes we went to the trading post at Zuni [fifty miles away] and sometimes to Grants [seventy miles away]. We would take our wool to Grants. It would take seven days when we took a wagon. Usually we would hook four horses onto a wagon. It would take four wagons to take in all our wool. That was the time when we owned a lot of sheep. In return for the wool we would bring back groceries like flour, salt, sugar, and baking powder.

In the past there used to be herbs and plants that would be higher than me when fully grown. Now I hardly see them any more. I don't see their seeds fall any more. We used to pray with cattail pollen. The men would go into the water and get the pollen. Now we hardly see cattails. The pollen was used to keep us all in health. We would put it into little antelope-hide bags. It was protection against evil. We would have little horses and sheep in the pollen bags. That kept the horses and sheep healthy and was a protection for them.

Corn was an important food for us. We used to grind it with the *tse das-jah* [grinding stone] and make Navajo cake. We didn't have modern grinders. We also made kneel-down bread. At harvesttime we used to take corn ears off the stalks while our parents went banana hunting [the fruit-buds on the yucca plant are called "bananas"]. We would take the seeds out of the bananas and cut them open to dry out in the sun. We also scraped kernels off fresh corn and scraped out pumpkins to dry in the sun.

They used to tell us to take care of the hogan and not play with toys that are useless. So I didn't play games. It's not like today. Today kids are always playing. That is why we, the People, are forgetting our traditional ways. If the parents didn't let their kids play and taught them about the ways of the People at a young age, maybe they would remember. My parents always told me to stay at home and work. That's how I was raised. Today I think it was worth it. I am thankful that they taught me these things. When I was married I was able to make my own living. Now I am here by myself. My kids are all married and have kids. Sometimes I'm lonely for kids.

My grandfather was a good man. He taught me many good things. He was really my great-grandfather. He used to tell me how to make tools. He told me how to make a bowl. Take a juniper branch that has a big knot in

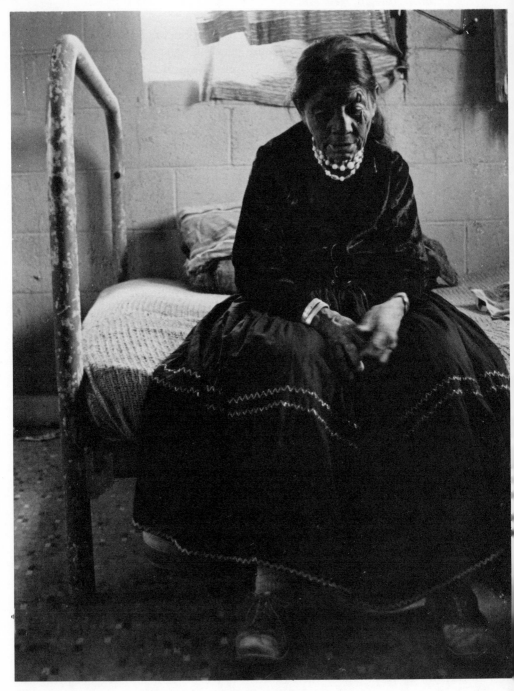

Alice Garcia

the middle of it. Chop off the branch on both sides of the knot. Fire out the insides by making a hole in the knot and put hot pebbles in the hole. The hole will get bigger. The inside turns black from the hot pebbles. Then you remove the pebbles so that it is like a bowl. I forget what they called it. That's what they used to make all their food in. The same was done to make a ladle, but the knot was at the end of the juniper branch.

Mud jugs were made to carry water, and were also used to boil or cook food. They were black. Back in the old days there weren't dishes like today. We made them from mud. Forks were made with sticks that had three points sticking out from them. Spoons were made from juniper twigs. My grandfather told me these things when he was really old.

My grandfather also used to tell me to jump into the snow early in the morning so I could be tough and strong and have tough hands so I could weave, grind, spin wool, card wool, and work outside without getting blisters. They used to know when you didn't work by looking at your hands. If they were skinny and thin that meant you didn't work. I believe it. My hands aren't soft and don't have any fingernails. That's how it is when you weave, grind, spin, and work outdoors. If you don't work, you have liquid hands.

I am always up early in the morning. I never sleep till noon. They used to say, "Never sleep when the sun is out and hot. Do some work around the house where you live." I think it's true. I don't sleep in the daytime—even when I come home from a night sing [a religious ceremony that lasts all night]. People tell me that I look young. I tell them that it is because I respect the old ways. Some people that are younger than me already have white hair because they don't respect the old sayings. "Don't wash with hot or warm water. Use cold water or you'll have wrinkles on your face." That's what my father always used to tell me.

When you are walking, don't walk lazily. Walk like you want to go someplace. When I want to go to the trading post, I walk. If somebody wants to give me a ride, they give me a ride. Sometimes I walk for miles before someone gives me a ride. But I like walking. When I ride in a car, I get sick. I don't like the odors it gives off.

Every morning we would get up and bring back water from the nearby waterhole. Today the white people say the water is no good for you. We used to drink whatever we got from the waterhole. We didn't get sick. Today, if you drink a cupful you get sick in the head.

Money was different in those days. It wasn't paper money then. It was like silver plates and really light. It was easy to carry. Today, if you carry just four quarters it's heavy and it bothers you. But in those days people really didn't care for money. All their value was in their sheep. If you didn't have any sheep that meant you were lazy. So, if you want people to know

you are a hard worker, own sheep. A wealthy person is known by his sheep and horses. There was a sacred chant for the sheep and horses. Corn pollen is a sacred thing. There are four kinds: white, yellow, blue, and dark reddish. The old ones prayed every morning using the corn pollen. Now they don't do it any more.

I used to herd sheep for my father's people, the Spaniards. I learned a little bit of their language, but I forgot it all. When I came home from herding sheep at noon, they would cook for me. I got thirty dollars a month. In those days things were cheap and that was enough money. I really enjoyed herding sheep for them. Blankets were also cheap. These days all things are too expensive.

Sometimes I wish it were still the old days. The planting season then was great. When we planted we wouldn't have to wait very long until the plants were big and ready to be picked. But now the rain has gone away. It is because we don't respect it. We don't give it pollen. We have forgotten the

old ways. Maybe if we go back to them the rain will return, but I don't think so.

The old people used to say that in the year 2000 all sorts of things will happen. A long time ago they predicted things like the Navajo people forgetting the old ways, forgetting clan relationships, and becoming Anglo instead of Navajo. I think these things are coming true. When these things do happen, the people will see it, but it will be too late. There is no going back to the old ways. The old medicine men told each other stories about these things. I was the only child that listened to these stories. While the other kids played around, I listened and didn't make fun of the stories. I tried to put them all in my head.

My grandfather said that when you are young, you go through many bitternesses. But you can't get around old age. Someday after I am dead you will find out what I mean. Old age is a big log—you can't step over it.

My grandfather made a pouch bag that hung around his neck. He kept a knife and an arrowhead and other useful things in it. He died with it still on him. A person who died of old age was never buried in the past. The body was just left under a tree or between its branches with some twigs covering it. Nothing ever bothered it or ate it. No trace of the body was left after a time. Now there are funeral services for them and they are buried in a casket which is probably made of gold. In the old days this type of thing was done in secret. Even that is forgotten now.

I never made fun of old people even if they looked funny or walked funny. That is where we are all going someday. Have more respect for everybody. If you don't respect others you won't live as long. If you respect others you will go through old age easily.

Be more understanding of kids or they might not want to be near you. Teach them what is right and what is wrong. Listen to them. If you hate children, you will have more of them. That's why I like children. But I only had three, and two of them died. I would like to adopt a child, but I'm sure nobody would want to give a child away.

A long time ago people always used to tell their kids to live and work a good life. These days the parents are slaves to their children. The children are the ones who tell the parents what to do. The children who have gone to school say "shut up" to their parents in English. In the old days kids didn't talk back to their parents, even if they were being scolded.

If somebody tells you of their old ways, respect them and listen to them so that you won't forget what you really are. These days when you're talking to young people about these things, they just laugh about it or make fun of it. We tell them about the clans, but they just laugh about it so you really can't teach them anything. They don't want clans. In the old days we used to respect all this, but I think because we have gotten into the white world, they don't respect it any more. But it is good that they are learning the white man's ways because that is where they are going.

I'm really proud of the kids who are going to school. In the old days the girls wore dresses, but these days they only wear pants. The boys wore their hair short, but now they wear it long and shaggy. But it's good for them.

And to you students—never think or bother with something that has to do with bad stuff or something that will lead you into temptation. It will never do good for you.

"We don't clean houses.
We put out fires."

CARL ANDERSON

Carl Anderson was born on October 8, 1890, in Sweden. He and his family immigrated to this country, arriving at Ellis Island in 1891. They moved to Illinois, where Carl has been a pin setter in a bowling alley, and has worked on railroad steam engines checking the headlights and oil levels. After he and his fellow employees went on strike against the railroad, he became an employee of the fire department in Galesburg, Illinois. He remained there from 1926 until his retirement twenty-five years ago.

He warns young people against taking up fire fighting as a career if they think it's a romantic, exciting life. "You have to be prepared to take a great deal of physical punishment. I remember once that we fought a huge gas fire for thirty-two hours. There was almost no relief. It was in the 1940s during the winter near Christmas time. I'd ask a kid if he thought he would want to do something like that."

Carl became an American citizen shortly before World War I, in which he fought. "I went to Camp Dodge in Iowa. One day one of the officers said, 'Will any foreign-born people step forward.' I stepped up and they took me off for questioning. Four officers ques-

tioned me at a time. *They wanted to know if I knew German sym-
pathizers and if I was really ready to fight for the United States. I
just kept saying that Sweden was nothing to me. I felt American.*

"They let me go then, and several days later, one of the officers
came and got me off the firing range. They took me into the office
and explained to me that they had a Norwegian recruit who refused to fight for the United States. He had six hundred acres of
land and three thousand dollars in the bank. The officer wanted me
to talk to him and explain that the government would take away his
land and deport him if he refused to fight.

"I started talking to him, but he was stubborn. He kept refusing
to fight, and I was getting pretty mad at his whole attitude. Finally
I said, 'Well, it looks like you don't care whether you protect what
you've worked for. You're a fool, because in the old country you
could never get what you have here.'

"I turned around to leave and I said to the officer, 'Hell, you
don't want him in the Army. He's likely to shoot you in the back.' I
was out of the building when the officer called me back.

"'Private Anderson,' he said. 'Come back. I can speak Swedish as
well as you. We just wanted to make sure that you felt a strong loy-
alty for this country.' They swore me in as a citizen before I
shipped out for France."

—ALLEN BYRD, RICKY JONES, GERALD CRAWFORD,
CARROLL VANSKIKI, KEVIN LAWSON, JEFF BAINTER,
RICK ENGLAND, JIM DUNN, BOB STRONG.
—SHERYL LEE HINMAN, ADVISER,
LOMBARD JUNIOR HIGH SCHOOL.

MY FATHER CAME to the United States to better himself financially. He came over first in 1890 and he hoped to save enough to bring
over my mother and me, but in those days he was only getting a dollar a
day. He couldn't get enough so his sister's husband paid. We left. We got in
a wooden boat and started out over the North Sea. I was just a baby, but
years later my aunt told me this story about the crossing. It seems that a ty-
phoon came up. The ship was tossing all around. My mother dropped me
on the deck and I began to slide away from her. The captain saved me from
going over the side. Then he got everyone down into the hold. Eventually
we arrived in Liverpool. From there we went to Ellis Island. There I know

we had to have a physical exam and we had to be able to say who would take care of us here—that was my father.

I went through Ellis Island a second time, too. You see, my mother never did forget Sweden. She went back several times. She left America and took me with her when I was only six. We stayed there a year, but by the time I was ready to return I had forgotten all my English. The second crossing was really terrifying. The engine on the boat stopped. The sea was bad and the whole ship began to roll back and forth. We floated for hours. I was hanging tight onto a side of the boat trying to keep from rolling around. People were down on their knees praying. I was old enough to understand that these adults were afraid we were going to die. Ellis Island was just one more frightening, confusing place. And then I had to start school here with no real understanding of English. My mother never did learn to speak English. I spoke to her in Swedish up to her dying day. She went back to Sweden three more times but she always returned to America. This was where the children lived. She came back for us. My father never did make

Interviewers from Lombard Junior High School

Carl Anderson

enough money to return himself. Times were too tough. I actually had to go to work to help support the family when I was fourteen.

I was a call boy for the railroad. I had to get on a bike and ride around to the homes of the engine men when they were needed. I would work about six hours a night doing that. Nowadays, they can just telephone a person.

My next job at the yard was making out requisitions for the trains. I had to give each train a certain amount of oil. It was all figured out by a formula according to how many miles the train was going to travel. In the whole time I held that job I never made a single mistake on a requisition. I always had things figured just right. The bosses didn't hardly want to take me off that job because I did it so well, but finally I got an advancement. I went to work on the headlights. They had to be filled with kerosene. I inspected them, cleaned them, and changed the whole works. I'd climb around on fifty to sixty engines a night cleaning. Back then there were five thousand men employed at the rail yards. There were no factories around. When the strike came and I was blacklisted for taking part in it, I was in a tight place. I'd went out on strike against the railroads in the '22 strike. I'd been an inspector of beef in the packing department. See, I worked on the railroad when you was nothing but a slave. You worked twelve hours a night and got $77.50 a month and you couldn't make ends meet. When Woodrow Wilson got in, they made it sixteen hours long and eight hours for the shop men. The company was gonna go broke because they had to have a third shift. Then they hired in mechanics that were no good—just sponging off the Government. They had a lot of misfits there. I guess they had to call a strike to get rid of them. Our union didn't really have the money it needed and the strike lasted a long time, so they broke us and we lost, but it cost them.

So I looked around here for different jobs, but I always got laid off, so this fella says, "Why don'tcha get in the fire department? There's a opening there." So I happened to know the alderman in the seventh ward. He knew I went out on strike 'cause he went out on strike himself. I got to him and he spoke a good word for me. I had to show him I was the right kind of man. They want to know your record and all that, you know. Politics is a funny deal. They want to know how many friends you got, what lodges you belong to, and all that stuff. Course, I'd been here all my life and I was a taxpayer and all. There are a lot of things connected with it, you know. You gotta have the right kind of pull to get in. If you don't have, you don't get in. I was hired under a mayor that the strikers put in office.

Fireman's a hard job. It takes at least a year to learn all the streets, your hydrants and all that. You don't learn that in one day. People don't realize what a fireman's job is. They hate to see us sit around; they don't know we're on guard duty. It's nerve-racking job 'cause you gotta be on the alert all the time and you gotta know where you're going when you go. If I had my life to live over again, I'd never be a fireman. I'll tell you that right now. Too dangerous.

Every time a fire truck goes out, you got traffic to contend with. A lot of times if you get there you're lucky, 'cause this traffic's getting worse every day. I often wonder, when the truck goes down Main Street, how they get by. There's so many cars. And there's so much arson and false alarms in this country. People don't realize the danger when they turn in a false alarm. There were many times I wanted to quit—but there was no place to go. In the railroad, I was blackballed for the rest of my life. I even stood trial over in Peoria for the strike in '22. They gave us a good talking to over there. I was never insulted in my life until then.

While I was with the railroad, I did the job as well as I could. I figure if a man's gonna go to work he should do his job. Otherwise he's hurting the organization and himself with it. The only way a person can get anything is to work for it. The only time I wasn't working was during the strike of '22. If I hadn't had good recommendations, I wouldn't have had other job offers, would I? What's the first thing an employer asks you—"Where'd you work last?" They want your boss's reference. The most important thing in life is to do your job well because if you don't, you're building up a bad reputation that'll follow you around. But if you've done your job well, you can stand up for your rights at work.

But I started out in the fire department on the tiller. That's the aerial ladder that used to be drawn by horse and buggy, but they replaced the horses with a Mack truck. It had hard rubber tires on it. They weren't very wide, and they had the streetcar tracks run through here in them days. I got caught in one of them tracks at Seminary and Main. See, the guy in the front of the truck made a turn first. Then just about when I got to the intersection, I had to use good judgment so I could follow him around the curve. The wheel got caught in the track, and I had to let go fast. If I hadn't let loose it would a broke both my arms. Joe Anderson saw it all and said, "My God, you got a soothsayer's job there." I said, "You're tellin' me!"

In my life's experience as a fireman, I've had four close calls. I was in a foul-up on Lombard Street, January 4, 1936. That's when we had the deep snow, the deepest snow we ever had that I can remember of, and I'm up in the eighties, when a fella knows what he's talkin' about. The snow looked like walls on the highways. You couldn't cross a field or nothing. Course, in town it wasn't so bad except it was in ruts all the time.

We got into a rut goin' to 67 South Whitesboro. It happened to be a false alarm. Somebody turned it in. We got to Lombard and South and a big tow truck hit us in the middle when we crossed the intersection. I flew thirty feet in the air; it demolished the fire truck. The switchman come around there and wanted to pick me up. I said, "Don't pick me up. I might have a broken back." I hit right across my hips, see. So I was off forty-three days, fourteen in the hospital. When the boy in the tow truck opened the door, he went skidding right out on his head. It laid his scalp back and broke his jaw in three places, and he was unconscious I think five days.

When I thought I felt like I was all right, I took a chance 'n' went back and signed the papers that I was okay. Course they carry insurance on you and all that. Then I was playing cards with some friends when all of a sudden it felt like a needle went up my back. I said, "Uh huh, sumpin' wrong here!" So I went to a chiropractor. Chiropractor Tucker, he looked me over. The tail bone was bent in. That was causing the pain. It set off the nerve. It took about fifty treatments before he got that back right. Boy, it was painful. I'd signed papers, and I was back to work so I couldn't collect nothing. It cost me fifty dollars. It was only a dollar a treatment in them days. I mean to say, these false alarms are bad things. People don't realize when they're turning in a false alarm that somebody's life's in danger. It might be the fireman will get killed before he gets there. That could have been my

The Galesburg Fire Department with which Carl Anderson served

fate. I was just a lucky guy. That time I was knocked off the truck, I had a lot of clothes on. That saved me. The first driver, that steering wheel rammed into his stomach. A couple of years later he died of cancer. For these false alarms there ought to be a stiff fine. Down near Quincy two firemen got killed going to a false alarm.

The next bad experience I had was on a four-story building. It had been on fire twice before. We all surmised the man might have set it on fire himself to collect insurance. I was the last man coming down a ladder from the fourth floor. There was a traffic cop outside and said to the chief, "I believe that wall over there is cracking." The chief hightailed it on over and told us all to get down. I was the last one down. I got down just in time, and I backed up and hit the curb. Down I went. The wall buckled in the middle; it jackknifed kinda. The bricks was piled up on me clear to my waistline. If it hadn't a jackknifed, it would have killed us all. It would have buried us. But when you're fighting a fire, you don't have your mind on what's gonna happen. You're just thinking about putting out the fire.

I'll tell you another thing what happened to us. We went out here to Rock Island Avenue to one of them cheap houses—just a wooden house. When we got out there the whole house was full of smoke. Well, we figured there must be a stuffed-up furnace. So we thought, "We can't get in it 'cause we can't eat that smoke." We didn't have no gas masks like they do today. So we pried the window open in the basement to air it out. Then we went through the window. We finally had to shovel the fire out the window 'cause if we poured water in there, it would have cracked the furnace. We took down the pipe that led to the chimney, and it was all stopped up. Looked in the chimney and it was all stopped up too. Now this happened about three o'clock in the morning. Then here come the owners. They'd been out on a party somewheres, I suppose. They found the house and the furnace all tore apart and everything. One of them says, "Ain't you gonna clean it?"

I said, "We don't clean houses. We put out fires." And I says, "What kinda man are you anyhow?" I said, "You smothered that fire and you shoulda had that furnace cleaned. Every year you should have your furnace cleaned. It was careless on your part. Maybe you'll know better next time. But don't ask a fireman to clean out your furnace 'cause they don't do that. They put out fires."

You get into some awful jams. All the fires are difficult. I went to one fire on Phillips Street one day. They had a big attic, and we wanted to spray water there with the big fire hose. The chief sent me in toward the house and the woman had locked the door on me. She wasn't gonna let me in. I says, "Lady, you better let me in or I'll get the ax. All we're trying to do is save you a lotta damage." People get so excited it's pitiful. They just go crazy. Once a little eight-year-old boy went in to take a bath. There was a gas burner in the bathroom. He locked the door and had the gas burner going. He burned up all the oxygen. We found him dead in the bathtub. The parents got excited. They should have knocked the door down. Instead they called us. By the time we got there it was too late.

And once I seen two drunks that got burnt up in bed. They were cigarette smokers. And then there was a Mexican guy who wanted to put a fire in his cookstove. It used kerosene but he tried gasoline. It made him a human torch. I had to hold a lead [hose] over him, because he was just a skeleton laying there. I had to hold the hose to wipe off the body. We didn't want to scrape the flesh off his bones, but his head was just a skull. The worst sight I've ever seen.

Fires start with somebody's carelessness mostly—like with little kids playing with matches. Once we found a kid out in a boxcar on Grand Avenue. It was during the Depression days when everybody was out of work and everything else, and these people lived in boxcars. Well, this kid, one afternoon, was playing with matches and started a fire. We found him as a skeleton down in the corner. That's the most important thing—keeping matches away from the little tots.

In the old library they had a fire up in the attic, so I got up on top of the roof. It was tile. I had to put a hole in it so we could get a hose in. After we got the hose in, I smelled formaldehyde. That was used for fumigation of the books. The assistant chief—he was one of those guys who knows it all— he came up. I says, "Where you going?"

He says, "I'm going down there."

"No, you can't go down there. You won't have no eyes if you go down there." He was one of those bullheaded guys. He stuck his head down there, and he came back up quick, too. There were tears rolling down from his eyes. All we could do was drown the fire—there was a lot of water damage. We couldn't go in because this bottle had tipped over during the fire, and it had formaldehyde in it. How I happened to know it was because I used to use it when I inspected in the railroad depot packing department. When a car came in with diphtheria or smallpox or any of them contagious diseases, we'd set that car out, and we'd put a few drops of formaldehyde into the coach for twenty-four hours sealed up tight. And that would kill all the germs, see. That's how I happened to know that there was formaldehyde in the library. But this guy wouldn't listen. So when we got back to the station, I said, "Maybe you'll listen from now on. You don't know everything, yet. You've been in the fire department longer than I have. You're assistant chief and all that, but remember one thing. There's always someone who knows more than you do." He didn't like that too well, but he went to the doctor about six weeks for his eyes. You learn something everyday. I could still learn. You know, you got some guys that think they know it all, but they don't.

People need to realize we're equal. I've had people come to me and say, "He was born in Sweden" as if to say, "You're no good."

I say, "Who in the heck do you think you are? Who brought you over here in the first place? Your forefathers. You're foreign blood. You may have been born here, but you're foreign blood. You can't take that away. You're poking fun at a guy that did something that your forefathers did for you. Does being born here make you better? Not one bit better. You don't understand the principle of America. Nobody's above anybody else. Just read the Bible. There was only one man on earth above anyone else, and they crucified him!"

"Friends are lots nicer than money."

MARY MOORE

A little annoyance like the heating stove blowing up and settling black soot all over her six-room house, or the bathtub overflowing in the back of her house did not upset Mary Ann Moore (though these accidents postponed some of our visits with her), for she did not reach her nineties by letting hardships, misfortunes, or loss of family and friends defeat her. Handicapped in eyesight at birth, plagued with sickness in her youth, and never becoming very strong, she has continued year by year with determination and faith in God working to serve others.

She thinks there is nothing remarkable in what she's done—"I just did what had to be done"—or that at ninety-four she still does all her own work, even washing on the washboard her household linens soiled by the soot. What she can't understand is why she has outlived so many of her contemporaries, two sons, and three grand-children.

Mary was born on October 7, 1881, just a few miles from her present home in Phillipsburg, Missouri. After her husband died of TB in 1913, she worked at many jobs to raise her four boys. "Ever'body

was awful good to help," she said, "and that made it awful handy."
In turn Mary was always ready to help those less fortunate.

—TERRY BRANDT, DONNA SCOTT, DIANA FOREMAN,
NANCY HONSSINGER, DORIS BRELOWSKI, SALLY MOORE,
DOUG SHARP, TERESA REED.
—ELLEN MASSEY, ADVISER TO BITTERSWEET.

I THINK WE'VE got to do everything we can and then trust the Lord. We got to do our part. That's the way I've got by and I'll be ninety-four this October.

When I was born my mother was only seventeen. She was young. My father went after the doctor on horseback. He never got back until after I was born. Well, the woman was so nervous and scared she touched her finger in my eye. And I never had no sight in it at all. I never could see anything out of it.

I just went to the third reader in school. I didn't get no education and I didn't get to go all the time when I went. My mother and father worked lots and we didn't make no money. I heard somebody say when we had this cleaning done here after my stove blew up the other day, that a woman could get ten dollars a day now for work. My mother worked cleaning houses for people at a dollar a day. Then when she quilted a quilt—she was an awful good quilter, now—she got three dollars. To quilt a whole quilt for three dollars! Well, now lots of times she had to keep me at home to take care of the little brother. I just raised him. He just died here about a month ago. I was so in hopes he'd live to be the last one, but he didn't. He went on. But I got to be with him when he was sick and talk over lots of things and it made it nice that he could go that way. We always shared and that made it awful nice.

But that's the reason I didn't get no education. I had to stay with the little one. I wanted, here about forty years back, to go to school at Springfield and learn to be a missionary. I can talk pretty good, and I can do quite a bit of work in a church and such as that. Of course the boys, they didn't want me to. So I listened.

When I was still at home my daddy was cranky. He wouldn't let me go with nobody because there weren't no boy that would suit him. One time I was working at my aunt's. There was a young man there and I was talking to him. I never thought nothing about it. He just come in talking and putting away the dishes. Well, that night after prayer meeting, he wanted to go home with me. I never thought nothing about it, so I let him go. And I'll

Mary Moore

Mary Moore with interviewers from Bittersweet

tell you now I got a whipping! And I'll tell you now my daddy told him, too! Oh my! Well, he wasn't a bad boy. When I finally come on to some boy he would let come, that's who I married. I lived with him till he died and I had the children.

I was eighteen when I got married at home, right down here about three miles by a Baptist preacher. My mother now was only fifteen when she married, but now listen, she was a big girl. She was tall and her father had died and they didn't have much of a way to make a living. They didn't live too far from here, only about a mile. She got the chance to get married and her sister had married at fifteen. But you know, that's all right because lots of girls know more at fifteen than at eighteen.

When Mr. Moore died he was only thirty-four years old and I was thirty-three. He's been gone that long now. The boys were three, six, and nine, and I was pregnant with another baby. He was born in September after his father died in May. Well, now, I went through then more than I thought I could bear. I thought how in the world can I make it? How could I? Well, you know whenever you make up your mind, you can do anything. It don't make any difference what it is, we can do it. We've got to do things that way.

After he died, I moved over there in one of the first houses ever built in Phillipsburg. It wasn't a very good one. It was cold. I lived there and my brothers brought me wood. One time I got kind of low on wood, and someone knocked at the door. It was the Baptist preacher. He said, "Mrs. Moore, ain't your wood about out?" I said, "Yes, but the boys will think about it." But he said, "I'll have the wood here before noon." I saw him saw it up. He sawed many a load of wood for me whenever he'd come and there wasn't any wood on the woodpile. And you know, that was awful nice.

I went to work. I worked a long time at the hotel. We had a good hotel here then and we'd have about thirty-eight men on Monday and Tuesday. I worked there a long time. I got my baby took care of and I worked.

Well then, after that I washed for a living. I washed clothes on the board for there was no other way then. I'm very particular about my washings. I had people from away bring their washings to me, afraid I didn't have all I could do.

So we got along. We were on a farm some and went right along with the crops and we had cows and things and we just went ahead and made a living. I drove a cultivator—drove the team for my boy to plow for two years because he was too little to plow the corn and drive the team too. When noon'd come, we'd go to the house and he'd take care of the horse and feed the hogs, and I'd get dinner. You know, a lot of time my dishes'd go two or three days and I didn't wash them. If we got real busy plowing, why, we went ahead plowing. And when we come in of a night, why, I milked and the boys took care of the horses and things and we got by.

We didn't need much. It didn't make any difference if we just had butter and bread and something that we raised on a farm, why we just had what we needed.

Now I've got nine grandchildren and twelve great-grandchildren. When I was a girl, about sixteen, my mother and everyone didn't think I would live for I was poorly. Here I've outlived my mother and my father, my husband, my brothers and sisters, and some younger ones. I couldn't understand that. Many times I wondered why that was.

I want to stay here in the Ozarks as long as I live, because I have my home and everything here, and that's what I want to do is stay here and trust the Lord.

I never had no education, but I can read the Bible as good as anybody. There's some words I can't pronounce, but there's a lot you can't either. I'll spell them and go right on as best I can.

I think it's important to teach little children to read the Bible. I remember when I went to school, the teacher got up and sang a song, and everyone would help her. Then she led in prayer. Any more they ain't allowed to use the Bible at school. Ain't that something?

Ever' day keeps coming along and the time goes on. I'm real glad that the Lord has blessed me like He has so I could work and sew and wash. Now I washed all my things this morning—all the curtains and bedspreads that got black when the stove blew up. You know, I still wash on the board. They're much nicer that way—cleaner and whiter. It took five washings to get everything all clean again. I ironed, I do all that along with all this other work and I seem to get along as fast as anybody does.

I've had lots of friends in my life. I think a real friend is a friend in need —someone you can always talk to. I'll tell you I had one lady here in Phillipsburg and she's dead now, but I could go to her and tell her anything in the world and ask her to do anything in the world and she'd do it. And my boy, he thought just as much of her as I did. Now she was a friend to us whenever I was down and got lonesome and didn't know what I was going to do. I'd just go to her and we'd get down and pray and we'd pray and then talk. And I'd go home all right. I never did hear anything that I ever told her that she'd told. You take a real friend and tell them something and they'll keep it.

Friends are lots nicer than money. You know you can spend your money, but friendship is always there. Now you take a real friend; at any time of day or night they're a friend to you. They'd do anything for you that's right. Now that's what we ought to be careful about in particular is to always do what's right. And you want to be fair if you can because that is the way to get by. You've got friends. Well, just stay with them and get more.

I've always tried to help out whenever I could. I've always done a lot of setting up and a lot of taking care of sick people. I've went and set up night after night and cared for the sick a lot here in the Burg. Today if people would sit up like we used to, they wouldn't have to hire anybody to stay or take care of you.

We used to sit up with and care for the dead, 'cause we loved them. When they had the funeral, there was a lot of help, 'cause the people then lived that way. But now we have some people that never go. I don't know why. Some say they can't. Some say they have to work. There's a lot of excuses and that's the way it goes. But used to they really cared for one another. Let one get sick, and over there's one coming and over here's one coming. They're coming to see what they can do. They may be awful poor but they've just got the poor ways like everyone else has and they'll just help you the best they can. When everybody was there, that's all that was

required. They took care of you when you died. Showed lots of respect.
Prayed lots of prayers. Sang lots of good songs—the good old-time songs.

I'll tell you one story. There's a lady died back over in here. She had been
real bad sick for a couple of weeks. The fever and flu, you know. And they
hadn't doctors. She was awful bad. I went to see her several times. When
she died, she died in her nightgown, and it was her wish when she died that
I would dress her. When I got there some of the folks were there but they
hadn't touched her. So I bathed her and I dressed her. She had her clothes
made and had them all ready. I got her ready. The next day it was awful
bad—a big snow was on. Oh, it was awful deep, awful bad. When I went
that night the boy got a mare and saddled her and I rode the mare and he
led her, and he went through the woods because the snow was so bad and
the road was so slick you couldn't go.

I could tell you another case. There was this man and he was a real good
man with a good wife and a good family. He got sick of pneumonia fever
and the doctor came and said, "He is going to die if he doesn't get his bed

sheets changed and cleaned because that fever is so strong, it ain't going to leave." Now they were good people but they just didn't know no better how to care for the sick. Well, the doctor came to my house and he knocked on the door. He said, "Mrs. Moore, I want to get you to go to this place and change them sheets. They think a lot of you and they won't get mad when you ask them." So I went and I said to the wife to come into the kitchen and I said, "We're going to have to change him and you and I can do that." And she said, "Oh no, we can't do that." And I said, "Oh yes, when it's depending on life or death, you can do anything. Yes, we can do it." We sat him in a big chair, put something over him and we changed the bed and we changed him. We pulled off everything he had on and bathed him some. We put on clean clothes and put him back and he said, "Oh, how much better that feels." And I took all them things home and washed them and took them back. Now that was one of my neighbors and he was a good man. He worked hard. They had had a lot of bad luck. Well, this man got well and he worked for me after that a many a day. And you know, so many times when people get sick, it's the way they are took care of that causes them to live or die.

My neighbors was awful nice to me when I was hard up. A neighbor came to me one time and said, "Ain't your children getting kind of short on clothes to wear to Sunday school?" I said, "Yes, why, they are. It seems like everything's kind of come up and seems like I got as much as I could." Well, he wrote a letter to the lodge that their father belonged to. He told them to get some money here to them children for some clothes. And you know, it come! You know when things come along that way makes it awful handy and awful nice.

We can do things for children, too. I think it pays us as we go along to find a little boy or a little girl that's poor and do a good deed. I'm favoritive to boys and all my children are boys. I didn't have no little girls. I love little girls, but you let a little boy come along and I'll have him in a minute—just kind of natural for me.

I've seen boys go astray, I know because of the way they was treated at home. There's a family lived right back down here and the man got awful mean to the little boy and he called him Pig. Lots of nights he wouldn't let that little boy in the house. He was little then. My boy was working away as an electrician. He come home and I told him about it. He just went and told that boy, he said, "Now listen. Any time your dad don't let you come in, you come and Mother'll fix you a bed." And I did. He lived there a long time and I got so that when I baked pies or cake, I always saved him a piece. Then a long time after that he met one of my boys and said, "Is your mother still living?" He said, "Yes, she's still living." He said, "Tell her I want to see her." He came and he said, "Mary, I love you. I think so often about how many times you give me pie. Nobody else ever baked me pie." And of course, I just took a big cry and was glad I done it. He said, "Oh, I'll never forget you, it don't make any difference how long I live." That done me a lot of good then to hear him say that. We always can do something good if we only will.

I think parents should be with their children all they can. I had four boys. I had to help them some about the milking—kind of oversee the boys. That shows them how to work. I always went with my boys whenever they went to do work. Then we got it done without a fuss. My brother said after my boys was grown, he said he wished his boys would work good like mine did. His wife said if he'd went with them like I had, they would. It does help a child to go with them. I didn't mind it any.

And I'll tell you what, I could give anybody a little bit of advice on taking care of children. I've heard this: "Don't spare the rod." Now you know what I'd do if I was raising my boys over? I wouldn't whip them a time. You could sit down and talk to them boys and have them sit down in a chair and talk some good talk to them. And they'd soon get till they'd be loving you a lot better and they wouldn't be trying to do that. And right at first they would have known that you had them under control. When they want to do something that isn't right, talk to them and give them advice. And you live what you tell them.

And I think women should stay home with their children. Did you ever think about the knocks and cuffs them poor children get without no mother to see about them? They're just unlucky. Lots of times they don't get fed and they cry themselves to sleep.

I'd say the main thing in life is try to be yourselves, and if you are yourself and do what you think is right, you can talk to others and show them the way. If you join them just to be in the crowd even when you don't like it and go on with them and do what they're doing, then there's no doing nothing with them because they'll say, "Why, you done just what I done. You ain't no better than I am." But if you don't like what they're doing, go right on being yourself. It won't take them but a few minutes to notice how you're acting. There'll be somebody say something and sometimes they'll giggle and laugh, make fun. But you go on and show them what you can do and it ain't long till they see. And when they see you don't behave in that way, they'll be after you for advice. You may get awful blue and get dishearted and think, "Oh, I can't do nothing for them. There ain't no use in me to try." Then God's working on you. Right then he's showing you what to do. If you give way and do what the crowd does, you aren't no better than they are. You may think that you're trying to do something that you can't do. But you can if you're strong enough to just stay with it. People may slight you. They even may try not to be seen with you. They'd rather not. But you just go on and you can do good work. It ain't long till they see.

I'm sorry I couldn't visit with you the other day when you called, but my cousin's funeral was that day. I was poorly and couldn't go because it was away and all, but out of respect for him, I didn't think I ought to visit with you young people that day. I was glad you could come today instead. It makes it nice to visit like this and remember lots of things I haven't thought about for a while. If there's anything I can help you with, do come back. Good-by and God bless you.

"I'd rather be on the end going out than the end coming in."

LYMAN GUPTILL

Lyman Guptill lives in Trescott, Maine, in a two-room house which he built himself. Born on the fifth of May, 1899, in Machiasport, he has lived in Maine all his life. His mother and her family were from Nova Scotia, but he's not sure of his father's family, as his father and mother were parted when he was seven or eight. His father, a Civil War veteran, farmer, and "horse dickerer," died in 1914 in a veterans' hospital. Lyme felt so strongly that he must provide a home for his mother that he sacrificed not only continuing his education beyond the eighth grade, but also having a family of his own later in life.

When Lyme was twelve he held his first job at the Whiting Saw Mill. For forty days he worked ten hours per day, earning only forty dollars for the entire job. He worked at the mill at many different tasks on and off for about thirty years. Due to his integrity he was always able to find a job at the mill and elsewhere whenever he needed to. Another job Lyme held was at a sardine canning factory. He worked for six or seven seasons, including two seasons on the night shift.

During the Depression, Lyme peddled fish and clams. He sold his land bit by bit, and finally his house, and then bought the land he now lives on, hoping to survive as a farmer. At first he sold the wood he cut from his property, and then he began raising cattle and sheep as well as some vegetables. By utilizing his produce and selling the surplus he became almost self-sufficient.

His mother died when he was fifty and he then married a widowed woman with children of her own. His son-in-law wants Lyme to come live with him, but at this point Lyme has decided to live on his own. This is due to the fact that Lyme's goals in life were to have a home of his own, to pay his bills, and, most of all, to be independent.

Lyme's life is a conglomeration of many different experiences and he considers himself a "jack of all trades, master of none." This, however, seems to be a rather demeaning title because it doesn't take into account the warmth and charm he displays when sharing himself and his experiences with others.

—JOSHUA BEADLE, RICHARD DACOSTA, DAVID ENKE, NICK MANDLEKERN, STEVEN OAKLANDER, CARL SWEENEY, ANDREW WALLACE, DEBRA FARBER, HOLLY EVERHART, LISA FIDLER, DEBRA JACOBY, NANCY JENSEN, MARGIE KLAVER, LINDA MICHALOVSKY, NANCY OYER, JEFF RITTER, NANCY ROBERTS, LISA SHULOCK, JANE UTIGER. PHOTOGRAPHS BY JEFF RITTER, LISA SHULOCK. —DIANA COHEN, ADVISER, TRAILSIDE COUNTRY SCHOOL.

IF I WAS YOUNG growing up, I'd have an education like the rest of them. I'd have a high school diploma and go out and get a job. I would take a choice of the jobs that I wanted if I was going to work; and, if I could do it, I could get into a job with the rest of them that paid good wages, and I would have more recreation and entertainment and the like of that. Or I could save my money. I could have my choice.

Now I only had the eighth grade education, but at that time you would learn a trade on your own. You could be a carpenter, you could be a plumber, you could be a bookkeeper or something like that. You never had to have no high school diploma to show. If you were capable of doing your work, they'd hire you. But today it's different. You've got to have that certificate to show what you have done in school. That's the first thing they'll ask you for when you go for a job in a shoe factory or in anything. I

know that for a fact 'cause I worked up to the State School [for the re-
tarded] a couple of different times. I worked on one of the farms there and
I worked around the buildings for a winter. I had an uncle that lived up
there. I got through on that job and I was staying there with my uncle a
while, and we were out to Portland and we come up to the office of some
pulp company. My uncle says to me just for fun, he says, "Go in," he says,
"and ask them for a job. See what they'll say."

Well, I did it just to find out myself. I didn't want no job. But I went in
and asked them how they was fixed for help. They asked me where I was
from, how old I was, and if ever I done any of it. I told them I'd done
woods work and the likes of that. Wanted to know what my education was.
Told them eighth grade was as far as I went to school. He says, "I'm sorry
we haven't any vacancy right now," he says, "but in business now there's a
lot of things that you have to have in order to fit the job." He says, "Such as
a high school diploma and things like that."

I says, "I understand."

He says, "I'm sorry."

I says, "I'm sorry I found it out. I thank you very much. I didn't want no
job. I just came in to find out."

But what you do—that's your judgment. As you go along and see things,
it will be for you to make your choice of what you think's the best. That
would be the nearest I could come to it. You have many opportunities, city
jobs and different things to do, and you're the ones that got to make your
choice. You prefer what suits you best. What you'd rather do. But if you're
on a job you don't like and you have to stay on it, why, it's not too good.
I've had those kind of jobs where the time passed so slow it seemed like the
day would never go.

The first job I had when I was twelve. I worked at the Whiting Saw Mill.
I was taking shucks away from the planer where they planed them herring
box tops. Lugged the little kindlings out from the edging saws where they
cut the edges off them and fitted them into covers and bottoms for the
cases. Ten hours a day in the fall of the year. Went in the dark and went
back home in the dark about five miles each way in the night and morning
—dollar a day—didn't get paid till we got done either. Worked forty days.
The richest I ever was was when I got the forty dollars. I worked in saw-
mills off and on—not steady—for thirty year. And I worked in a sardine
factory. It was all handwork at the time. Giving the crates to the packers,
taking back empty ones; and I worked on the flaking machine where they
flaked the fish, cleaned the floors up and whatever there was to do. Just
common labor.

All the work I ever did was always common work of all kinds. And I did
anything that was the handiest to me. Any job that was available, why, I

Lyman Guptill

took it. I never was fussy what I did. It was all in a day's work. It was a day's pay I was after. I worked up in the mill in the spring of the year. And there would be slack times in the mill, you know. They'd send me over to the house to saw firewood. They'd have to have it sawed and cut up. I had a secondhanded Ford truck that I used to haul out wood with, and I made a sawing machine out of it after a while to saw firewood on; you know, a circular saw. I had it on the rear wheels of the truck. Jacked the truck up and the tires on the truck would run the pulleys and make your saw go. Nice rig to saw wood with, too.

I didn't really mind what I did. There was no "best" to them. But I will say I never took a job that I disliked so bad that I didn't want to do it. I always found something else to do. There's no law that will hold you to a job. I'd even leave before I'd do that. I'd do factory or some other work. I used to shift. I never had no particular place to work. I'd work in the mill for a while. Then if the factory started up in good shape and I could make more money in the factory, I'd go to the factory. I worked in the canning plant cutting out sardine cans six or seven seasons. I worked on the night crew two years. They used to run the night crew when the Russians were bringing in fish. Then, of course, machinery took the place of a lot of that stuff and they didn't need as many laborers. I worked on a tin slitter [cutting out sardine cans]. The presses that cut the cans was a press you had to pump with your foot. That was good work. They do it all by machinery now. Have for a number of years. They got automatic can pressers in there now. They put the tin in and they just chump-chump-chump-chump, and go down the chutes there dropping a box there on the other end and a light that tallies when they get a hundred in there. They got a hundred in there almost as quick as that. Three or four of them presses would cut as many of those cans as thirty-five foot pressmen back in them times, so you can see what that machine has done there. Used to have the tin upstairs. Bring down the tin in an elevator, put it on a bench, and shove it through the slit one sheet at a time with your thumbs. Now they bring down a thick stack and pack it into the machines, turn the switch and away she goes.

Then we had what they called the Depression. There was no jobs and you couldn't do much of anything to make a living. I managed. I peddled clams, I smelt fish, I found little jobs that I could make a living. Of course, I didn't have a family. That was a help. But anyway it got so that everything was tight. You couldn't do much of anything. That's when I bought this place here. No use to go away for a job because the jobs away were as bad as they was here. So I says to myself, I always could make a living on a farm. If you're on a farm you can most always make something that you can live on. Well, this place was laying idle here and I bargained for this and went to work myself. And I worked for myself since. It was not so easy in the beginning. No market for much of anything, and what there was on the place wasn't worth nothing to amount to anything. But I cut and peeled pulpwood and hauled it to East Machias and loaded it aboard freight cars for six dollars and a half a cord. I made a success of it and I kept building up my business here on the farm. I got into cattle, sheep. I raised potatoes, turnips, and I cut and peeled pulpwood in the summertime. They never used as much fertilizer in my younger days as they use now. Used to get the scoots from the factory to use for hayfields and the like of that for fertilizer. The scoots were the heads and tails off of the fish. Waste. That's what become of all of them. The farmers picked them all up from all the factories. Hauled them, spread their fields with them. And you could compost them with your barn dressing and stuff. You could make a mixture. They were good, but on your hayfields they were really good for only one year. You had to spread them every year. One crop and they were all gone. Your barn dressing and stuff like that would last longer. Herring skins were good too. Use them a lot. Now that all goes to the fertilizer and to make fish meal. Bag it up in bags. They use the fish meal mixed with grain for hen feed, use the fish meal to plant with. They've discovered a lot of uses for it.

And everybody around Lubec was burning firewood. I took my pulp-wood waste up. Instead of throwing it into the brush, I sawed it out and sawed it up for firewood and hauled it into Lubec, sold it. Six dollars a cord all ready for a stove. You couldn't get a cord cut for that now, but as I say, everything else was cheap. You got by all right. Back in them times, if you could earn three or four hundred dollars a year you could pay your bills. You could get by all right and have enough to eat and be comfortable. But you didn't have no luxuries and you had to make every cent count.

And when I began to work for myself the time flew by. I couldn't get work enough done in the day. The day was gone and it was very much more pleasurable to work for yourself. You were doing something that you wanted to do, and you worked full as hard or harder than you did for the other people, although I done a nice fair day's work when I worked for other people. And I had a chance to expand, which I did. To make more, you know. Make more business. Earn more, make more, buy things. Bought a tractor. I worked the tractor on the place some and kept expanding and I had more business than I could handle. Used to hire help at times. And I enjoyed it. Then when the thing commenced to turn, the help that you hired wasn't so good as it had been and they couldn't make you a profit, and they didn't intend to make you a profit. So I dropped the help and I run it alone as long as I could. I didn't feel like paying them for something they didn't earn, so I just did what I could do alone and kept cutting down on the business. Well, finally I'm where I am now. I don't work. Ain't got no business.

But I wanted a home, and I wanted to be situated so that I could pay my bills and own it and be independent; not be beholden to somebody else. I've done it. I don't owe nobody a penny. I was honest and I always had good credit. When I was working on a job and I got my money, I went and paid my bills and didn't just buy something that I thought I'd like to have. That's what kept me going is honesty, I guess. I always could go get credit, and I always could pay my bills.

And I had interest enough so that when I see done what somebody else could do, I could most always go to work and do it. I went to work and built a barn. Don't look too bad. I found it nice and usable. Like my house. I built my house. Don't look so good. Ain't got no nice finish on it, but it's comfortable. I don't have running water or electricity. I have a hand pump right in the sink there, and all I do is pump the pump. I got plenty of time here to do it [laughter]. That don't put me out none. And I have a flush here. Like anybody else, flush. But I have to run my water from the pump into a pail and fill my toilet tank when I empty it. But I have plenty of time to do that. I guess you'd call it old-fashioned and unhandy. You probably wouldn't want to live that way. If you was working on a job and had to get there a certain time in the morning, you wouldn't have as much time to do the stuff that I'm doing. You could do it but it would be "extry." If you had electricity, you could press the button and do it a lot quicker. Wouldn't be too much time spent at it. But I've never had it. That makes a lot of difference. Got used to this way and my home was always common, as you see here. There's been times that I would like to have a little more in it, look a little better, more up to date, but I'm comfortable and I don't have any desire for it. If I won some money on a contest or something like that, why, I'd use what I wanted to use of it and I would take the rest and I'd put it into something where it would do people some good. Some kind of an organization or something; cancer research, heart fund or a school of some

Lyman Guptill with interviewers from the Trailside Country School

kind for people that couldn't afford it. I'd find something to do with it where it would do some good. I would start passing it out, perhaps, to people. I'd make little presents of it. I'd make some good use of it. But I don't want anything special. I might like to have an electric light line in here so's I could have a television. But then again I can't see why it would be worthwhile for me to spend that much for the time I'd watch it. I'd rather put it into something else that would benefit other people.

So I do a little work around here—I saw my wood for winter, take care of my property here, keep it in repair—there's always something to do on the place; and I go to the store about every day. If somebody don't drop in and I don't have nothing to do, why, I jump in my car and go somewhere for a little while if I feel I'd like to talk to somebody. If I don't I just set here and relax and don't do anything.

I planned in my retiring age to make some trips, see some of the country. I've had nice offers, too, only I haven't got the spirit to start. 'Fraid I'm too old. 'Fraid I'm too late. But I meet a lot of new friends and they take a liking to me, I guess. I'm a little hard to get acquainted with; that is it takes time, I don't get acquainted too quick. Usually when I'm making friends I keep them. They take a liking to me and I do them. I tell them the truth and they appreciate it, I guess. Not scart to trust me, and that's worth a lot.

Long as I get enough to pay my bills then that's all I care about. As a fellow says, I ain't gonna take nothing with me. I never had no desire to hoard money and I still don't.

Now I have a son-in-law, nice home; I could go to Portland if I wanted to where I wouldn't have to do nothing. I'd get around a lot, but it would be misery to me. They might want me to go somewhere sometime. I wouldn't want to say no, that I was too lame, and keep them home. Here I can do as I'm a mind to. If I'm too lame, I can set in the chair here. As long as I ain't so lame as what I can get around and take care of myself, it's better for me here. If I was disabled so I couldn't get around, I'd *have* to go somewhere, but till I am, I'm gonna stay here.

As a fellow says, you're never too old to learn something. I'm learning a lot right here amongst you people today. Getting an idea how you live and how you do, and some what you like. I guess I'm different from other people in a lot of ways. I'm sort of odd, I guess. Of course, I'm alone a lot. That's why I'm so interested in the people now. I learn a lot as an older man. I learn a lot every day. Now I enjoy you here; I'm learning a lot from you, in my opinion. I see that you're out seeking something for a lifetime probably. I'm telling you the truth, what I think and how I know it. I don't ask you to take it or believe it. As you go along, it will come to you perhaps. Maybe times that you'll remember some of the things I told you same as I have when things have been told to me. No harm done; won't hurt you none. It might do you some good. Never can tell. Future is quite a thing to look into.

[But there are a lot of things that confuse me today. Things aren't made as well, and I don't understand that.] Now, that stove right there is an example of that. That's an old Glenwood stove there. You can get a new one today, I guess. But I've had that stove fifty years and it was secondhanded when I bought it. But it wasn't hurt none. As good as new. Now, you can't go buy a stove today that will last you fifty years; or if you can, you'll have to tell me where you could buy it. None that I know of that they manufacture now would last that long. They won't heat the same. The stoves you get today are insulated or cased in so the heat all comes from the top. You build a fire in that stove of mine and you can set in front of it, you can set where that girl's setting, sit behind it, the end of it, and feel the heat from it there and on the top, too. Just use a couple of sticks at a time. Good, nice dry wood. Two sticks in there with the stove all shut up tight and that little thermometer on the wall will be seventy. If I want to make a pan of biscuits or boiled potatoes where I got to have more fire, why, I put a little more wood into the stove and open it up a little bit and get my oven hotter. Then it's a little too uncomfortable and you've got to open the door a little for a while [laughter].

There was one stove that they used to demonstrate. They used to come around with a wagon and a pair of mules on it. I think that was the Kalamazoo if I remember right. That and Home Comfort and Glenwood were the best stoves. But this cart was an old-fashioned cart with wagon wheels with steel tires, heavy wheels. They'd take the stove covers, thrash them on those wagon tires—try to break them, you know. They'd get a maul and they'd pound them with a maul [laughter]. It's true, it's true. They'd dump the whole thing right out on the ground. And they couldn't break it. And that's the way they demonstrated them. Today I think if you'd go to R. H. Rodgers in Machias there and take an eight-pound maul and go to work on it, it would look like a wrecked car.

And now the way the thing is in the city, I'd take my choice here. Wouldn't want to be in the city because I'd be uneasy. What they tell me in the city is that your neighbor that lived alongside of you walks right by you and you wouldn't dare to say hello because you don't know who they are or what they are. That wouldn't do with me. Now you take here. No matter what the stranger is that comes along you're gonna say hello to him. I am anyway. Just for courtesy. They all do around here. Always did. I couldn't pass anybody. I'd be ashamed. Just for courtesy. [More and more are moving here from the city for that reason.] They're getting in these country places. We got a lot of neighbors all around here everywhere. A few years ago there wasn't none. They're coming in from other places, settling. They bought up just about all the land all around. Somebody owns just about all the land. Not too much land for sale.

But it doesn't bother me. No, I like it. I like people, I like company. I don't get lonely. When they commence to come in here, I make friends with them all. They're real nice; they're all nice. They even drop in, see if I'm all right, and that means a lot to me. It really does.

I wouldn't know how to get along in a city the way things are now. I wouldn't know how to tackle it. I'll tell you what I think. I think we've got an awful beautiful country but now we haven't got no one to run it. What the results will be, your guess is as good as mine. I don't want to discourage you, but it would be a dull-looking future for me to be looking into if I was young and knew as much as I do now. I won't see it but I'm wondering just the same. It seems to be getting worse instead of better again. To be honest with you, I'd rather be on the end going out than the end coming in. I don't want to discourage you and make you feel that way. That's the way I see it

and I can't see it no different. Now I may be way, way wrong, but that's the way I see it and that's honest.

But there's no use to git scart. The only thing you can do is face it, do the best you can, if you can, to improve it, to make it better. Part of it is there's more people to be dishonest. You get right in your towns or you get right in any kind of business, you'll find a lot of it today. I suppose they don't care for themselves. They haven't got no respect for themselves or they wouldn't do it. They know right from wrong. There might be a few that hasn't had the chance, that was an orphan or something like that, but still in all they picked it up on the outside, I think.

Now you hear a lot of people say the young people don't care today. That's a mistake in my thinking. The young people do care. But there's a lot of old people who say the young people don't care nothing about you. That all they want when you're gone is what you've got left. There are some that way, but all the young people that I've met has used me nice. I'm surprised, really surprised, that they care. You can tell by the things they do. I can see their good quality in little things that they do. The way they act and the like of that. They really care. You can't make me think they don't. Now take them few that don't care. I don't think they've got the respect and care for themselves. They might be discouraged in some way or something, I don't know. There's something that's turning them that way. They must have a cause. I'll tell you what makes me think that way a good deal. We used to go to town, and we used to tie our horses up at the blacksmith shop. There was an old man and a young man was working on the roads, and they got in an argument, and the young man hit the old man with a shovel. And the talk was that they thought that was an awful thing for a young man to hit an old man with a shovel. Which it was, probably. But I happened to go into the blacksmith shop—of course that's where you got all your news at that time—and they was talking about it. The old fellow there was a truck-man; Patty Ryan, they called him. I never said a word and he didn't. He stood right alongside of me and after they got through talking saying those awful things, he says, "Anybody that would do anything like that," he says, "they've got a cause." [Laughter.] He says, "What would I want to hit Lyme Guptill with a shovel for," he said, "if I didn't have a cause?" [Laughter.] I think poor old Patty was quite right, don't you? If that young feller hadn't had some cause, I don't think he would have hit him with a shovel. Course, it was kind of a rude thing to do, I suppose! [Laughter.]

The way I look at it, it's a challenge to set things right again. You've got to get together. People's got to get together. Work together. Straighten it out. Get it a-going right. You've got quite a job on your hands because they've put it wrong so long now. You've got a lot to straighten out.

"It makes shivers go up your back."

MARY AND JOHN LAFAVE

Mary LaFave was born on February 2, 1909. Her mother was a Chippewa Indian and her father was a white man who had been adopted by the tribe. She attended a public school until the sixth grade, and then went to a boarding school in Hayward, Wisconsin, for two years. She and her husband John now live in Cloquet, Minnesota.

—THOMAS PEACOCK AND JAMES WHITE

MARY LAFAVE: My mother was a full-blooded Indian. Her maiden name was Liza Keene. She was Catholic. But both of her parents were pagan. All of her people on that side were pagan. There was a family of ten, and she was the only one that wasn't.

We went over and saw my mother's father and mother in 1918. My grandfather died in 1918. He had cancer of the back. A bear had caught him when he was young and scratched his back. He developed cancer there and that's what he died from. This happened when he was young but as he got older it got bigger and bigger, I suppose. They only spoke Chippewa, and that's all I learned until I went to school and was taught English. I went to the public school till I was in sixth grade.

We didn't know what discrimination was at one time, but when we went to school at the public school, we knew. I know they used to call us squaws and big Indian, and, boy, we'd get mad. After a while the white kids wouldn't even bother. After the sixth grade, I went to Hayward. It was a boarding school. They furnished us food, and we stayed there nine months. Then we had permission to go back to the reservation till the end of vacation. Then in the fall they'd come after us.

We weren't allowed to speak Chippewa, but us girls used to speak Chippewa when we were alone. Anytime the employees heard us speak Chippewa, they'd punish us. Oh, they'd give us demerits. Then we couldn't go to town on Saturday. If we had more than five demerits we had to stay and work them off on Saturday afternoon. We had the military style there. We used to have to march to the dining hall and march back, all in formation; and we'd have to drill about fifteen minutes before we ate.

I remember when I was an officer there and we had to take these kids in and sign them in and take their names. And then we had to see that they were cleaned up and had their haircuts. Nobody was allowed to have long hair. The girls, too, their hair was cut short 'cause it was easy to keep clean.

[For subjects] we had English, geography. We never did have Indian history. Oh, we had some, but it was always bad about Indians, you know. Never anything good. That they were hostile and all that.

And they had a farm on the Indian school, and they'd keep some of the children in the summer, and they kept the farm and canned.

Anyway, that was my schooling and how I learned to speak English.

Now my mother became Catholic when she married my dad. I have two other sisters. I was born February 2, 1909. And when I was a kid my dad used to tell us all about the Indian religion. He was no Indian himself, but he was raised by the Indians. He had full knowledge of the Indian way of life, and he could talk it, but, still, he wasn't an Indian; he was a white man. He was adopted by the Indians and the one he claimed to be his mother had light hair and was light complected, and, during the war with the Sioux, he said they were riding down the river and when they'd see him with his mother, they didn't bother them because they were so light. He had red hair. And the Sioux didn't bother them.

My dad used to work for the town. He drove a school wagon—a covered wagon.

I didn't think it was too bad [back then] because my father was a farmer and he had a good house. He kept things there, a lot of food. Oh, there was potatoes and cabbage and carrots and things like that, you know. So we weren't too bad off. We never knew a day's poverty when we were kids.

And Indian children respected their elders. They never made fun of anyone. They were real good children at that time—well, they're still good children, but I mean they respected their elders in every way. We were told to respect our elders and not make fun of other people.

I remember a lot of happiness and a lot of rituals. In one, we went into a wigwam. There was nothing going on in there, but, boy, you should see the pretty things they had up. Nice blankets and nice beadwork they had up in there around the inside of the wigwam. I don't know if they just done this for people to see, but I sure thought it was pretty. They had beaded belts and everything up there. They had deerskins that were tanned. They had some kind of baskets where they used to keep their tobacco. There was great big beadwork that they put over their shoulders.

Another time I went to a wake and we stayed a couple nights there. They'd have great big water drums.

JOHN LAFAVE: They are hollow and they got water in there and they pound on them all night long and they tell Indian stories. They go around in a big circle. One tells a story, then another one, then another one.

MARY: We stayed there two nights and then they had the funeral. They have big feasts every night and they put a mat on the floor, and they eat on the floor. They have rice, and maybe deer meat and dumplings, Indian hominy.

JOHN: They never carry a body out through a door, always through a window and feet first. And when someone is buried, you take all the clothes, make a bundle, and put it into the casket.

MARY: And they have a little pot for tea and a pot for something else. And that head beater tells the body which way to go, not to look back, and whenever you get to this river to go across it. It was really something to hear, how they chant these songs. It makes shivers go up your back and your hair stand on end. It's beautiful all right.

JOHN: At the grave, every fall they'd put something near it, like sugar. In the spring of the year, they'd put sugar and, in the fall of the year, they'd put wild rice and raisins and then sometimes they'd put tobacco. A big bunch of boys would go and pick up the tobacco. The chief told me, "If you want that rice and things, go get it. That's what it's there for, to eat."

MARY: I remember a lot about those days.

My aunt used to go out to the sugarbush, used to make sugar. And they had to go about four miles to get to the sugarbush. That's what they called it. And I know several times us girls went out there to help her to carry sap to these great big kettles they had. And they stirred these kettles to make their syrup. They'd have to boil it a length of time before it can be syrup.

They had to have so many gallons of that sap before it could make a gallon of syrup. It's a tedious job, but good if you have a lot of help. They'd go to every tree and empty it into the buckets and then they'd bring it over to the big kettles. Make a lot of friends that way.

You know, a lot of Indians, even though they're Catholic, still cling to their old ways. I think it's good. I think that in this day and age these Indians should know the good ways of living they had. Of course, the Indians always had good ways of living. They lived out in the open, never hardly stayed in the house. I don't know why some of the white people say the Indians are dirty. I don't think they were dirty. They had water! And I'm sure that if the Indians nowadays went back to some of their old ways, I think it would be better in some ways.

JOHN: If they don't follow it now, it'll die out anyway. Later on it will die off. Some has already.

"We've always been the hewers of wood and the drawers of water."

MABEL MURPHY

Mabel M. Lucas Murphy was born on January 4, 1894, in Sweet Springs, Missouri, one of five girls and three boys born to Stephen and Alice Murray Lucas. Mrs. Murphy began attending the Banner Schoolhouse in Jennings (at that time in the Oklahoma Territory) at the age of six. She walked two and a half miles to school each morning.

At the age of nineteen, she married Fred S. Holly, by whom she had four daughters and four sons. While her children were young she began her training to become a registered nurse, but discontinued her education after becoming a practical nurse in order to support her family and herself when her husband left her.

In 1939, Mabel moved to Los Angeles to care for her ill mother. She did not return east as she had planned after her mother's death, but remained in California working as a cook and maid for a family in Beverly Hills. She intended to build a home for delinquent boys and purchased two parcels of land in Dos Palos, but when she was unable to obtain the funds to continue her plan, she built her home there nine years later.

Since that time she has remarried and is currently very involved in community affairs and crafts. She is a minister in the National Alliance of Truth Seekers, and the founder of the local crafts club, her own specialties being handmade quilts and hairpin lace.

—BILLIE SORIANO. PHOTOGRAPHS BY NANCY RENTON.
—NANCY RENTON, ADVISER FOR WESTSIDE RIF PROJECT.

MY GRANDMOTHER on my father's side was a black African. She was born and reared in Louisville, Kentucky, on a big plantation. Her boss's name was Larsh. My grandmother was a daughter of eight children. When she got to be sixteen years old my great-grandmother put a long dress on her. That let the white man know that she's coming to womanhood and she's eligible to be placed in a house, or a cabin, as they called it, to raise children. Mr. Larsh came by one Saturday and said to my great-grandmother, "Hannah, I see you got a long dress on Marianne."

She said, "Yes, she's comin' to womanhood now."

He said, "Well, I've got a youngster over here that's a nice strapping young man. I want to put them in a cabin and raise me some young'uns."

Now, my great-grandmother hated to give her up but she did. My grandmother had eight children by this man.

And then this same boss man came by again. He said, "Marianne, give your baby to Sara"—that was her other sister—"and come and go with me." She gave her baby to Sara and came to the door. Then they called jackets a bass. He said, "You'd better get a bass and put on." So she reached back and got her a little jacket to put on. When she got outside there was ninety-nine other people outside. They were going on this travel from Louisville, Kentucky, to St. Louis, Missouri. They didn't know it, but they were going there to be sold. He was taking a hundred slaves over to sell them. My grandmother, nursing her baby, walked all the way. They walked in the daytime and then they'd rest at night. Oxen would carry the food and the bedclothing that they'd bed down with.

When they got to St. Louis, my grandmother's breasts had swollen and were so sore they put her on the block first. She tried to step up on this block and she couldn't. So they helped her up on the block because her bust was swollen so. The boss man tore her clothes all off to show how big she was. She said she just cried. They sold her for one thousand dollars. They sold her to this man, George Lucas.

He and his wife took her immediately to their plantation out in Missouri because she was suffering. They put her with another Negro man. His name —everybody that worked for this man, their last name was Lucas—was Steven Lucas. That was my father's father. They had eight children, so that made my grandmother the mother of sixteen children. We didn't know her real age, but as well as we could count she lived to be ninety-five years old before she passed. She was living in Oklahoma when she passed. Slavery was over. She saw a lot of children and men mistreated while she was under slavery.

My father was twelve years old when freedom was declared. He died in 1919. I forget now how old Papa was but I have it in our Bible. He wasn't big enough to know all about it, but he saw men whipped. They'd whip them with fifty lashes or a hundred lashes. He saw the babies eat out of a trough like they were pigs. They had a yard mamma that took care of white and colored because the white men had had babies by their colored slaves. Some of them was white and some was brown and some was black. This yard lady took care of them and she fed them just like she'd feed pigs in a trough. Then when they got to be six and seven years old they went somewhere else and somebody else took care of them. They just wore one little bit of jacket. They didn't have no underskirt, no panties, no shoes on. They had a place where they slept. When they got bigger they had another place to sleep. And so on, until they were grown up and able to get out and work like other people. So it was bad.

My father was a very brave man. He married a Cherokee Indian, so my mother was an Indian. He never allowed us to say we were afraid of anything. He'd always tell us, "No, you have no need to be afraid of nothing. If you show fear, you are defeated. If you stand up and be brave, you can master it." We used to live in Oklahoma where the Indians would come through sometimes on their horses. Sometimes we'd want to be afraid of them. He'd tell us, "No, don't be afraid. Now you just watch when they come by this time." So my dad wouldn't take no gun or no weapon or nothing. He'd just walk out and offer them rest. They'd fall off of their horses. They'd say, "Hm, shake hand." They never did offer to fight my dad. We lived in the early part of the Indian fights in Oklahoma. We never were attacked by them. They'd come by and a lot of times they would want food. My mother would feed them; then they'd go on about their business. They never did harm us, because my mother was Cherokee anyway. Her hair was down to her waist, and when they took one look at her they knew she was Indian. My father always treated them kind. They never done us any harm.

I think people should stay as near as they could to the Golden Rule. Maybe some people see it different from how I see it. I still say kindness rules the world. If we love each other, well, I don't think we'll do anything

Mabel Murphy

wrong to each other. So, young people should learn to love good, and do good whenever they can. I don't know just how to put it, but I'd like to place a lot of young people in interesting things that are good for them. Like music. I believe in music and entertainment. I think they should have just as much privilege to enjoy life as the elderly people. They're young and they should enjoy life, but there's a nice clean way to enjoy life. That's what I believe. I don't believe in dope and smoking and drinking. To me that's— I'll tell you this, I've never saw a person that drank get prettier or have any more wealth or live to a beautiful old age. They always wither away. They don't help themselves and they can't help nobody else. So I would to God that they just never smoke, never drink, and never use pills. Now if I could see the young generation minus that I think it would be a beautiful world. I'd like to see them grow up and get married.

If boys want to get with girls, there's a decent way for them to do it. They don't have to lower their morals. Girls don't have to throw themselves away and have babies before it's time or ruin their health by disease. There's a nice, decent, clean way for everything to be done. I think marriage is one of the greatest things. If they want a family, have a family. I'd like to see them with farms if they want to farm. If they didn't want to farm, I'd like to see them with a nice business in town, and live respectable and decent. The Bible tells us, "Do all things decent and in order." If people done that they'd do fine.

But my advice to you younger people is to always be energetic, clean-minded, and prepare yourself efficient for whatever task is set before you. A lot of young people nowadays don't want to do this or that because they don't want to. I am very thankful that I have learned to do so many things. I've plowed, I've planted, I harrowed, I stacked hay. I'd know how to do anything on a farm if I was sent today. I'd know how to make an excellent crop. Those that don't want to do that, let them learn how to sew, how to cook, how to can, how to be secretaries, how to be stenographers, or how to be teachers. Let them accomplish something.

You can do it. I made up my mind that my children would all get an education and have a chance at a decent life—better than the one I had. Now Omar has the largest bicycle shop in St. Louis. He's doing great. My other son, he loved to cook and he was handy around the house and he liked medicine. He wanted to be a doctor. I wasn't able to send him to medical school so he became a male nurse. He went to the extent. My oldest daughter is a registered nurse. My next daughter is a clerical clerk in Los Angeles and a social worker now. My next daughter is a clerical clerk in Los Angeles. My other daughter is a teacher in Berkeley. So they all have nice jobs. My baby boy, he's an automobile mechanic. One of the best. He works at Bayshore in San Francisco. My next son is a cook on the railroad for twenty-seven years. He'll graduate from there in about three years. Maurice, Omar, Fred, and Alfred was my boys. Wylene, Theeta, Yanona, and Flora are my girls. They all have nice jobs and I thank God for them. I let them choose their position as far as I was able to put them through school.

Don't give up, always try. If you try you can accomplish whatever you undertake. If we want to do anything bad enough, we'll do it. It's just like a lot of times I'll get something in the middle of the floor. "Oh, I wish I could move that, but it's just so heavy." I may go back and attempt two or three times to move it. Next time I think, "Well, I'm gonna move this chair," so I just reach down and pick it up and it's gone. Someday I would like to finish school. And I want to write a book of poetry and at least a dozen songs and put them on the market. I'll do it someday. If you want to do anything bad enough you can do it. You don't have to depend on handouts and government charity. I think welfare is making a mess. I wish the Government would give everybody that isn't working, that needs work, I wish they would give them a job. The Government has money. If they haven't got money, they have ways of making money. I'm sick of handouts. I'll tell you why. That makes lazy people. Don't you agree with me? If I'm gonna sit here, "Honey go get me this, honey go get me that, I need this," and if every want that I want materializes, I'm just gonna sit here. I'll be old and forgotten in a little while. Because it stops me from moving around. It stops me from getting up, being interested in my own welfare. So I say forget about handouts.

Now with my eight children, when my husband left me, he told me, "Now go downtown and get on the county 'cause I don't want to be bothered with you and all the kids." I went down and talked to the lady. She made it so bad for me. She wrote to my people in Oklahoma and told them I was walking the streets and needed food. That just disturbed them. They wrote me and said, "Why didn't you tell me this and that?"

I went back to this lady and I said, "Listen, I don't mind you telling the truth on me, but never have I walked the streets hungry and left my children hungry. I work every day. That lie you told, I should take you to jail for it. If I have to eat dirt with the chickens, I'll never ask for help again." And I didn't. I never got any help, never asked for no help. I don't need what she had. It wasn't hers no way.

I believe in giving, don't get me wrong. There's a certain amount of stuff that should be given. This surplus stuff in the fields that lays there and wastes, I believe that we should utilize that. But I don't believe that every this and that and the other should be handed to you.

Money is important to a certain degree, but the love of money has caused many a person to be asleep in their grave today. So, I don't value money as I do kindness and love. I'll tell you why. I worked, I'll say fifty years, and got very little money. And if it hadn't been for my kindness and being nice to people I wouldn't have gotten a lot of things that I did get. I used to work when my children were small, especially when my baby boy was born. My husband left me and the eight children. I had to work the best I could, where I could and when I could. So I put my baby in a market basket and went to work for a lady, she was an Italian. I washed and ironed for her. One whole day I washed, the next day I'd go back and iron. I got two dollars each day that I went. I had to carry my baby in the basket and pay my carfare and do this washing and ironing. I don't say it because it's me but I could *iron*. I didn't mess up, I didn't leave no catfaces, I *ironed* her clothes. I had from twenty-five to forty-five dresses to iron for her and her children. She had six girls, and they were beautiful girls and they were all in school. She was wealthy and she could dress them well. So, we had ruffles and laces galore to iron. So I ironed for her, and she was good to me in return.

I live here and have a nice garden. If it's a flower garden or if it's a vegetable garden or if it's a fruit orchard, and my fruit is plentiful and I have abundance, I think I should share with not *one* neighbor; I think any neighbor that comes by I should share with. Now that's the way I feel. I don't think I should sell all my stuff. I have made better than a hundred quilts with fingerwork, mental work, and endurance. And I haven't sold but two or three. I give them away. Or I do them for you if you do something for me. I think I should share with my fellow man. If I share with them, I'm sure they would share with me. Just like I have some neighbors now. There's not much I can give them because they are better fixed financially than I am, but they share with me and I share with them. The world is narrow of that, though, now. Real wealth to me is health and happiness and a moderate amount of finance to get along. If you've got your health and if you are loved by other people—if you love people other people will love you. I think if we love each other and are kind to each other regardless of circumstances we can always be happy. We can always have and share with each other.

I have worked with the schools uptown. I have worked with the white churches, the white schools, the black churches, and the black schools. I have tried my best to get people to see on eye level that color don't mean anything. I have worked in a home in Dos Palos where this woman couldn't help herself, but she needed help and I was a practical nurse. The doctor asked her to hire me to take care of her because I was able to take care of her. So she did. She said, "Well, Holly, you can come and work for me, but I've never let a colored person eat in my house."

I said, "Well, let's don't fall out about that because color don't mean anything. All you need is my service."

She cried a little bit about my sitting down at the table with her. But I told her, "I'm human."

She said, "You should be out there in the field with all the other darkies. You shouldn't be here in the house with me."

I said, "Well, when I go to the field, there's just about as many white darkies as there are black ones. So I work wherever I go or wherever I'm sent." We talked and I put my arms around her and I said, "Now, you may not love me, but I love you."

After that she was my dearest friend, and we got along lovely from then on. She even wanted to let me live with her. She said, "You won't ever have to buy a home, you can always live with me." She divided her silver and her crocheting and her dishes out of her china closet. She did all that before she passed on. She thought there wasn't nobody in the world like Holly. I stayed with her until the moment she passed.

I think if people would forget about color . . . we didn't make ourselves, God made us. I'm one person on the earth that loves people. When we moved to Kansas and Oklahoma, we had different people to encounter. They didn't have schools then like they have now. All different nationalities went to the same school. We went to the same churches. We didn't know color. I never heard my mother separate color. Never. We were the only dark people in the school and there weren't but three of us children. The rest was Bohemian, Indians, Germans, Irish, Dutch. We were the only three Negroes. We didn't have any Mexicans then in our school. But after all's said and done, everybody was just lovely and we never heard no names called and no separation or nothing.

The change came in 1907, when they began to sit Negroes in one school and whites in another. They began to separate them then. I was nine when that first separation came about. Their reason I couldn't dare tell you. It was done by the Government. My father fought it until he died. He was a teacher there, and he based his whole body and soul on reading, writing, arithmetic, and spelling. He was an excellent speller, and he was a mathematician from head to foot; and grammar, he was the very best in grammar. And he thought the separation would be bad for education. But one person trying to fight it down couldn't win. You know we couldn't drink where they drank, we couldn't go to their shows, and we couldn't go to the white churches. We were all separated. Clear up until, I guess 1962, somewhere like that. I guess you know when they had that freedom train going from Mississippi to Washington, D.C.? Well that was the next turnover. So I guess people will get together now and act like people. I've been in thirty-two states of the United States. I've been to Washington, D.C., Seattle, Washington, and Victoria, British Columbia. My father told me never to go south because the whites in the south were different to where we lived. My father felt like I was too good a person to be treated like they treated people in the south. You had to go around to the back to eat, you had to do this, and you had to do that. He thought that was terrible and I thought it was worse.

But I have been south. I worked for some people in Los Angeles. They took me to the Carlsbad Caverns. I was the only Negro in five hundred whites. I went with Mr. and Mrs. Asbury. I slept in the hotel room with them; they kept me with them all the time. I ate at the tables with them. Therefore, I didn't have to go around to the kitchen. That was the only way I traveled through the south.

I hear it's different now. They have given the Negroes a chance to equalize themselves. They let them eat in eating places, and we can stay in motels where we used to couldn't stay. We are considered humans just like they are. They should have considered that a long time ago. I don't see any black marks on our money. I don't see why we can't purchase a nice hotel or anywhere we want to sleep. We are just as clean as any of the other people. We know how to take baths. We were reared clean. I'm glad that they have changed a lot of the southern ways.

We should learn kindness and equalization. Learn that God don't love the white man no better than he love the black man. He made us all. He loves us all.

I feel like God has made the plan, if people would follow through. The Bible says, "Be ye kind to one another, tenderhearted, forgiving one another, even as God has for Christ's sake forgiven you." I feel like if people would follow the Divine Plan we wouldn't have much worry at all. Don't you think?

I had a fellow come to my door one time and he was talking on some business. I said to him, "Sir, don't you think you are prejudiced in your heart toward us?"

He said, "Mrs. Murphy, down in my heart, truthfully speaking, you couldn't have asked a better question. Yes, I am prejudiced."

I said, "Well, if I scrub a thousand years, I couldn't make myself white like you. And if you were painted a thousand years you wouldn't be black like me. So why not forget color? All I'm asking for"—that's when this stink was going around here—"is something be done about that cesspool. The health authorities have told me that it's against the law for that open sewer to be in our faces like that."

He said, "I'll do my best."

When it boiled down to his last say, they asked him, "Well, did you smell the stink down there in that area?"

He said, "Yes, I smelled it. It was pretty bad. I think they can take it." In other words, this is a black area and they think black people can endure anything. But they just won't. Our babies—I was keeping babies then—at six or seven o'clock in the evening, when the stink would come in, they'd vomit up all their milk. I fought like mad for a change. We're getting it; we didn't get it right then, but we're getting it. They're putting a sewer in now.

I'm gonna say this, you may not agree with me. They call themselves freeing the black man, but to me they've never freed us. We've always been the hewers of wood and the drawers of water. We've always been commanded by the white or the Irish or the Mexicans or whoever was hiring us. So, to me, material freedom to the black man has never come. The only freedom we have is with our heavenly father. We are free to pray wherever we are because we can pray without opening our mouth and we can serve God without going to church. But I say that's the only freedom that we have, is with God. Spiritual freedom, not material freedom, not governmental freedom. But we live and we move and breathe. It's the heavenly father that grants us that privilege. Now, that may be kinda tough and maybe some of my people wouldn't like to hear me say it, but it's the truth within me. That's the way I see it.

I want to be counted a woman like any other woman. Like the President's wife. I'm just as good as she is, but never could I make them believe that. I'm just as clean as she is, I'm just as friendly as she is, and I'm just as obedient, I feel like, to God as she is. But people would never believe that because I'm not the President's wife.

"I used to swing on the telephone wires."

SUSORINE BON

Mrs. Bon was born in Leadville, Colorado, January 11, 1909. Her parents immigrated to America from Italy to farm; her father arrived first in 1906 and her mother joined him a year later. Mrs. Bon went to school in a one-room schoolhouse, and later taught in that same school. She married in 1934. They never had any children of their own. Mr. Bon died in 1970 and since then Mrs. Bon has worked for many people in the valley not so much for the money but rather to be doing something. She lives in the house that she and her husband built when they first moved to Carbondale, a simple white house with an immaculate yard. Until just a few days ago, a huge willow tree stood behind her house. She had planted that tree about eighteen years ago and it was very special to her. As she said, "Well, one day it's up and another day it's down," and she went on to tell us about getting her lawn trimmed for the winter.

—LIZ ELLIS, TONY GREENLEAF, JACKIE BERWIND.
—NITA BUNNELL, ADVISER, COLORADO ROCKY MOUNTAIN SCHOOL.

I JUST CAME BACK from Italy a week ago. [My mother and father came to America from Italy before I was born. I've kept up with my family there all my life.] I don't have a single relative here, except brothers and sisters and Mother and Dad. No uncles, no aunts, no grandpa, no grandma, no nothing. And I always had it in the back of my mind that someday I'd go back there and meet some of my relatives, and I got a chance. My brother-in-law and sister were going and they asked me if I wanted to go. So we went and we visited real well. I still have the dialect and they still speak it so we were able to converse right along. They were so surprised we could speak the dialect and they said, "Why, you speak it a lot better than we do here. How come you were born in America and you can speak the dialect better than we can?" And here everybody thought this dialect wasn't worth anything. If I hadn't had that, I couldn't have visited with my relatives.

It's a mixture between French and Italian is what it is. And everyone up and down the valley spoke it. My mother never did really learn English. Oh, she could buy groceries. She could do little things like that but she could never get out and carry on a conversation in English.

Dad came to America because everything was pretty poor over there. They had opened some of these mines in Leadville, but Dad [and the others who came] didn't like the mines, so they came on down and farmed. This valley was all new then, and they went to farming and they were all good workers. The whole valley up and down here was all these Italian people. The kids today don't like to farm, so they let them go—and see what happened to our valley? This used to be quite a farming community. Little by little the farms got sold and now there's not much farming done any more.

I'm disappointed about what they did to the valley here. Oh, this used to be a good valley. It was very noted for its potatoes, and they used to ship carload and carload of cattle out of here. And quite a lot of sheep, also. Wasn't one of the nicest valleys, of course. The work was tedious and your patches were small. And the country is kinda up and down. And then it has to be irrigated. Not like over in France and Italy where I went. And if you had a brown spot in one of your fields, you heard about it from the other farmers. You got told. But it was a good valley.

My dad lived on a little ranch on the west side of the Stage Coach Inn. And you wouldn't even know it used to be a little farm now 'cause they let all those trees grow back. And here we worked so hard to grub those trees and pick those rocks. Oh, I picked a lot of rocks in my time. When we were kids, I remember we said we'd never pick out any of those rocks when we grew up and did our own farming. Well, I had to eat those words, 'cause I couldn't stand rocks on my field. I used to get out there by myself a lot of the time and pick 'em.

I was born in Leadville. I was about five when I came to Carbondale. We lived a little ways from Marble; Prospect, they call it. We lived there two years. I remember in the winter when there was enough snow, my older sister and I used to swing on the telephone wires. And another thing that I remember—there was a little crick going by with real clear water and I remember one day Mother had churned the butter and something happened to the lid and the thing spilled down the crick and you could see all these little balls of butter down there. I don't know why I remember that.

When we first moved there, the old cabin just had dirt on top. When it started raining, you would throw up some more dirt. Then grass would sometimes grow up on top in the summertime. And then Dad built a new house. He cut down his own logs, and I was pretty small but I did help him skid some. You did it with a horse then. And then he bought two old houses up at Spring Gulch and tore them down piece by piece and brought them down, and every day after school and Saturdays we had to take nails out of the timber so that he could use it to build. Except for the logs, there was nothing new in it.

My father was a farmer. We loaded potatoes on the wagon and in the winter on a sled. Then we used to sort them with the old shaker-sorter. In the wintertime, I'd load the sorters and sort potatoes. Course, we raised hay for the cattle, always had cattle and grain. Some of the grain was sold; some was fed to the hogs. I was seven when Dad put me on the dump rake raking hay.

We tried to raise all we could. You had to get your salt, coffee, sugar, and your spices, and I don't know what else we bought. We didn't buy bread! We used to trade the wheat for flour once a year. My dad would make a trip to Glenwood. There was a mill down there. Dad would take down a half a ton or a ton of grain and trade it for flour and then we'd stack it someplace. According to Mother, the older the flour was, the better the bread it made. So we made our own bread. We butchered our own pork, cured it, made sausage. Never thought of going to town to buy a steak. And we used to raise our own beef. Course, we didn't have freezers in those days. Had to can it, brine it, and keep it in the cellar. Put the meat in the brine for so long and then hang it up to dry. Then it's just like jerky. And we cured all the hams and bacon. We used to pickle the head—put them in vinegar and spices. It was good, if you like it. I used to pickle the tongue and the kidneys so we could eat it in the summer. At home, when I was a kid, I used to hate liver because we had to eat up all that liver, heart, and all that stuff.

Susorine Bon

A lot of these people now, they're going back to the organic stuff. Well, we had all that when we were on the ranch and we still do here. You know, I don't like corn that I buy at the store. I can't eat it because I'm used to going out to the garden picking it, put it in the pot, come home, and boil it. And it tastes a lot better, I don't care what you say! I wouldn't think of buying peas or beans in the store fresh. They look so wilted and dried to me. I wouldn't want them because we always picked them fresh and ate them right after we picked them. We were really organic people. We ate everything from the garden and we milked our own cows. Everything was fresh and pure.

I went to school in Carbondale. There was a little country school, eight grades. I don't care what they say, I still think our country school is the best little school that you could get. You had individual attention, as much as you wanted. And I rode horseback to high school in Carbondale. It was fun in the winter, four miles. Our pencils and papers were furnished and we were not supposed to get more than one pencil a month and one tablet a month. But I could make mine last quite a few months. I don't think I had more than two pencils during the term. Same with paper. We were very conservative with paper, and if we didn't need a whole sheet we cut it in two—and wrote on both sides of the paper, too. And then always save the paper that came back. Like in arithmetic if you wanted to work out your problem you used that for scrap paper. We didn't have just sheets and sheets of paper like the kids do now. It seems so funny to see them just waste things. We were taught to conserve things so much and it's still hard for me to see people waste things. I can't throw anything away yet. I won't throw anything away even though I'm all by myself now. If I have a potato left over or a little bit of vegetable or anything, oh, I put it in the icebox. Well, especially now with iceboxes, or refrigerators, you can save 'em.

When I finished my high school, I went to summer school and I taught school that fall. I went back and taught at the little country school I had gone to for all those years.

When I started teaching school, I stayed at home and I still worked at home. I helped milk and I did the washing on Saturdays. I always gave Mother a little bit of money and she sure seemed to appreciate it. She never had any money of her own as she didn't always get the cream checks. That's one way we got money on those farms. We always milked a bunch of cows and sold cream and then we had a little money; and, then we raised chickens and we could trade our eggs for groceries.

But on the farms everybody worked. You'd come home and do chores. I wanted so bad to play basketball, 'cause I was a tomboy, and they had a girl's team of basketball, believe it or not. I wanted so bad to play, but I couldn't stay for practice after school. I had to go home and do the chores; get the milk, haul in the wood, and the coal.

There wasn't much time for entertainment, and not much in the way of entertainment anyway. I had several best friends—they were from Basalt— and once in a great while we could take our horses and go stay with them overnight. It was quite an adventure in those days. There was no shows, nothing, no picnics. We didn't even get to go to church because our nearest church was in Glenwood and it took all day to go. Never had much toys to play with. We had some old, old sardine cans and blocks and not even very many dolls. I remember the first doll that I ever got was when one of our teachers brought all the girls a doll. They cost about twenty-five cents in those days. That was my first doll that I remember. I remember we had an old wooden doll, too. We didn't have a lot of time to play. Folks believed in making us work. When I was five years old I had to go herd cows. I was to stay with them at all times so they wouldn't get too far away. I would play while I was herding them cows. I'd swing on some trees or bend some over and then they'd spring back and you ride 'em. Just things like that. In a way I'm glad I lived then. I was Dad's hired man. We never got to start school till the crops was all in. Dad had to have us at home. Mother never had very much say so; Dad always let everything suit himself and he never asked anybody anything. He was the boss, and that was the way it went.

He didn't even have to talk to us, all he had to do was look at us. He was very, very strict. We could get away a lot with Mother, but we never got away with anything from Dad and never had any money either as far as that goes. I remember, I think I was six or seven years old, they used to drive a derrick horse. They had a derrick that they stacked their hay with; they have a little rope going through and a horse at the end. Anyhow, I drove that derrick horse and I made a dollar a day and Dad took it all! That was my very first money and he took every bit of it. He always did that. That may have something to do with the way I watch my money now.

Maybe I didn't have the misfortune not to save any money, but I don't like the idea of people living off somebody else entirely. In years way back, when they didn't have welfare, everybody took care of their own. They all got by. But now it takes so much money. Everytime I look around the Government's asking for more. Where are they gonna get the money? All the young people are going to have to pay everything. How they gonna do it? It's really going to burden them. Oh, the taxes are terrible. I pay enough taxes on that house and my car, and insurance—sheesh, takes a lot of money.

But if you try real hard, you can save. Little bit at a time. It don't come fast, but you can save. I still save money and I can't use all I have coming in. I hate to throw it away. Still conservative. Get what I want. But I just don't buy everything. Unless I get sick and stay sick, I'll probably never use it all. I get a little social security. And also I clean house for people. This is just because I, well, especially in the winter—what do you want me to do here? I like handwork. I make afghans and I sew and I embroider but my eyes are so bad I can't do it very long. The days are too long doing nothing all day. I had a little time on my hands when I wasn't helping my husband, so I got out and did a little work and I liked it. A little money to spend and so I just kept on doing and will as long as I'm able. And I can get out and do a little work in the yard in the summer, and I love it, and they say it's good therapy to get out there and work. Let me tell you something. People who say they can't find work, it's not that they can't find work; it's just that they don't want it. Out here there's no excuse for people not working. I like anything that's got dirt involved in it. Even cleaning house. I'd rather work outside than inside but I have to work inside a little bit, too. I can be real disgusted and down and just go out in the dirt and I'm all right. It's good therapy. Or if you don't feel good and you think you've got a headache or something just get outside and it just kind of evaporates. You forget.

I still like to work. I still like to go cut potatoes because I still like to go cut potatoes. That seems silly, but I always like to do it. And that's one of the hardest jobs on a ranch. But I still like to do it. Course, I'm getting a little old and it's getting a little hard for me. But to me it never was a punishment. I can do any kind of work on a farm. I could use all the machinery. And we had horse machinery, we didn't have tractors. I never learned to drive the tractor because we didn't have one. [Laughs.] But it wouldn't be impossible 'cause I drove cars and trucks all the time. You have to learn to

Interviewers from the Colorado Rocky Mountain School

like the soil and get what you can out of it. You have to work lots, and try to enjoy your work. Don't say, "Oh, I hate to do that. I wish I didn't have to." Just do it. I worked because I wanted. If I didn't want to work, I wouldn't have to work nowadays. Even cleaning house. Seems like an awful lowly job. But I like to do it. I like to see the results after it's clean, looks nice. People always tell me I'm crazy to do that kind of work. Maybe I am. [Laughs.] But if it's good for me, why should I worry? People turn my kind of job down because they think it's too lowly. They don't want to do it. It's more peaceful. I dunno, there's something about it. I like it.

And I'd be the last to tell young people to scorn that kind of work and go to college instead. Sometimes I think there's no use in going to college because you often can't get a job when you come out anyway. A lot of people are too particular of what they're going to do. "Oh, this I won't do, that I won't do." But you get on some of the machines, your trucks and your bulldozers. They'll bring you more money than your college students will. There's a lot of outside work you can do. And it pays big money. You should never get discouraged; just keep on working. A lot of us are pulling for you. Sure there's a generation gap and, if you ask me, it's bigger than ever. Some of these older people, oh, especially the real old people, think kids today are not much. I have a little more hope for you, though. I heard that in our generation trouble went on all the time. But I think you'll find that if you are pleasant, and do speak to the older people, and, you know, recognize them, I think you'll get quite a ways there. When I see an old man or woman, I always say either hello, good morning, or how are you? whatever. And try to ask them something or talk to them. They like to be talked to. They are so neglected already. You know, when you get old nobody wants to talk to you any more. Make it a point. Always talk to the old people. If you don't want to, why, say hello or good morning. It doesn't cost you anything. But it sure goes a long way. They like that. That's what you live for—to be needed by someone. And they think it's great, especially when you younger kids talk to them. It really impresses them. Just do more of it. Sure won't hurt anything. Especially the older people. And they're the ones that think kids today have gone to the dogs. The kids are no different, it's just the way they're brought up and treated.

Once I was teaching in Basalt and the first year I taught up there, we had one principal and every one of those kids were so well behaved and everything went like clockwork and nothing was out of order. Then the next year we had another principal and all hell broke loose! They practically tore the building down. And it was no different, they were the same kids. I guess it was the way they were treated. But kids still need discipline. I think they like it, too. They don't like it when they can do anything they want. I don't know how you kids were brought up, but don't you think you want discipline? Don't you like to be told "no" once in a while? It's good for you. You have to have discipline. I saw too much then. I said it's not the kids, it's whoever's above them. That makes a difference. My opinion is that the kids are kids, it's the way you discipline them and how you bring them up. And that's all it is.

Now I can't say I like rock music. In fact, I don't like any music that's loud. But we did things in our day that our parents didn't like and they thought we were going to the dogs, and that's always been. And I made up my mind it wasn't so because my parents thought that we kids were going to the dogs then. Now there's another generation and now they're all going to the dogs. But they're not. Not really. The times are just different and you have different opportunities. I don't think the world will come to an end because of that.

"Life is too sweet."

JOSEPH VENTIRO

Joseph Ventiro was born in Manila, the Philippine Islands, in 1902. He was raised there and worked as student and teacher in the Philippine School of Arts and Trades, graduating in 1923. He served as the driving instructor for four years until he left America on June 11, 1927.

His first job in America was washing pots and pans. He then worked as a porter and a card dealer until World War II broke out and he was given the opportunity to follow the trade for which he trained. He became a journeyman machinist in the local union and worked at his trade for nearly thirty years until he retired in 1971.

He now spends his time reading, tending his house plants and aquariums of tropical fish, and occasionally serving as a card dealer.

—GILLIAN D. STORK. PHOTOGRAPHS BY GILLIAN D. STORK.
—MARCIA PERLSTEIN AND JUDY BEBELAAR, ADVISERS FOR
OPPORTUNITY II HIGH SCHOOL, SAN FRANCISCO, CALIFORNIA.

WHAT I REALLY MISS [about the way things used to be] is that the people don't enjoy walking around any more. That freedom. It seems to me that people are scared to go out—especially at nighttime. What I really miss is just like in the good old days—you could see couples and families, ten or eleven o'clock at night, window-shopping on Market Street hand in hand—you know, lovers—they window-shop. Now you don't see those things any more because they're all scared.

Me, I stay busy here at home. Now that I'm retired, I have plenty of free time. If I'm not reading, I do something around the house or do some exercises to keep me fit. Just sitting down and doing nothing is waste of time for me. I have to keep myself busy. [But I can't tell you young people that.] You can't tell the young people to fill their leisure time with something that *you* want because *everything* they do is part of their growing up. You can't say that the young people are wasting their leisure time because they have to have time to think. It's part of their life now. They got to have their leisure time because they have to think. It's part of their growing up. So you can't push them too hard on that. I think reading is a good substitution for TV. I say read a lot. [But I try not to criticize a lot of what they do in their leisure time.] Only thing is, you got to supervise them and tell them what is wrong and what is right.

Now I think school and colleges are very important because without them we'll have no rules and no guidance to our life. Schools will shape us or the young folks how to live their life. Especially in the advanced age now, the technology, we have to have more education to compete with the rest of the world. Without the school, you can't have no success. You can't because it's the school who provides the books, and who wrote those books came from the school that has taught how to read, how to write. The function of the school is to help us to lead a better life. You should at least be able to read. You can't even go down the street without having to read.

And school can help them to choose a career or life style that is helpful for them when they grow up. And, if they love to do the thing, then they will be happy.

[There are some other things I have noticed in my life that might be helpful to young people. There are some things I believe that I would like to see them care about:]

I think the environment is just like your home. If it's in order and it's beautiful, then you'll have a healthy life. So our environment has a lot of influence in our life. A good environment is a healthy life.

What I have learned about Nature is [that it is] just like a human being. You got to treat them with love. Then it will return a hundredfold if not a thousand. It has been a good provider to me. My age—that's the proof.

I believe that no one has ever lived all these years without Nature. Look around. You can see Nature is all around us. We can't live without it. The scenery and everything—it's part of Nature. When it rains, the sunshine— you can see it. You know with your eyes. Love, and then it will return to you back. Nature is like that. You got to treat it just like a human being, like I say. Another human being, you got to treat them with kindness and with respect. Then it will return that love to you. You can't abuse Nature because you're only hurting yourself. We should protect the land.

Another thing we should protect is trust. Trust is a precious thing. We should regard it very dearly. You have to trust the other people because without trust we can't live. It's so dear that you really have to value it—to trust other people. You are taking a chance by trusting somebody you don't know, but right at the beginning you have to trust somebody that they would accept your trust in good faith.

Trust and friendship goes hand in hand. Without the one, you can't have the other. And to have friends, you have to be one. First you have to show that you're a friend. Just like the old adage says, "No man is an island." You can't live alone by yourself. You got to have friends. And to keep them you got to be a friend all the time and love them. You got to take a little bit, you know, little hurt sometimes. You can't always be on top, you know. We have to forgive a little to keep our friends.

You have to also protect your health, for that is your wealth—not money. If you have your health, you are wealthy. That's all I can say.

Success and money are two different things. You can have a lot of money without success. You can be a poor man but still successful to your endeavor. I wouldn't say that money is the root of all evil [like some people]. It might lead you to it. [But it's not the most important thing to me. One thing important to me has been religion.] God is not three letters to me. I don't know about other people. I haven't seen Him, but I believe in Him. And about religion, it has helped me a lot, and it has been a part of my life; because to me, I believe there is no religion that teaches bad things, like to kill or to rob. And to have a religion, it's something that guides you in your life. How to get along with the other human being. And without religion, 1 think you are just like a ship in the middle of the ocean without a rudder. You have no chart, you have no compass to guide you in the storm in your life. You don't know where to go.

If we don't have faith, with everything we do we can't trust—we can't love. I believe it—that there is a guiding in our life. We can't just guide

Gillian Stork and Joseph Ventiro

without somebody's help. Because, like I said, I believe in God. I believe there *is* somebody.

[Religion is a good teacher. The best advice I can give young folks is based in religion and in my living—my experiences. It is] to be more considerate to the other people. I guess that's the main thing. Because if you have no consideration to the other people, you'll find you'll always be in trouble. Love your neighbor. Be considerate to other people and show respect and love, especially to their elders. In other words, I have to give part of my life and my thought and my love to the other human being. I believe that if you don't do it, you have never lived, just like the saying is, "A person has never lived who much received and never gave." Because we haven't asked to be born. And, since we're here, we got to make our best, to get along with one another, to survive.

I believe if I reach the end and I have done nothing—especially to my loved ones—to make them happy, then I have not accomplished anything.

How do I feel about death? Death is the ugliest thing in the world, and I believe it's the ugliest word, too. Life is too sweet. There is nothing so ugly as death. There's tears on it. The family cries and so on. Even the plants, when their time comes—or animals—makes you feel bad.

And death is mysterious. I was on the highway in 1923 driving a touring car going someplace. Suddenly a black butterfly appeared in front of me from nowhere. I shooed it away many a time, but it kept on coming back flying around me. This incident lasted for about ten to fifteen minutes before it finally flew away. And you know what? When I got back from the trip, my uncle, the husband of the oldest sister of my mother, had died at the time of that butterfly incident.

Here is another. And this happened about August or September of 1927 somewhere in Santa Cruz, California. This was a summer resort and this was my first job here in America. I was hired as a second cook—vegetable man, dishwasher, and pot washer. There were two entrances to get into the kitchen, and one of them was the door to the dining room of the resort, and the other one was the back door of the kitchen that leads to the back porch, which was used as a work place. And this porch was enclosed with a screen wire and a screen door. Bear this picture in mind a moment and listen to this. One afternoon I was helping Ethel, the head waitress, to make some marinades. She was pouring the oil in the bowl and I was doing the beating of the stuff. Suddenly a big black butterfly stopped near me for a moment before it flew away. Noticing it and knowing what a bad omen a black butterfly brings me, the first thing that crossed in my mind was my mother. Was she dying? Or already dead? Then the tears began to appear in my eyes. Ethel asked me what I was crying about. I told her that the black butterfly was a bad omen for me. I excused myself and went to my room. I opened the door, threw myself in bed, and I let it go and cried as I have never before. That night I wrote my mother. Pour out my heart to her . . . how much I love her, ask her to forgive me for my mistakes and short-comings to her. And I hoped that my letter was not late to let her know of my love for her. This happening might seem unbelievable, but listen to this. Soon after, I got a letter from home—they cross each other on the Pacific Ocean—letting me know that my grandmother died. So there is that big black butterfly.

And here's the latest. One afternoon at work while I was at rest and my machine was doing the work, there was an instant that I felt unconscious of the noise and the surrounding in the shop. And I began to be saying to myself, "Mother, on your way up to heaven, say 'hello' for me to Father." You know that when I got home that evening there was a telegram from home, the Philippines, notifying me that my mother just died. Really, they're all true.

Death is the ugliest thing there is. And I don't want to think about it, but if it comes, I can't say no. But still I say life is too sweet, and I will hold onto it as long as I can.

I want to be remembered. Why should I not? I want to be remembered that I loved my loved ones; that they will miss me; that I have not failed them; that I have given them the love that they wanted, that they deserved.

"We had music every day."

ANNA HAGLIND

Anna Haglind was born May 19, 1893, in Howe, Indiana, the youngest of six children in her family. She was raised in Howe, and attended Lima High School (the first commissioned high school in Indiana), Western College for Women in Oxford, Ohio, and graduated from Indiana University in 1914.

After teaching for a year in Sturgis, Michigan, Mrs. Haglind returned to Howe and taught at Lima High School until she joined the National Headquarters of the Red Cross at the end of World War I. She worked for the Red Cross for four years and then returned to Indiana to teach at Brighton High School in Howe. She married her husband, Harry Haglind, there and they had two children. When her husband died in 1941, Mrs. Haglind returned to teaching until she retired. She now resides with her daughter in Michigan City, Indiana.

—LAURA HIGDON.
—MELBA HOWENSTINE, ADVISER FOR RIF PROJECT
IN MICHIGAN CITY, INDIANA.

WE DON'T KNOW people as well here as I knew everybody in the town where I lived. I still take the little county paper. The one thing that seems strange to me is that I don't know everyone that lives there any more. But, I used to know everybody and everybody knew me and my family. But, here now, up and down this street, I don't know anybody but you, except one other family and I know them just to speak to them. I don't know the people next door. The larger the community that you live in, the fewer the people you come in contact with. We came into this community as strangers and, after five years, I feel pretty much a stranger yet. I think that Mary, my daughter, and Lee, my son-in-law, have a good many acquaintances; and, of course, the children going to school here are getting acquainted. They have their playmates. But in a tiny town like the town I lived in of about five hundred people, of course, I knew everybody. I knew everybody all around in every direction. I knew who lived where and all about them. But I don't any more. I can go to the grocery store and see lots of people, but not see anyone I know. It didn't used to be that way. I used to know everybody.

I still own and care for the home in which I was born, but I live with my daughter now instead of staying there. I don't want [my daughter and her husband] to think, "Oh, of course we had to have Grandma with us all those years." I hope they won't feel that way. For instance, one night I said something about someone that was in a home. I said, "I suppose that's where I should be." And Mike said, "Not as long as we're here to take care of you." And that made me feel very good. It made me feel that they wanted me. But, I think you can overdo a good thing and I have begun to feel that eighty-two years is a long time to live. [Soft laugh, a pause, and then softly, "I'd be willing to go anytime."]

Death is inevitable. Death and taxes. We are here, I suppose, to accomplish certain things. When that is over, then we die and someone else comes on in our places. I don't spend much time thinking about it. I know that it isn't too far off, but that doesn't make me dwell upon it. I just feel very fortunate to have been cared for in this home by my own people rather than in an institution. The thing that I am grateful for is that when I wake up each morning I can think. I feel so sorry for those people that have to live on and on and can't think. I am lucky to be able to think and take care of my own business, and be financially able to help with my own care here.

And I know that I will be remembered by some of my pupils as their teacher, because that is part of the compensation you get from teaching. Fifty years ago about the only thing a woman could do was teach if she worked outside her home. She could teach or do housework or be a secretary. All of my training tended toward teaching, so that's what I did. And I would advocate it. I think the field is overcrowded now, probably, but there are great satisfactions in teaching. And they go on. Even at my age I am experiencing some of the wonderful satisfactions of gratitude of pupils. Really the only way a teacher is paid is through the gratitude of the pupils she has taught. There is sort of, well, not an adulation exactly, but through the visits you have with them you realize that you have had some influence on their lives. Those are compensations you get while you are here. And I suppose you are thought of afterward, just as a teacher that I had meant so much to me. When I think of her now, it is of my association with her. She was very much alive, full of fun. I think of those times.

[And I think of my father. You know,] the environment influences everything we do in our lives. Nature is an excellent teacher. It teaches us a lot about life, about birth and growth, death and rebirth.

I began learning very young from land and from nature because my father was a naturalist. He was a great planter. He had an orchard. He planted both trees, vegetables, and flowers. Everything that grew he loved to plant. He carried a pocketful of black walnuts and a stick and he would put his stick down into the ground and put a black walnut in. The result was that there are a great many valuable black walnut trees around my home.

He was a great fisherman. In those days the rivers were very clear. They were not polluted. He preferred to have us fish and swim in the rivers because these had running waters. He did not like the small lakes. Now our rivers are polluted and you seldom see a child living near my home town swimming in the river.

I enjoy the environment around here. I think it is beautiful. I love the trees and the green everywhere. I enjoy the lake; it is ever-changing. I hope the big oak trees and the big pines out on the other side of the house can be preserved.

If you want your children and grandchildren to enjoy what you had, you should be interested in seeing that the land is preserved and cared for. We can protect the land by caring for our immediate surroundings and through legal channels. By voting we can help preserve the land the way we want it to be.

Of course, I have always thought our government was superior in every way. I have never had any real reason to change that feeling. My father was an English church school boy and he came to this country. He moved to the town where we lived so he could bring his boys up in a church school. He did just that. It would be very difficult for me to be enthusiastic about a

Laura Higdon and Anna Haglind

government that wouldn't allow people that privilege. Real independence is being able to live as I want to without any interference with my family or religious life.

I wish there were more flags out. I think we have so much that we probably are not appreciative. We have things that are bad that we will have to work and make them better. When we were asked to help feed the hungry in the world, there was no lack of desire on our part, but our problem was finding a route for the money we could give to get it to the people that needed it.

I think the people of America used to be very generous. Now it seems they are disillusioned a good bit because so many times the money that they want used generously is used by a few selfishly and it doesn't get where they want it to go. [There is so much dishonesty now that it worries me.] Crime [worries me]. I don't read a lot about it, but I hear about it on television. I feel sorry for the older people in the cities. One of our neighbors stays here and drives into Chicago each day to see her husband rather than stay in her own home. She has to travel far to go to see him. She is probably afraid to stay alone, and I think that is too bad.

There seems to be no way to keep people out. If they want to get in, they get in. It worries me. I keep the doors locked when I am alone here, but some people don't. I feel that we are pretty safe as long as there is a car in the driveway, for then no one can drive in to carry things away. But when the car is gone, I think the door should be locked so someone couldn't step in the house and just help themselves.

I never used to think anything about these problems. They probably existed, but I never knew anything about it because I lived in a little town. Our only communication was through the local newspaper and the wire service. We didn't have telephones, radio, television, etc. I never really knew there were problems. Now as I read I learn that there were a great many problems as I was growing up, but I didn't know about them. I still don't know too much about problems because my life has been too protected. I guess that's why I am an optimist, a person that thinks everything will turn out all right. At different times during my life, we have had difficult economic conditions, but we've survived.

I hate to see economic conditions affecting the schools, though. When I was growing up, I had an opportunity to take so many subjects. For instance, I had Latin all through high school. I had math all the way through and had at least three years of history. Then I had a year of government and state history. And, of course, four years of English. But we also had music every day. We had a regular music teacher. We had vocal music every day. I learned the basis of my music knowledge concerning the opera, the symphony, our great soloists, and musicians through that course. Some days we sang. Some days we studied, but we had music every day.

We had art, but not as consistently as we had music. The result is that I know very little about art and have very little interest in it because I have no foundation for it.

I don't like to see the children having to give up opportunities like that because of this depression. If it causes them to have lacks in their education, I feel very sorry about that. If I had more money, I would probably use it to educate deserving children. I've been fortunate in always' having enough for my needs, but that is not real wealth. I've not had that, but I've had enough. Much depends on what people do with their wealth. If they use it selfishly, for crimes, violence, or unworthy things, I think that is too bad. But, for people who have accumulated great wealth, dividing it so that a great many people benefit from it . . . For example, when I was growing up there was a man, a very wealthy man by the name of Andrew Carnegie. He left money to build libraries in small communities. Now, in the county seat of my little home community, we have a Carnegie Library. That has been a tremendous influence for good. There are people in churches that have used their money to build schools and equip them. I think when we use wealth to benefit people, that is a fine thing. I'm sorry I don't have any more.

The advice I would give my grandchildren about money would be to take care of it, so that when they want some they will have it. [And to remember that] success and money are not the same thing. You can be very successful in the thing you choose to do and this would be a great satisfaction to you even though it did not yield a lot of money.

I presume that we all have goals we set as we're being educated and maturing. When we have reached some of those goals—in my case it was the rearing and educating of my daughters—and when they were both married and in homes of their own and raising families, I began to feel that I had accomplished my goals.

If you are a career woman, you would look back with satisfaction on your career. If you are a mother, you look with great satisfaction on your children and grandchildren and the kinds of homes they make.

I'm not worried too much about the future. I think children are being prepared. I think they are being prepared to meet any problems they will have in the future and have some means of solving them. I'm an optimist in that I don't think we have ever surrendered to government enough that our lives have been dictated to and ruined.

"Idle brains
are the devil's workshop."

MOZELLA JAMES

Mozella James, seventy, was born in Flatonia, Texas, and has lived in Lockhart, Texas, for the last five years. She has three brothers and five sisters, and believes strongly that many of the problems of today would be cured if there were a revival of the close family life and community togetherness that she remembers so well from her childhood.

An intensely religious woman, she has taught Sunday school since 1930, and she has been a leader of her church's Missionary Society for thirty-one years.

Like so many people today, she is cautious when confronting strangers: "You just can't trust people like before because everything is different now. You could pass along on the road, pick up someone, and be happy to pick them up. But now things are so dangerous you can't afford to pick up a person. But God knows your heart. He understands why you leave them on the highway."

Among people she knows, she is an energetic force for kindness and good.

—SHAELA LEGGETT, CINDY SCHAEFER, JILL FRIZZELL,

SHELLY WILMS, MIKE ADCOCK, BROOK HARRISON.
PHOTOGRAPHS BY LAURA JOHANNES.
—BETTY JOHANNES, ADVISER, PLUM CREEK PRESS,
LOCKHART INTERMEDIATE SCHOOL.

ME BEING the oldest girl and the fourth child in the family, all the work was on me and Mother. I can remember when I was nine years old, that's when I started to cooking and I had to get up on a box to even make up the corn bread. I could really make good corn bread. I'd always put a little flour in, put my soda in, my good old milk, and had cream to put in to make it nice and rich and put about three or four eggs in and make it. And then pull it out of the oven and it looked like cake and it was really good with molasses and butter and with ham and good bacon that we raised. This meat that we get now don't taste at all like when we was coming up. Yes, we'd take that corn meal and pour the hot water on there and we'd take it in our hand and mold it, you know. Then we would cook it and eat it with our greens. I like it with chitlins sometimes. That's when we killed the hog. We'd clean those intestines, let water run all through them, clean them all out real good. Then after we got them all cleaned, then we'd set them in a big crock and let them sit overnight with salt in it. Then we'd put them on the stove and cook them. Take some flour and eggs, just like you make pancakes. Had that batter real thin and cut them chitlins all up and put them there and fry them. Fried chitlins.

But I had to take care of my sisters and brothers. I was a mother to them, too, you know, and I had to do the washing and the cleaning. In those days we had a rub board. You put your clothes in a big round tub, and we had a rub board and we would rub the clothes to and fro. We didn't have detergent like we have now. My mother made lye soap from the grease that was left of the killed hog. Then we had a big old black washpot that we'd put wood all around and we'd start that to burning and we'd put all those clothes down in there and have a broom handle and we'd punch all those clothes down there with the lye soap in them and take them out, rench them through two or three waters and hang them out on the line. We didn't know what a dryer was in those days. The sun dried our clothes when I was small like you all.

For ironing we had a wood stove that we put these black smoothing irons on. We'd sit them up on the stove, grab them hot, and had a plank that was covered all over, and we'd lay that on the eating table and would do the ironing on that. That's the way we did our ironing.

We were lucky to have very little sickness in our family, but what sickness we had we had to care for ourselves. I had a brother that had rheumatism, they called it rheumatism then. And when he got to the age of fifteen years old, he got a scratch on his second finger and his blood poisoned him and killed him. He died when he was fifteen years old. But so far as any disease, we didn't have any in our family. We got sick sometimes, but we had home remedies. We had a weed that would grow called hoarhound. And my mother would let it grow upside of the fence close to the kitchen. That's what she would take when we would have fever or had cold. She'd take that root and make a tea out of it; even for fever, she'd take vinegar and take a brown paper bag and put that in there and put it to the fever.

It seemed like when I got grown, I'd already reared a family. But, when I was a little girl like y'all, I started to sewing. I was nine years old. The first garment I made, they had this what you call flannin and we wore gray flannin petticoats to school. The first hem I put in, I put it in crooked. Oh, I just didn't know how to put it in and when I got it in, it was just going this way and that way. So my mother had me take it out and pinned it at each seam and told me to put it in all around. So from that day to this day I been sewing for the public and I have been very successful. My mother brought me up to that. I started this sewing by hand. Then I begged my mother to let me sew on her sewing machine which you would tread with your foot, and she would let me make some underclothes first. Then I learned to cut out dresses and things; I learned to cut without a pattern. Never did use a pattern until I got married. I didn't know what a pattern was. But of course, when I went to high school in Houston, naturally I taken sewing there, and they had patterns there. And the teacher that I had, she asked me who taught me how to sew. I could sew so well.

I went to school out in the country through the ninth grade. That's as far as it went. After I finished ninth grade, then I went on to Houston to attend Booker T. Washington High School, and I finished there. Then I married up. My country school, those was the best old days. We started going to school at the age of seven. We didn't have no kindergarten and all like that. Our parents at home learned us our alphabet. We wasn't able to paper up our house or have paneling or anything on our house, so our kitchen was always papered with newspapers. My mother would tape it up so we'd get the large headlines, you know, and we children would ask, "Mamma, what is this?"

She'd say, "That's a B." That's where we learned to read—in the kitchen on the newspapers that my mother had up.

Then when we started school we had little buckets that we would put our lunch in. Course my parents were good farmers and we raised our living. And we would take our nice pork sausage when they had killed hogs, and we'd have that and have our baked sweet potatoes that we raised on the farm. Put them in there. And my mother would always bake teacakes and we'd put a little jar in there with syrup molasses and we would take our dinner to school. We had our good little pals that we would share our lunch with. My mother always told us, "Always think of those that are less fortunate." Their parents couldn't provide for them. I'd always, after I got up, put extra in there for them.

That was some of our school; and we didn't have things on our playground to play with. We didn't know anything to do but play church, or play little ring plays. The boys would play baseball and we'd go up the holler and have church. School would take up and the bell would ring. We wouldn't hear it, we was down there preaching and singing and having such a good time. The teacher'd have to send somebody down there and tell us to come.

I liked all of my teachers except one. When I was a child, I always would faint-off—I believe we called it faint-off—and I would faint. One morning I didn't feel well at all. I was just sick when I went to school. So we had to recite the sixth table, and I just sit down and my teacher thought I was sullen. I don't know why she thought that, but that's what she said, and she whipped me. They used to have these here switches they called rattan. You'd go out in the woods and get these switches, and she whipped me and I just sit there, they say, and didn't do nothing. She whipped me, cut the blood out of my leg. And so some of the children went to crying and went and told the other teacher. We had just two teachers in that school. So he came in there, said, "What's the trouble?"

She says, "She's sullen."

The children were crying, "Mozella's not sullin', she's sick, 'cause she told me this morning she was sick." And I have cried about that so many times. I said if I ever got grown, I was gonna whup that woman. Now that's what I said when I was little. [Laughs.] But that was the saddest experience I've ever had in school.

My father was a farmer and my father only went to the fifth grade in school. But my mother, she taught school for two or three years, and when they got married, they built a house, and started the family, and started to buying land. Everybody was eager to get a home back there and land. Then, they bought land from five dollars a acre on up. At my father's death, he had bought up a thousand acres of land. He had bought up that much land. But, all between times, he had a cotton gin. He raised cotton and peanuts, too. He raised peanuts like everything. And he had lotsa hog, lotsa cattle, and chickens and turkeys, and all of that; and he had a molasses mill. That's when people would raise the cane, and they'd bring it there in wagonloads, and they had a mill that would grind them stalks of cane so the juice would come out. And the mill was drawn by horses or mules. Then they take and had a large pan with a wood furnace under there, and made molasses. I knew how to make it when I was a kid coming up. I learned from my father. And it was a happy life there on the farm. He was very successful and he reared up his nine children. Three of the girls are teaching now. They went to college and they're teaching.

But as children, when we came in from school, we always had something to do. We would pick peanuts, chop cotton, pick cotton, harvest corn, and all such as that. Once we were going over to the farm to chop cotton. We'd go in a wagon drawn by mules. We children were all in there. So we had to go through a creek. And my brother, just for fun, instead of going down the road, he let the wagon go up on the hill from the side and that turned us

Left to Right: Shaela Leggett, Shelly Wilms, Cindy Schaefer, Jill Frizzell, Mike Adcock; Back: Mozella James, Brook Harrison

out in the water. We all got wet. Then they got us out and got back on the wagon and went on and chopped cotton in those wet clothes. But we didn't tell our parents about it, no. That brother that turned us over, we thought so much of our brother; that was fun for him. My brothers would see that we didn't get drownded. But he was always doing something funny.

I miss all that hard work, but I'm thankful that I came up with it; made me appreciate what's going on now.

Most of our free time was on Sunday afternoon. We only had church service twice a month. Then, that afternoon, our little friends would come

over and we'd play church. We would all go down to the tank [pond] and our brothers would be the preachers. We'd have about ten or twelve, and we'd go down and play just like they played at church. We'd take some old clothes and put on and two of the boys would take the girls and the boys by the hand, and the preacher that we would have would go out in the water first, and they would perform just like they did in church. The preacher would say, "I baptize you in the name of the Father, the Son, and the Holy Ghost," and duck us under the water!

But it was mighty little waste of time that we had. My parents were, I don't know, they just always had something for us to do. They always taught us, "Idle brains was the devil's workshop," and they used to keep us busy. Say, "Well, I want you to keep busy doing something, if it's nothing but picking up wood chips and putting them back in the same place. Do something, keep busy." That's the kind of parents we had and I'm proud and thankful 'cause we didn't have all that wasted time going up and down the street. Wasn't streets out in the pasture anyway!

Then on the nineteenth of June, we looked forward to a great day. You know, the blacks was once in slavery. They was slaves. The white man was over them. They would sell the people off just like you see them selling cattle. "This is a fine group of boys," and all like that. So, Abraham Lincoln issued the proclamation and he freed the Negroes and all, and so it was on the first of January, but the white man kept the colored man and worked them until the nineteenth of June, when they freed them. Some of them left with nothing but their clothes on. My mother-in-law was in slavery. She was a little girl. So thanks to the good Lord, the black have come from a long way.

We got it through God. They knew it was God, and they prayed to God and through their prayer, God heard them, just like He did way back in the Bible in Pharaoh's time. And if you pray to God, He will bring things out in its own time. And the time came when the Negroes was more equal. Now after the freedom, they have a freedom of speech and freedom to go places where I wasn't even allowed to go. After this integration went in effect, the children could go to all of the cafes. They could go to the theaters together, all be together, ride in the same coaches on our train, and the bus, go to the same school, same college. They have more freedom than I had. And I hope now they have it, they'll guard it. It's precious.

I'm sure all of you have accepted Jesus Christ, haven't you? You believe that there's a God and you put Him in front of you and ask Him to guide you and direct you, and you love one another? Do unto others as you wish to be done by. Don't do anything to your little friends that you wouldn't want them to do; that's a guideline for your life. Don't ever take anything, don't steal anything from no one and respect elderly people.

I think why people don't help one another so much, they've got too involved with self. Everybody's for self, seem like, and they don't help one another like they used to. It used to be, when we was a girl, if it was a girl that didn't have a dress, didn't have clothes to wear to Sunday school, we would share with her. But people's not too concerned about one another. They have too much of the worldly things to look to now, forward to.

Wealth is all right. God put everything here and it's all right to have plenty. But don't make it your major. Don't put it before God. Don't serve money. You make this a better place to live, work, and provide something for your future. When you young people grow up, especially when you marry, look out to have a home and work and try to save; try to have a family that you may have that love and peace. The Lord bless you with a family, with children. Rear them up in the way that God will be pleased, and they will make you happy.

"I felt so cheap riding in the fire truck."

BELLE FESSENDEN

Belle Fessenden was born Arabelle Bailey in 1889 in Lowell, Massachusetts. She married her husband in 1908 and raised five children, two boys and three girls. Their family has now grown to eighteen grandchildren, forty-eight great-grandchildren, and two great-great-grandchildren, and Mrs. Fessenden thinks there will be more. She now resides in Brookline, New Hampshire, where she has spent all but eight years of her life.

—INTERVIEW BY PETER FAIT, JANICE RIFF, DARBY NORTHWAY, MARYBETH SHUTT, JOAN SOMMERS, AND DAN WADLEIGH.
PHOTOGRAPHS BY PETER FAIT.
—DAVE CAWLEY AND AUDREY NORTHWAY, ADVISERS FOR SPILE.

I HAVE five children and eighteen grandchildren and forty-eight great-grandchildren. We had a reunion here, oh, four years ago. Really and truly, it was a wonderful thing to see those children of all ages right up to college down to kindergarten. They're beautiful. I don't think a family is a family without children. I worship all of them, but I can see what a vast difference it is today. There's too many temptations for them. They're not satisfied.

My boys used to make water wheels in the brook down there. They'd spend a whole day making water wheels in the brook, you know. And that'd be their fun. And they never asked to go anywhere, you know; they were satisfied. And the girls would have their schoolmates come and play but it's different today. I don't know hardly anybody in town now. So many are gone. Wish they hadn't left.

We used to have the icehouse here. We had quarries, it was a busy town. Lots of work for everybody. Trains ran in here twice a day. A freight train came in here and got carloads and carloads of ice every day and took them to Massachusetts.

My husband, he worked all hours. The trains used to come in here at quarter of seven at night. And he was the station agent, so he had to be there. He also owned the grain store. He worked in the office. He worked there a pretty little of the time. Ya, it was a big place. We sold grain, hay, and we started to put in meat, fish, and stuff to sell to the help. We didn't put in meats or fish or stuff like that until the last few years the mill was running. They had about thirty-five men working there and they used to want to get stuff on credit. Well, they'd go up the store and my husband's father, O. D. Fessenden, he would give them the money to go and get it instead of charging it. Well, finally, we used to go in to Boston every week, my husband and I, and he'd pick out the fish and the fruits, oranges and bananas, and stuff, and he said, "We're gonna put in some stuff for those men." And then they had a meat room there, and it's still there. They sold meat—now this is the truth, you won't believe it but it's the God's truth—twenty-five cents a pound we used to get for steak. We never knew what hamburg was in those days. Didn't have it in those days. Now we live on hamburg. But it's mighty handy to have . . . Course back then there was an awful lot of deer, and a lot of woodchucks in the daytime.

Deer meat is nice. We used to get deer right up here on this hill. And, my husband always took coon up there. I said, "I'll try to cook one," but I asked my mother-in-law how she cooked it and she told me: "Well, I put it in the

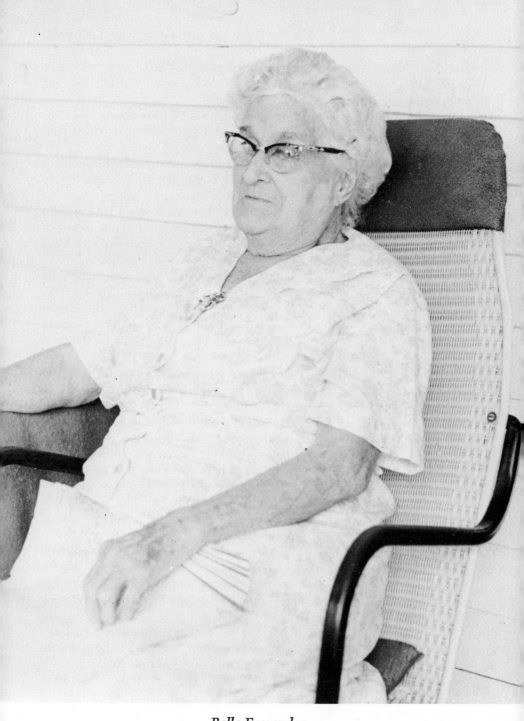

Belle Fessenden

pan . . ." And when I got it in the pan it looked just like a little baby, you know? Little feet, and of course it had the head cut off and all that, but oh dear, I couldn't touch it! I couldn't touch it.

I suppose God gave them to us to help out, but I can't see it. I used to even cry when our pigs had to be slaughtered. I hate to see them killed. You know you get attached to them. But, that's how we get by.

Once in a while we'd go to the grocery store and if we saw something extra that we thought we wanted, we would buy it. But always cash. Today we live on credit most of us. We have to. That's the way it works.

And they used to have a lot of trading in those days. We'd take eggs to the store, you see, and they'd take our eggs for groceries and that was a help. And people would bring in different things from their farm into the stores and they'd take that in the place of groceries.

But it's gone. Everything's gone, really. The ice industry went out as the years went by and the electric refrigerator came in, you know. The business went down and then somebody burned the icehouse. It was the largest icehouse under one roof in the world. It was a huge one, beautiful. And we used to have tourists come there. Every Sunday they'd come up on the train from Boston, and it was really interesting.

There was a big sawmill. That's where we got the lumber to build our house with; and then a big cooper shop there where they made barrels. You see there was work for everybody in those days. And they'd make barrels there by the thousands. Every day in the week they'd make loads of them. And the mill was running and selling lumber, you know. It was wonderful, really. Then they had this grist mill here and the farmers would bring their grain and have it ground. I wish we could have preserved that for the children of today to see how they ground their grain. It was really interesting.

And then, over here we had a platform at the depot. They used to load peaches. We had peach farms here up on Townsend Hill, and you should see the hundreds of bushels of peaches they raised there. Honest and truly.

And when my father was a blacksmith here, we had a nice blacksmith shop. He used to shoe all the horses for the ice company and all the farmers. I used to love to go down and shoo the flies off the horses. We had cows and horses and pigs and hens and turkeys here. We had an interesting life.

There's an awful lot to see in life, I think, with animals and nature. But a lot of the children say that's dead, that's not fun. We used to have a barn full of hay for the animals, and we had a nun come up from Worcester. We loved her. She was a darling and she was kind of shy. My father was a wonderful man and he said, "Now we're all going to jump down into the hayloft, but be careful, don't fall." In those days they had long skirts. We all got down fine and then that poor darling, she took a leap and her skirt caught, and it tore it all off. She was a good sport, but we all felt so bad, you know.

And in the fall we picked chestnuts and the walnuts, you know and the butternuts, the town was full. And after a frost then they'd go and get them and they'd put them in our attic where it was dry and those butternuts were something delicious, let me tell you. Or if you wanted to make a cake, you know, they were just lovely. And we had walnuts. We'd go out in the cow pasture and get a whole pail of them. Of course today, chestnuts are gone, very few walnuts are left, and I guess no butternuts that I know of.

And May flowering was one of our big hobbies in the spring. All the family done it. This hill right across the road here, there was no trees and no brush, and I would take my grandmother's old shawl and I'd put it right down on the ground and we'd fill it up in no time. Ship them into Boston. Twenty cents a bunch we used be paid for them. I say to some of my children today, "Why don't you go May flowering?" Or my children used to walk way up on Townsend Hill and pick strawberries. They always had to walk. They had no other way of going. They got eight cents a box for picking them. That's all they'd give in those days you know. But they loved it.

And they'd walk up and get the mail every night for their father—the paper and the mail. All of us walked just about everywhere. There were no tarred roads at all; all dirt roads and sidewalks. The Fessendens used to furnish the horse and the man, and we'd plow the sidewalks out every winter. Then going by here they'd plow out the roads with two horses and a big sled and a log tied on behind to make a path. My children would get on board that sled and they'd have a great time.

There weren't many cars, though. The first car that got in the family that had the windows instead of snap-on curtains, I was scared to death to ride in it. I was afraid something might happen and the windows would break and we'd all get killed. I was foolish, but I tell you it was an awful feeling because we had always ridden in the open cars. My husband drove for his father, but he never would own a car. He wouldn't allow one on the place. He'd drive a horse. Once I rode with him and he was supposed to turn a corner, but instead of that he ran right square into a stone wall and ruined his car. Well, that was the last time I went to ride with him. He just didn't want to drive. He wasn't interested.

I have an old car out in the barn—an old fire engine—that's an antique that my grandson from Chelmsford is storing here for the time being. It's one that Eldo use to drive. It's seen a lot of use, but he loves it. He takes the kids to ride here in town. He took me uptown one day in it. Oh dear, an old woman like me, you know, I felt so cheap riding in that fire truck. But I

Interviewer with Belle Fessenden

went just the same. We had a great time. It's put out a great many forest fires here in Brookline.

And haying time in Brookline used to be so wonderful for the young boys going to school. It gave them work. The farmers would cut their hay and they'd hire the boys, you know, to help work it and that gave them something to do besides hanging around on the streets. And today the poor boys don't have that job. You don't have those things to do. That's gone. I don't know. I know people enjoy life, and I know the world has changed and we have to change with it. I realize that. But I can see where I think some things could still be changed for the better. I really do. But that's only my idea of it. I used to love life.

"It took a full month until we reached Auschwitz."

DIANA GALANTE GOLDEN

Diana Galante Golden was born in 1922 on the isle of Rhodes. At the age of twenty-two her community was invaded by German soldiers who deported everyone. Diana ended up in Auschwitz, a concentration camp located in Upper Silesia. Her memories of those horrifying years in the camp are still very vivid.

After the liberation of the camps by the Russians, Diana immigrated to the United States. She settled on the West Coast, where she was taken in by relatives. America, the land of opportunity and freedom, was everything she'd ever dreamed it would be. Diana considers America her home, for better or for worse.

—LESLIE SEMLER. PHOTOGRAPHS BY PAUL MILLER.
—SHIRLEY TANZER, ADVISER, OREGON JEWISH
ORAL HISTORY PROJECT.

I WAS BORN on the isle of Rhodes, which at that time belonged to Italy, and I was also raised there. There was quite a large Jewish community there. I would say, at the peak, there were ten thousand. The rest were Greeks, Turks, and Roman Catholics. We had a peaceful coexistence.

The Jewish community was like a self-imposed ghetto. In other words, the Jews lived in one separate section, and it was like a big family, many interrelated. The synagogue was in walking distance, the school was within walking distance, and we all went. All the Jewish children went to the Jewish Parochial School; however, all the studies were done in Italian. We did have Hebrew and Bible studies every day.

It was the Mussolini regime. The island was under Italian rule, and at that time fascism went all the way up before it tumbled down [laugh]. We were not persecuted, we were not mistreated. However, in 1936 or 1937 when all this trouble began, I would say when Mussolini allied himself with Hitler, then the anti-Semitism began, and the press, little by little, took various steps against the Jews. It was mostly in the press at the beginning.

I was born in 1922 so I was already about fourteen or fifteen years old when this anti-Semitism began. Right at the time the Italians occupied Ethiopia is when the thing started to go bad for us. Great Britain and America sanctioned Italy because they occupied Ethiopia. Mussolini found Hitler, or Hitler found Mussolini, as an ally, so he started to follow the same path as Hitler, and the very first thing was to immediately take it out against the Jews.

The newspaper and radio [started it]. They wrote something not very kind towards the Jews. They would say that we exploited other people, that the world was in trouble because the Jews were dominating the banking system throughout the world. In other words, we were pictured as vultures living on other people's blood.

It is all very clear in my mind. Until the day I die, I will never forget it. It was a horror. First they asked all the men fourteen years and up to present themselves to a certain building, with the pretext that they would go and work in the field to build trenches close to the beach. They were asked to come and work in the fields. The Germans issued identification cards to every citizen there and we all had our pictures on the card; and, of course, we were labeled as Jews.

There was a curfew. Everyone on the island had to have an identification card. In the first place we had food rations and we had to have cards, but when the Germans took over we also had to have our pictures in there so they knew exactly. They had the books stating who was Jewish, who was Turk. In other words, they could round up everybody in a matter of hours.

The island was small, we were all concentrated in one spot anyway. So they asked all the men to come, and they knew how many were of that age, and they also stated that for every man who was missing they would kill five of the ones there. So, of course, we were very scared to say the least. We were terrified because we knew they meant they killed indiscriminately; we knew that. So my father and all the men who were anywhere between fourteen and sixty-five, they all went there. They kept them there overnight and the next morning another bulletin came out saying that all the women and children should go and join them. And for every family or every person who was missing they would kill ten men at random. Most women had either a son or husband or both, and nephews. I mean all our families were there. Of course we wouldn't want to jeopardize anyone's life, be it family, friends, or neighbors. So we all went there, and they did ask us to bring some food for a couple of days, and clothing. No luggage, we had to carry everything in knapsacks. That's all we could carry, nothing else.

We knew the end was coming for us. Although we did not have radios, we were aware that there were concentration camps and they were deporting people from Germany to Poland. There were concentration camps in Germany, all over Europe. We knew the plans of Hitler, not in detail, but we knew that they were persecuting the Jews. That they were taking all their possessions, all the property, whatever they had, and they were putting them in concentration camps. But we didn't know what was going on inside them. I don't think that any human being can imagine that things like that could exist in this century, and could have been done by people who were supposedly educated and very high in science. We could not imagine that they could have such beastialities and such heartlessness.

[And we had no defense.] We in the island of Rhodes did not even possess a gun. The only thing we had was a table knife to cut bread. That's the extent of it. We did not have a radio, we were not allowed. When the Germans took over, all the radios were confiscated.

We were afraid of spies. We knew that they would resort to any means to spy on us. So we could not fight them. They were all armed. They were all with submachine guns and we were really very tired through the war. We had many bombings, many homes were destroyed, many people had died already, and we were all in hunger. We didn't have much food left because there was a blockade. In other words, what was raised on the island was not enough for everybody. And we, the Jews, did not possess any land to plant anything. The commerce was in our hands. Banks belonged to Jews. Most stores—clothing, shoes, or necessities for the home—were owned by Jews; but, when it came to farming, for instance, there was not a Jewish man who was in farming. So we didn't have any food. The only thing we had was gold, chains or watches or bracelets for instance, and oriental carpets. So we used to trade. The older farmers were either Greek or Turks, and we used to give them a gold chain, or some nice crystal, or some nice silver spoons, or flatware, or vases. Whatever we had that had intrinsic value we used to exchange.

Everyone was terrorized, really. In order to save their own skin, no one showed any emotion or complained or asked, "Why are you doing this to the Jewish population?" Nobody lifted a finger to save us. They couldn't. It would have meant jeopardizing their lives and, if you think that another person would jeopardize their lives for the Jews, that was not the case. Even if they felt sorry for us, they couldn't do anything.

I'm not bitter, really, because I don't think it was really possible to help unless you were an idealist who said, "I'm going to risk my life and save a Jew." There was no love between us anyway. Rather I must admit that there was plenty of envy. They felt that if the Jews were out of the island, then they would get all the things from the Jews, which they did. After we left many people heard that we were all exterminated, so they went and lived in our homes.

So we all went to the police station and we were kept there for three days. Then they asked us to go to the port. They sounded the siren and everybody went. There was not a soul in the streets. We marched from the police station to the port. They put us in two boats. We were 2,500 persons at the time. That's all that were left in Rhodes, with the exception of about eight or ten persons left because they still had Turkish citizenship, so they were protected by the Turkish Consul. The rest of us were all Italians and we had no rights since the island was already in the hands of the Nazis. They took our papers, identification cards; one by one, they inspected everybody, and there was no one missing.

It took a full month until we reached Auschwitz. We stayed about eight or nine days on the boat and we reached Peiraievs [Piraeus], which is the main port near Athens in Greece. We disembarked from there and walked for about three miles, and they took us to a detention camp where we stayed for two days. Then we were brought back again, not to the port, but to a railroad. We were put into boxcars and it was written there in French that it could carry forty horses, and there were seventy-seven in our boxcar. There were others with a hundred persons inside and there was just a little window in that boxcar, and it was in the heat of summer. It took us fifteen days after that to arrive in Auschwitz. We went through Greece, Yugoslavia, Bulgaria, Hungary, Czechoslovakia, and we finally arrived in Auschwitz on August 16.

It was a horror. Many died. My father died. He was not together with me. He was in the next car. My grandmother died. We were all full of lice. During the day, the train would stop a couple of times and we were all sent out with big sticks, "Hurry, hurry," and we had to do the personal means in the middle of the fields. Men, women, and children, like animals. Many people were sick. Many had dysentery because the water that they gave us came from a barrel. There was this barrel in each boxcar and the barrel contained olives before. They were not washed properly so that the water was rancid. It tasted terrible and it smelled terrible, but that was the only water we had to drink. One man in each boxcar took care of distributing the water. As smelly and horrible as it was, we were all very thirsty. By the fifth day many people were dying already. Before we went they gave each of us a little piece of bread, about the size of a hamburger bun, and that was all the food for about four or five days, when they gave us another little bun and some raisins.

At every stop they went around saying, "Is there anyone dead?" They used to say, *"Kaputt, kaputt.* Bring them out." They put my father in his own coat and four persons carried the body out and they gave them shovels and all they could do was to just dig a shallow grave and to leave him there. He was buried in Yugoslavia. My grandmother died a few hours after and she was buried someplace in Greece. Those were the only two members of my family who died during the trip. My mother was very sick, but still living when we arrived in Auschwitz. Many died, I don't know how many really.

We were all crying. We were praying that if the intention was to kill us, that the end would be coming very quickly, that they would do us a favor by just rounding us all up and putting dynamite in the boxcar, or just put all of us in the fields and shoot us like you shoot birds.

We prayed. In each boxcar there was someone to lead. In the morning we would all say the prayers. When the boxcar used to open we knew that they were coming with the whips, so a man used to say, "Let us all say the Shema, let us all pray together." We were full of lice, our bodies, our hair. It was just sickening. Many people were sick with diarrhea and doing their personal functions of the body right there sitting in all that stench. We thought that death was the sweetest thing that would happen to us because of the suffering. To know all of a sudden that you are dehumanized you lose all kinds of self-respect. We all had our own privacy in our own homes, in our own rooms, and all of a sudden you are doing your very private needs in front of other people, and you feel naked altogether. And you're also demoralized because you are treated worse than an animal, and you know their intention is to kill us. Well, they may as well kill us in one shot. Then it will be over quickly rather than this continued suffering hour after hour. I'm afraid of suffering. I pray still that, when my time comes, whenever it is, whether it's in three minutes or three years or in three days, I pray to God that it may be quick.

The camp was the separation point. My mother's sister was blind. I was holding her by the hand. My mother was with my little brother. At that time he was eleven years of age and my other two sisters, we kind of stuck together. We held hand in hand. There were several officers of the S.S. inspecting everyone as we came out of the boxcar. They were looking at us, and separating. He asked me to let my aunt go and I did not do so because she was blind. She would not know what to do. So I signaled to him that she could not see and he came with the back of his hand. He slapped my face and threw me to the ground, and he grabbed another woman who was standing there and asked her to take the hand of this blind woman, and he pushed them all away. And that was the last time I saw my mother and my brother. This was the very last time that I saw this part of my family. They were looking at us and the ones who were separated in one side were all young men and women who could work, do something. They had no use for children, for elderly men and women. They felt that they were useless people because they were in such a state that they couldn't produce anything. So we never saw them again, and those who were not in the working camp where we were sent were all sent to different barracks and exterminated. They would send them to the showers telling them that they were going to take a shower, giving them what you would call a piece of soap. And instead of water coming from the shower, some kind of poison gas came and they all were dead, or nearly dead, and the floor opened and they all were thrown down in another chamber where all the gold of their mouth was extracted, if they had gold teeth, by a crew of prisoners. And then they put them in ovens and they also made soap from the ashes. They extracted everything they could out of the cadavers.

We were sent to a working camp. We walked two or three miles and it was nighttime. We didn't know where we were. We knew we already entered the camp because I remember the heading in German which meant work makes you worthy of living, that's the translation. We thought in the beginning that we would be put in some kind of camp or compound where we would be taking care of ourselves. We would be left alone, separated from everyone and everybody, maybe in huts, maybe in barracks. We were just like a bunch of sheep. We did not demonstrate. We were just a bunch of scared people and all we wanted was to be as small as we could in order to be left alone. We really couldn't do any harm to them. We didn't do any harm to anyone.

There were barracks, barracks, barracks, as far as the eye could see. And all the barracks were separated one side to another with electric wires. There were no walls to separate one row of barracks from another row. All there was was barbed wire and it was all electrified. So, if someone chose to hang onto the wires, in a minute or two the person was electrocuted. Everyday there were several who committed suicide by that. We couldn't go anyplace, we couldn't escape. That was impossible.

[Our living quarters were] all dirt. There was no cement, no grass; the floors were all dirt. There were wooden barracks and there were three cots, in other words, three layers. No mattress, no pillow, nothing. I would say that the cots were about the size of a double bed and we had to sleep ten there. Ten girls lined up like sardines. We couldn't lay flat, we couldn't lay any other way, just on our sides. All clothing was taken from us completely. Then we were processed into another room and all our hair was completely shaved from every part of our body. In a way that was good because we were full of lice and that was one way to get rid of it. So we were shaved, and in another room we were given a piece of soap, which was sand put together with something, and we were told that we were going to take a shower. The water was very cold and, within two minutes, by the time we put the soap on and scraped our bodies, the water was off and that was that. And, if we would say something, some other women came who were the leaders—the capos, we used to call them—and who would whip us out of the showers. They threw clothing at each one of us, as we got out of the showers, no towels to wipe off, nothing; just a piece of clothes, a dress or a nightgown, whatever came into our hands. They had piles of clothes from other inmates, and that was the only piece of clothing we had on; no underwear, nothing.

For a week we did not work. They took us to the barracks and they said, "This is your place." There were thousands of inmates already there, but the barracks were occupied by Polish women; Jewish, of course. Well, by this time, they were like animals. They had been in camps since 1940. So, by this time, those who survived were so hardened that they looked at us with hostility. We could not communicate with them because we did not speak Yiddish, and they could not comprehend why we Jewish persons could not speak Yiddish. They wanted to be reassured that we were Jewish. We told them in Hebrew and quite a few of them could speak Hebrew. So we spoke whatever we could in Hebrew, or we recited the Shema. We told them about Pessach or Rosh Hashana or Yom Kippur, words that only a Jewish person would be acquainted with. They were very surprised because we didn't speak Yiddish so we told them that we were Italians, and they called us Italianos. Then other women came the second day, some French-women, and some from Belgium. At that time they already knew what was happening, where we were, what was the procedure there and they told us to forget about the others. They said, "If they are not in this camp with you, don't hope to see them." That's all. They pointed towards the high chimneys with flames coming out and they said, "They are being gassed and cremated." They said it very clearly, "It's a horrible thing to tell you that, but that is the fate of all those who don't come to this side." Many could not accept that and within a week about sixty or seventy of our girls were dead already from shock. They fell apart. We were all weak to begin with from the months in that horrible train. We were weak, but especially those who did not have sisters, who did not have cousins, who were alone. When I think about it I wonder, "How did I survive? What made me stronger than others?" And I really find myself answering to myself that it was feeling for my sisters. I had to live for them, they had to live for me, so we lived for each other. We knew that if I gave up that they would give up, and they thought the same. I mean, individually, each of us gave each other the strength to do our very best; in other words, not to give up. To try to live, to survive. Many tried and they just couldn't. There was typhus. There was trench mouth. They could not open their mouth, it was full of canker sores, so they just couldn't eat anything; so dead bodies were there like flies.

Every morning at four o'clock, it was still very dark, they used to call us to get up and we formed lines of four in a row. All lined up, and we were not allowed to touch one another. It was very cold, even though it was August. The nights were very cold, the days were very hot. All we had on was one little dress, nothing else, and our shoes. By this time many of the shoes sank in the mud and some of us didn't even have shoes any more. Those who didn't have shoes were able to get clogs, and they were very big clogs. Some women had very small feet and they couldn't even walk with those clogs on.

So we were there for about an hour standing in that cold, freezing, and the capo had her nice little warm bed with cotton sheets all over. They were all dressed nicely with leather boots. They were Jewish women but those were the ones who were really put to the test. They survived. They looked healthy because they ate well. They had a little room at the entrance of the barracks. It was heated. They had hair. They looked human. We no longer looked human. We looked like walking dead, like skeletons already.

We didn't dare talk to capos. We heard from French or Italian girls who were there who said that these women were the women of the guards of the camp, in other words, they were their mistresses. They had been inmates for a long time. Some of them, at one time or another, said they had borne children by the S.S. They had been made prostitutes, whether they wanted to or not. So by this time they didn't really care much about us. They said, "Well, I'm just trying to save myself; you do whatever you want."

Some of the girls, either from France or Italy or Greece, came and talked to us. They kind of gave us comfort; they couldn't give us anything else. They gave us the guidelines on how to survive. "Now that you are here it's up to you. If you just want to hang yourself on the wires, then you just go ahead and do it, that will be quick. But, if you want to survive, you have to be very, very strong to survive it. In other words, don't let it just completely demoralize you. That's what they want. They want to kill us by slow death. Now we just have to sweat it out. You give your sister your courage and she will return the courage. Find someone, even if you don't have anyone who's in your family here, and pledge life for each other." And, somehow, after the initial agony, some were determined to follow this. We would do our utmost not to die by our own hands, and that gave us courage.

After we were lined up there in the morning we were given a bowl of what they called coffee, but I think that all it was was boiled grain. It was something like colored water. That was all we had in the morning. We did not have any dishes. We didn't have spoons or forks, nothing. Everything was liquid anyway. At the entrance to the barracks they used to have so many containers—either rusty cans or whatever there was there. So we used to pile up to grab one because there were usually less containers than human beings. They were not cleaned up. They were rancid. For lunch they gave us another little bowl of soup. We could not keep anything. Even if we wanted to, there was no place to hide anything. We were wondering why they took our combs and brushes and they said, "You don't have hair, what do you need them for?"

The first week we didn't do anything. We just sat on the dirt, that's all. Then, in the second week, strange enough, we were in line and they took us to another camp. We picked up bricks. These bricks were out overnight and they were very cold. Each of us had to pick up three bricks, and we had to hold them against our stomach and we had to walk. These leaders—in front and in the back there were two German women who had the S.S. uniform— each had a German shepherd. We were told that all she had to do was to snap a finger and the German shepherd would tear us all apart, so not to try anything against the orders. So we had to walk for about two miles with those bricks, cold, cold, right against our stomachs. We arrived at the other side of camp, we left them there, and we walked back to our own camp. Then we went back there—take bricks from one place, put them in another, back and forth like that. Stupidity, but that was the punishment.

Later on they made us pick up squares of grass that grew in one part of the camp. It was cut by other inmates. All we had to do was lift it from the ground and take it back to another camp. I would say it was about two or three miles of walking back and forth and really we were so weak. We didn't have strength to walk but they told us we could sing. Now that was one thing that was never forbidden. They'd say, "Sing," and somehow they'd like to sing the Italian songs, I mean they'd like to hear them. They used to call us and tell us, "Italiano, you sing Italian songs." So we used to sing, whether we felt like singing or not. At least we were kind of cheering up ourselves.

It went on until the end of October like that. In the meantime, many died. By that time we'd already started to hear airplanes going by. We heard artillery, or whatever, cannons sounding from a distance, and planes flying overhead.

When we heard the siren we were asked to go in the barracks. We could not ask any questions. We knew they were probably Russian planes. We also knew that there were camps nearby which were occupied by citizens from Poland and Russia. A few times we saw from a distance many women in uniforms, walking. The women had hair. They had those striped uniforms with white. They had shoes. I mean they looked human, at least from a distance. They were clothed. They were not like us. Some of the other women who were inmates long before we were told us that these people were political prisoners. So the planes were looking at the camp. We were quite sure they were Russians, because they were closer than the British or the Americans. By that time already, by the end of September, they started to deport people out of the camp and into other camps. I assume that they were planning to evacuate as the Russian troops were approaching because after the war was over we heard that by the beginning of January there was no one left in that camp, just those who were near death. They couldn't walk, they couldn't do anything, so they left them to die without food.

At the very end we were lucky in one way because we were not asked to march into another camp. There were many who were forced to march for miles and miles. Many died, others were shot, others were left in the snow. By that time it had started to snow and many were frozen. Thousands died this way. We were fortunate because we were put in boxcars and taken to Germany. There at least they gave us a pair of boots, wooden boots— wooden soles and leather tops. They gave us a pair of panties which I could not believe, and a piece of clothing. We were in an extremely clean place. Each of us had a little tiny bunk all by ourselves. One in each bunk with a straw mattress. Although the place was all cement and the floors were wooden, it was all very clean.

After staying there until March, we heard plenty of bombings in the vicinity. At that time in Germany we worked in an ammunition factory. We were making holes in pieces which were part of machine guns. We worked one week at night and one week during the day and they gave us, I would say, two slices of bread per day and a bowl of soup which was much better. It was clean. We were guarded not by Jewish women but by S.S. women. We kept working there until the very end, which was sometime in April. Then we were locked in the barracks and they left us there for two days.

We thought really that they were going to blow us to pieces. Then, for some reason or another, they came back. They unlocked the doors and they put us back in the train. They took us for about twelve days, here and there, I don't know where we stopped really. They stopped in several places but nobody wanted us. Finally we ended up in Theresienstadt, which was in Czechoslovakia, and this Theresienstadt was a camp but it was guarded by Jews. There we were handed to Jewish guards and that was the last time we saw the S.S. women. That was April 25 or 26. Then, within a week, on May 8, we were liberated by Russians.

We were in camps until September, from place to place because we were Italian citizens and, since the Italians were allies with the Germans, they lost the war. They didn't have any means for us to return to Italy. So everybody else went home, and we did not. We were still sitting there in one camp or another. We arrived in September. Immediately we were put in touch with the Red Cross. We were asked to fill out all kinds of information regarding any relatives in any part of the world.

Finally, in September, we arrived in Italy along with Italian prisoners of war who were in Germany. We went to the Jewish Community Center in Bologna. We stayed in Milan for a few days but then we heard that there were other girls from Rhodes in Bologna so we went to join them. We lived in what was left of the Jewish Community Center in Bologna, which is the northern part of Italy. There was still a wing standing up; the other part was bombed down. They were very kind to us. They gave us a large room, and they put little cots with mattresses and bedding, and a little kitchen where we all could cook. They gave us identification cards in order to go once a day to a public restaurant and eat. We were entitled to one meal a day in the restaurant. The other meal we had to prepare ourselves.

In the meantime, as soon as we arrived in Milan, the Red Cross and the American Jewish Committee were able to get in touch with most of our relatives. Immediately we received—from the United States—packages. And also having relatives, they sent us a few dollars. They sent us clothing. Soap! Ivory soap was the very first we received. I remember we also received cans of Heinz beans, cans of beef that you can slice, like Spam. They were the very first ones to arrive; and Hershey chocolate bars. We started to gain weight rapidly but in a conspicuous way. From near starvation to overeating is a bad thing. We were eating too much and our stomachs were not used to that. Several of us landed in the hospital and were warned that we could die. So we were really lectured, and we were all sent to the hospital individually. Some of our stomachs looked four, five, six, seven, eight months pregnant. From the starvation and undernourishment, somehow the whole body's skinny but the stomach sticks out. It becomes bloated. I don't know what makes it such. It was terrible, but we were told that gradually, if we didn't overeat, we would return our bodies to normal functions. For instance, all the time in the concentration camp, none of us had our menstral period. It disappeared, and then gradually some returned sooner than others. Within seven or eight months after we were liberated, we began functioning normally. I myself, within a period of six months, gained a good twenty-five pounds. We were bloated really, our faces, our hands. We didn't look normal. We wanted to have a feeling of fullness with food all the time, so we kept eating continuously, whether we were hungry or not. We also wanted to take two or three baths a day, to take showers. Our elbows, our shoulders, some parts of our body, our feet, the ankles, the dirt was so embedded in our skin that we looked like miners, you know, coal miners. The dirt was there for months and months. And the hair was growing, slowly because of the deficiency of vitamins. We were all given vitamins. Little by little we returned to normal. They wanted to know where we had relatives and, if we didn't have anyone, we could go to Israel. My brother and sister at that time were in Tangier, which is Morocco. They got in touch with us through the Red Cross and they wanted us to go to Tangier and we did go.

The brother that I'm referring to left Rhodes in 1938. He was one of the last ones to leave the island. My sister Rachel was in Morocco with my aunt, from the age of ten. She departed in 1929 or 1930. My mother's sister took her there and she thought she wanted to educate her there, so she gave her a very good education. We got in touch with them, and we left, the three of us, for Tangier. From Tangier we corresponded with our relatives in the United States, in Los Angeles. They could bring one of us here. In the meantime, my younger sister met an American Jewish soldier in Bologna who came to the synagogue, and she already received a visa from her husband-to-be. While we were in Tangier, she received the visa and she was the very first one to come to the United States as a bride-to-be. She married within three weeks of her residence in New York; she married this young man to whom she's still married. My other relatives sent the visa for me. I arrived in the United States in February of 1948. Anyone who comes to the United States has to have a sponsor who will be responsible so that the newcomer will not be in need of welfare assistance. Someone had to be responsible for me and they paid for my voyage and I came to Los Angeles and lived with them for a year. Then I came to Seattle to visit other relatives. I liked Seattle very much. I liked the togetherness of the Jewish people there. At that time they all lived within a section. Most of them were Sephardic and they spoke Spanish and many of them knew my parents so I stayed in Seattle.

I came here with a heart full of love for my relatives, for this wonderful country. I did my very best to be on good terms with my relatives, with everyone with whom I came in contact. In other words, my attitude was one of co-operation and all I wanted to do was to learn the language and just be absorbed into society as a normal human being.

We all regarded the United States as a refuge where you had freedom of worship, where nobody would persecute you just because you happened to be a member of the Jewish faith. I did not become disenchanted in any way. People of my own faith were very kind, very good to me, my relatives especially. Within three weeks I started to work in a shirt factory and the people with whom I worked were all very kind. At that time really, they were all very much aware of survivors of concentration camps and the minute they saw the number on my arm, really I noted in their looks feeling sorry for me and tried to help in any way they could. In other words, "You went through plenty, we will make it up to you. You will suffer no more." So they were all very kind and my wish was to learn the language as fast as I could and immediately I started to attend night school for newcomers. We started with the ABCs. We were all foreigners from all over the world. My relatives were all very kind. I didn't have to come home and cook any dinner or do any housework. All they wanted me to do was to work, to be able to support myself, and go to school. That was all they wanted and really they have not regretted it. I knew I was their responsibility and I didn't want to have any behavior problems in any way that they would regret. Every day was like opening a new page of a book. The words I was learning, I was making very good progress really. I would ask everyone who came into contact with me, "Please correct me, tell me how to pronounce things." I was extremely eager to learn the language and within a year I was able tŏ communicate. I really realized that unless I spoke the language I would be an outsider.

Throughout the world the Americans were considered as the ones who saved the world, really. You have no idea of the misery, the tragedy, the persecution that the Nazis brought throughout Europe. From country to country all they did was kill, kill, torture, take whatever the country had in food, in objects of art, lives, everything. They were like vultures wherever they went. Then things changed. The Americans started to occupy. The Germans started to lose the war, things were not too good, and little by little they invaded France, they invaded Italy, so country by country, the hope and the prayer of every citizen in these countries were that the Americans should come and liberate. They were called the liberators. They were called the saviors of Europe. Unfortunately after quite a few years, they all forgot about it. Time takes care of everything really whether it's bad or good. We forgot everything, but really they should show some movies of what the Americans did for Europe in terms of good will and of help, material help and moral help. I don't forget it. Maybe some people do, but I do not. I have a very grateful feeling for the country, for the citizens, really.

Diana Galante Golden

They did a lot of good to the world at large. Whether they were Jewish or not, they helped everybody.

Now America is my home. I'm an American citizen, a proud one. In times of shame, of wrongdoings by politicians, does a mother divorce the children when they are bad? No. Do the children divorce the parents because they committed a wrongdoing? Well, America is my mother, or I am the child of America, let's say, for better and for worse, so I am here. If I can do something, my part, then I will do it. I love America, for better or for worse.

We have been going through a period of a very quick and radical change in moral values. The progress has been good in some ways and rather shameful in others, because, in the name of personal freedom, we have been doing things that really, if we looked deep in our hearts, we would not be proud of. We blame it all on progress, the mobility, the affluence of the citizens, the way of life. The center of life that was once the family is no longer the same, and when you break down the strength of the family base, it doesn't lead to good things, really. Again, I am referring to the time when for the sake of a sister I survived and she survived for my sake. I think we can try not to lose contact with each other. In other words, to still keep the family ties sacred, strong. Before committing an act of wrong, whatever it may be, a little one, a big one, ask how would it affect my family? Maybe that could stop someone from committing an immoral act. Anything, whether it's dope, whether it's committing adultery. According to the Bible, we should not live out of wedlock, a man and a woman; and now it seems like our society accepts it; or people choose to live like that instead of saying, "Well, it's better to get acquainted first before we get married, instead of getting a divorce." Well, that's one way to see it. I say don't get married. You don't have to live together. You don't have to share the same roof. You don't have to have sexual activity together, you know. You can talk clearly about the understandings of living together in wedlock, to know each other instead of rushing into marriage at a very young age, or rushing into marriage before being certain of each other. I'm not against divorce. If two people can't get along well together, I think that the best thing to do is just get a divorce. But, on the other hand, I say that people should not rush into marriage.

We Americans aren't perfect. Through the last few years we have been going through ups and downs. But this is my home. That's all I can say. I would not want to live anyplace but in this country.

"Red is the east for the sun."

ELIZABETH GURNO

Elizabeth Houle Gurno, a Chippewa Indian, was born in 1913 on the Fond Du Lac Reservation, near Duluth, Minnesota, and was raised by her grandparents. One of her most vivid memories of those days is that of a forest fire:

"I was only four or five years old but I remember it. My grandfather was a timber cruiser, and he was out in Brookston. He rode a horse out in the woods, and he knew that fire was out of control. And he raced to my mother's house and said, 'Go to the river!' So my mother, my grandmother, and my great-grandmother, we all took blankets and some food and left everything else just as it was. Went to the river hollering as we went to the other homes on the way to get down to the river. The young boys then cleared all the underbrush and turned up the dirt so that when we sat down, we were sitting in dirt. And my brothers stood waist deep in water and dunked blankets and traded and we had blankets on top of us. They'd dry out as fast as they'd put them on. And they'd throw pails of water at us and wet the ground all around as far as they could.

"I remember seeing Father Simon—he was a priest back then—

he had water blisters on his head, and he had the chalice to put the blessed sacrament in, and he had Coke and he blessed us with that and he said, 'You won't die. Don't be afraid.' But every kid is nosy. I lifted the blankets up and looked, and I could see the railroad track from the heat just buckling going like sort of a snake. And lumber and trees flying over us. And then there was a water tank, but below the water tank there were two barrels sitting there. And these men rolled this heavy barrel full of oil away. It was so hot that a man burned his hands, so it was near ready to explode. The water tank had a metal roof that just caved in. That's how hot it was. And the priest was blistered! He had great huge water blisters. He was very sick, and he had two black eyes. I thought, 'If this is the end of the world that I've heard about, then this is it.' But the next morning we were all there.

"Thousands of non-Indians burned to death, but not one Indian. They had the common sense that God gave them to go to the river like an animal. All the animals were there. There were bears swimming out there. I can remember seeing the bears. That was terrible. I hope I never have to live through anything like that again.

"And the cemetery—there was a cemetery right by the church. And the same man that rolled that barrel down the hill heard somebody hollering for help. He made three separate trips with wet blankets. He went up hollering in English and in Indian, 'Come this way! Come this way!' And he'd get to the church and it was all quiet. He said there was no church. He came down and told us the church was burnt. And when it was getting on towards morning, we heard this terrible screaming. Many voices. Not just one. Many. He went back up again. Went up three times and kept hollering in English and Indian, 'Come this way! The river is this way!' And it would be quiet. I don't know what ever happened. My grandmother always said that the dead were hollering. They were burning too. There wasn't anything left."

Mrs. Gurno was educated in elementary grades in Catholic schools, and went to high school at Flandreau Indian School in South Dakota, where she took training as a practical nurse. She married in 1935 and raised three children and now has eleven grandchildren and one great-grandchild. Mrs. Gurno goes to school "piecemeal" at the University of Minnesota, Duluth, and Bemidji State, where she became a certified Ojibwa (Chippewa) language teacher. She teaches in the high school at Cloquet and she teaches language also at the University of Minnesota, Duluth. She works as

a co-ordinator at the Cloquet high school and co-ordinates Indian
culture programs for both Indian and non-Indian students. She
likes to paint and do arts and crafts such as beading, birch bark
work, and some quilting.

—THOMAS PEACOCK AND JAMES WHITE.

MY MOTHER DIED when my sister was a year old, so I was
raised by Mr. and Mrs. La Prairie, two old, old people. And I have to give
credit to them. They raised four of us as Indians—Indian beliefs, rights,
and traditions. So I have kept it up these many years, and I in turn have
taught my children Indian things: like what living with other people means
to you. Respect them, but first of all respect yourself. Their property is just
as important to them as your property is to you. If you want viciousness to
reign the most, then that's the way to act and it will be returned exactly. Be
kind. There's a saying that an Indian will give you the shirt off his back,
and that is true. If you are in need of something, they give it to you—anything. That's a sign of love—not by words, but by actions.

We had fun when I was young. Grandpa made toys for us. We didn't
have many toys. There was no such thing as a dime store—no such thing as
money. But he made us a ball out of deer hide. This ball was covered with
deer hide and laced with deer hide like the balls you see now—more like a
softball. But in it, at the dead center, was a rock as round as he could find,
and he padded it all around with swamp moss, and it was packed hard. It
didn't take one day, it took *days* to make it. And he made several at one
time. And then he'd sew it with scraps that Grandma didn't have use for—
real buckskin.

And he'd carve out a bat for us out of cedar. They were nothing to what
kids have now, but they didn't cost a penny.

We played an awful lot of ball because my father was a ball player, and I
had a couple of uncles that were very active. Dad played with the White
Sox of 1910, and he always said, "I wish you had been born a boy, but I'm
glad you're you." So I played baseball with half the reservation boys.

And he made barrel hoop type things that we would roll from a certain
goal to another goal. I don't think you see that much any more.

And we created. We made paper dolls like they do now, but we used our
heads to do that. We made dolls out of buckskins. I had about eight little
buckskin dolls about six or seven inches tall. They each had an Indian
name. They went to bed the same time I did. My two older sisters had dolls

the same way. We only had one brother that lived with us. He was very sickly, so Grandpa catered to him. Made him a wagon out of what he found in the woods. Made the wheels and all. There wasn't one nail in these wagons that he made. He made him several. And we'd pull him in these wagons. That's how big they were.

There were a lot of kids there on the reservation. We spent our winters sliding down this big huge hill, which has since been cut down.

Of course we had to work. Grandpa had a small farm. We had cows and chickens. There was a lot of things to do. Raised potatoes and rutabagas and carrots. I worked hard as a child. Picked berries in the summertime and canned the old-fashioned way. Dried meat, dried fruit, vegetables. But along with it, at the end of the day, we knew that we would be rewarded with sugar cakes. That was always our reward. Or Grandpa might be lucky enough to have some things to barter, and he would bring back fresh fruit. That was a treat. He didn't have to go very far for it, but nevertheless, that was a treat.

And then we used to eat rabbits and porcupines. A porcupine can't hear. He runs with his nose to the ground for he only senses through vibrations. You can run down a porcupine and club him. And you can make a deadfall and kill a rabbit. And, of course, we'd eat venison. We'd eat every bit of it. Indians did not take animals and just take parts and throw the rest away. They never killed an animal unless they could use all of it. They ate the meat and used the hide for clothes and tents, and then used the bones for jewelry or for sewing needles. There was something that could be made even out of antlers. If they were cut a certain way, you could make a yoke and carry two buckets of water on the prongs. The weight was on your shoulders, and all you had to do was hang onto the pails.

The Indians survived with their hunting and their garden produce. And years ago there was plenty of wild rice. There was one lake we'd stay at while we were gathering. Camp there. And that's the only place we went to make rice. We had more than enough to bring home—say, ten big sacks of rice. But then they changed it. Now you can't take rice off that lake because the non-Indians that came said they were putting that aside for the ducks so the ducks would have some rice to eat. My dad said, "Since when did you ever see a duck sit on a rice stalk and eat rice, because he's not built that way. He scoops up from the water because he's built that way. The Almighty made him with a bill to scoop—not to perch on a rice stalk!"

Wild rice has always been our mainstay of life. If you have rice, you are not hungry. Indians believed that at one time or another, we came from the water. Therefore, anything in the water is edible. You can eat it if you know how to cook it.

And then we made maple sugar. They made maple sugar this year—the junior high and the senior high school. Some of the kids had never heard of it, so we proposed a project. And that's what we were teaching the kids. They thought that you went to the tree and just wiggled this little spigot and maple syrup would come out. It takes forty-three gallons of sap to make one gallon of syrup. You have to know how to do it. I think they learned a lot.

Indians took things from Mother Earth. She gave us maple syrup. But with the left hand, we thanked her. I still do this in my family. We had quite a ceremony about that when I was growing up. Same with rice. Even if you don't ask everybody on the reservation to come in and join you, you ask a few people to come in and you give thanks. And with this wild rice, you save up enough maple syrup or sugar to mix with it. Just the two things mixed together. You eat that. That's a thanksgiving for what Mother Nature has given to you. And you don't waste it. You take it and be thankful that you got it. And then you have a dance. I can remember going by horse and buggy up to a ceremony. That year the garden produce was terrific. It was beautiful. And they danced till morning and ate in between times. I remember that. It was a giveaway dance. That's a certain kind of dance they do. And they give away garden produce in baskets to the ones that they invited in to dance with.

There are many things in Indian life that nowadays you'd say don't make sense. We are associated with drums and feathers and that sort of thing. But all that makes sense to the Indians. A drum to the Indian has a place. I'd never deliberately walk up and give one a kick. It has a place. It's a symbol. That's *me*. Even though I'm a Catholic now, that's still part of me, of my heritage. My grandfather had a drum in the house. He never touched it. It had a place of respect. He'd always refer to it: "That is you and me." Nothing individual. It was all of us.

There's several types of drums. The *midé* drum, only the *midewiwin* men can touch the drum, and a woman, no matter who she is or how high in life she is, could not touch that drum. It's just never heard of.

Then there are water drums. Now water drums, you don't find them here because we are never in want of water. We have plenty of water. You go down south and you'll find your water drums because there they pray, they dance for water. Water is a necessity of life. Therefore, what water they do have, they fill half of their drum with water and that gives a different pitch. But we have our share of water up here.

And we have feathers. We are mostly associated with lots of feathers. But a feather in our culture has to be earned. We are born with one feather. That is a gift from our parents. Now my father told me that he was given a feather at his birth, and a blanket. And the blanket did not come from J. C. Penney. It was homemade out of rabbit hide. And the mother took nine months to make it. She finished her last stitch the day the baby was born. That was her gift to the baby.

Then, as the years go by, for a female, she put away her dolls at about twelve or thirteen or fourteen years old and said, "I'm through with dolls; I am entering womanhood," she then would be given another feather. Then she could wear both of them. When she married, she took one and fastened it over her right shoulder. Then, in the course of her lifetime, maybe she became a widow. She'd take this feather and put it on her left shoulder when she went out in public. It saved a lot of asking: "Are you a widow?" "Are you married?" But at the same time, she only mourned her husband one year. After that, she put the feather back up. Even though she had maybe nine kids, she still had the right to wear her two feathers up.

But a man is different. A man has to earn each feather. Now, he alone did not decide that he was entitled to a feather. He had to prove himself. Now he could be many things and earn feathers many ways, just like Boy Scouts. He could be a runner, a hunter, a scout, or send messages by blanket, or a provider of wood, which was essential to eating and warmth; or he could be a tent builder or bow and arrow maker. He earned credit like that, but he didn't decide that he was entitled to a feather. The elders of the tribe sat in council: "Did he earn this feather? How?" And then he had to show how he earned it. Well, then they'd give him the feather.

By the time he'd reach, say, forty—possibly younger—he could go out and kill a squirrel, cure the hide himself, eat the meat, and take the squirrel hide and make a bonnet type of hat and put the feathers on himself. He had to do his own. No one else could do it for him. I couldn't make you one, for example. He made his own and put all his own feathers on it.

And now these feathers weren't just crow feathers or robin. They were eagle. Years ago, eagles were plentiful, but as the non-Indians moved in with all their concrete, the eagles went other places. I remember my father telling that they'd go on eagle hunts up in the hills. This was when he was a little boy. And they'd sort of make a bet amongst themselves that they would gather the most feathers. Now you don't kill an eagle. You gather the feathers that he sheds. They call it molting. Once a year they molt and all the feathers fall to the ground for you to pick up. And they went up in the hills in what is now Duluth—all around in there. Michigan Street and Superior Street was nothing but a cedar swamp.

And then we decorated things with porcupine quills. Those quills are very dangerous, but then they were used to decorate anything made out of birch bark. The ends have to be bent. They can go through human flesh. They crawl. Very dangerous. They were dyed with chokecherries and raspberries for red, or pitch from the base of a balsam tree or a beech tree. That was boiled and it would be black. Whatever you had to dye, you'd stick it in that boiling water and then take it out and lay it to dry. The quills themselves are sort of a beige color. And they used them for decorating headbands and wristbands. And especially on birch bark baskets because they made a prettier design and were easier to work with. My grandmother had an art with birch bark that she chewed a design into the thin bark that my uncle would then in turn sew onto another basket. There are a few in a Chicago museum that she had done. She would fold the birch bark a certain way and chew on it, then unfold it and look at it, and if it didn't suit her right, she'd fold it up another way and chew on it. Just as quick. And she'd come out with the most beautiful designs: flowers, leaves. She did beautiful work.

And she worked in the true Indian spirit. An Indian always has several things in mind when he does things: first, that he's busy with his hands doing something and not wasting his or anybody else's time. Then, that he's making something useful and something beautiful to look at—not just an eyesore. And then that he's making something that will tell a story. It had to have meaning. For him to sit down and spend hours, there had to be a reason for it. In the end, it would tell something—like my headband. I have fixed roses on it. Took me a while to make it. It's pretty. It's going to be useful. But I can't wear it yet. I was born in 1913, and each rose represents ten years of my life, so when I am sixty, I will wear it. Until then, I can't.

The sacred colors are white, red, black, yellow, and blue. White is for the north, for the white snow. That, in turn, gives you strength. Red is the east for the sun. Yellow is for the south—for the heat that ripens our staff of life, the corn. And black is for the west. If a storm is coming, look to the west and there will be black clouds. The storm originates in the west. And blue represents man. So in doing any type of work, we try to include one or all of the colors depending on what we're making.

I think it's nice that the kids are trying to recover some of that now. I'm glad for them. But their mothers and fathers often don't know enough. That's where the hitch is. The mothers and fathers are going to have to be educated first. You don't read those things in books. You see, years back, it was a downright sin to be known as an Indian. It was something to be ashamed of. I couldn't go along with that because my grandmother spoke nothing but Chippewa. I lived in an Indian home. That's the way I breathed. The others picked up English. Then they in turn didn't want their children to speak Chippewa because the government agent told us that was wrong: "You don't look like a white man, but you got to live like one. You have to live like a white man now."

But I'm Indian. I believe Indian ways. They know I'm Indian and that's it. I cannot erase me. I'm here to stay.

But I think it's wonderful that the kids feel more firmly about Indian ways now. Life will be a little more meaningful for them. And I always stress respect, because that was taught to me from the year one. Respect your elders. They have lived longer than you have; therefore, they are wiser.

I think the kids are trying real hard, but they cannot learn overnight what for years has been driven out of them. I never was ashamed to be an Indian. I'm still Indian. Be the best darn Indian you can be. That's the way I look at it. In my eyes, that's right. And the kids are the same way. Some of these kids have beautiful thoughts.

"Don't come in here
with your mouth poked out."

SARAH ANN DUPEE

Sarah Ann Dupee was born May 25, 1898, in the small community of Bogart, Georgia. She lived with her mother and stepfather until the age of fifteen, when she moved to Athens, Georgia, to work in a private home.

At fifteen years of age, Sarah married to get away from what she describes as a very cruel stepfather. The early marriage lasted only a short time and Sarah continued to live and work in Athens.

At twenty years of age, she met and married John Dupee, a railroad porter, and they made their home in Evansville, Indiana, with their two children until he died in 1957. A grandson, Jason, was reared by Sarah and John.

Sarah's formal schooling in Bogart, Georgia, was only through the third grade, but she continued to teach herself and to read every "good" piece of literature she could get. Her home in the Lincoln Gardens has an extensive library. Some of her favorite quotations are from Edgar A. Guest, Booker T. Washington, Helen Steiner, and Abraham Lincoln.

A few of the quotations that she says have guided her life are:

"I will allow no man to drag me down so low as to make me hate him."

—Booker T. Washington

"I'd rather see a sermon than hear one any day, I'd rather one would walk with me than merely show the way."

—Edgar A. Guest

"I can see how it might be possible for a man to look down upon the earth and be an aetheist, but I cannot conceive how he could look up into the heavens and say there is no God."

—Abraham Lincoln

Sarah has traveled to many countries of the world and is known and respected by both young and old, black and white citizens of the Evansville community. She is a dear friend of the Mills Brothers.

Sarah has been a Sunday school teacher over fifty-five years at the Liberty Baptist Church, and children who pass through her classes can never forget the words and wisdom of a truly Christian woman.

At seventy-seven years of age, Sarah Dupee feels that what has made her the kind of person she is, is "working for the Man upstairs, and knowing good intelligent people."

She now lives in a four-room apartment in the Evansville Public Housing Lincoln Gardens area. Her home is a model for any apartment dweller. There is no other person who comes close to being like Sarah Ann Dupee.

—CLARRISA YOUNG AND BILLY SPERLING.
—MATTIE MILLER, ADVISER FOR GLENWOOD
SCHOOL, EVANSVILLE, INDIANA.

WHEN I WAS very young, I lived down in Georgia. Now get this, kids; if there's anything in the world that made me what I am today, it's how I started life. You know what's the trouble with the young people of today? Listen. Things, money, and power: those things are detrimental to anybody if you don't know how to use them. Believe me, children.

When I was about five, I didn't have what you kids have now. Look at you all—pretty, all dressed up. I had one dress, and I wore that dress all week long. I had a stepfather that wasn't quite so nice. You all got your fathers, haven't you? This stepfather used to come home with the Devil in him and he'd take it out on me. You all want to hear this old stuff? Okay. And sometime when he come in, he was kinda shook up and he'd take it out on me. And he used to say to my mother, "That little devil is not going to stay in *this* house tonight." I had a little dog. His name was Bill. And I knew then to go out and sleep with Bill on the porch. *How many* nights have I went out on that porch and slept with Bill.

And I'd hear my mother in the morning when she'd get up to go in there to cook breakfast. I'd hear her cooking breakfast, and I'd go around to the back door, and sometimes she'd take two biscuits with a piece of bacon in between and hand it out the door to me and I'd take it and go back around there and Bill and I would have breakfast. Never got bitter. Never. I'm thankful that [even] today I don't let things make me bitter. Okay?

When he'd leave, then, I'd go in the house. And my life was like that till I was about fourteen years old. Then I left home and went to work for some people up at Beauregard, Georgia. Well, I worked there and got myself started in working, and somebody saw me. And that's another thing, kids; when you're trying to learn how to do a job, do it *well*. It'll speak for you. It'll talk for you. I *learned* how to do things well. You don't slapdash. That don't say a thing for you. That says something for you, too, but something you don't like people to know about, you know? Okay?

So I grew up and began working in Athens, Georgia and this same stepfather was living way out in the country. [This story is] the reason I say don't get *bitter*. That's what's wrong with kids today. They're so ready to *fight*. And they say you're square if you *don't* fight. But sometimes, it's nice to be a square.

This lady that I was working for, she heard that my stepfather was sick. And she would go to the market on Wednesdays. My day off was on Thursday evenings. And I was going with a fine guy at that particular time who would let me drive his car. And this lady would buy sometimes three and four dozen of oranges—she'd heard me say that he had to have orange juice. And oatmeal. And I'd carry sometimes three and four boxes of that out there to him. And this lady was kind and nice. You get out of life what you put into it, children. Don't forget.

And you know, it was about a year that I went and took that out to him every Thursday. And one Thursday evening he looked at me—he always said I was the best friend he had—but you remember what I told you [about him] in the beginning? So he said to me one Thursday, he said, "Sarah, can I ask you something?"

I said, "You certainly can, Pa."

He said, "Would you forgive me for how I treated you when you were a little child?"

I said, "You didn't do anything to me when I was a child. I've always loved you, and I've always wanted to do things for you."

And when I said that, the tears just commenced to running out of his eyes. He said, "Bless your heart. I just don't see how you can do it because I know I was ugly to you when you were a child."

I said, "Well, I'll tell you this one thing. I can't help how you feel, but I know how *I* feel. I still love you." And before I got back the next week, he was dead.

And you see how lovely I can look back on things—that I didn't turn stone to stone? You do *good* for other people when they're ugly to you. [First] you learn to get along with yourself. If you can get along with yourself, you won't have no trouble with anybody else because you gonna have sense enough to know what to do when a thing like that comes up. See, I have to tell you these little stories that happened to *me*. [This next one,] you know this lady. I took her clothes down one day from out there on the line. Oh, kids, I could talk to you all from here to dark. They'd been hanging there *three days* right across my walk there. I went out there one morning and took them down, and I got some newspapers and put them on her stoop—she lives next door—and got some newspaper and put on top of them and got the pins from her line and put on top of the clothes.

She came home and saw her clothes taken down. She asked the neighbors —I won't repeat what she said, but it was *ugly*. Say who took her so-and-so clothes down. And the neighbors say, "I think Mrs. Dupee took 'em down."

And the language that she used I wouldn't want to say it out of my mouth. Then she came to my back door and she said *everything that she knew to say that was ugly*.

And I just stood there and looked at her. So when she finished, I said, "Have you finished?"

She said, "So-and-so *yes*, I've finished!"

I said, "Well, listen, Sweetie. I got something to tell you. [Whenever] your clothes hang in front of my door three days, I *will* be taking 'em down." And that's all I said, and came back in the house.

And the neighbors commenced to calling me over the phone telling me how beautiful I handled that: "Mrs. Dupee, it was *great*."

You know what happened to the lady? Two weeks later she came to my back door there and asked could she come in.

I said, "Yes."

She said [crying], "Mrs. Dupee, you made me feel like a dog and I'm sorry I talked to you so ugly. Mrs. Dupee, can you forgive me for what I said?"

I said, "Sure. I forgave you when you said it." 'Cause I did. And she was as *nice*. You can't put out fire with fire. You know that, don't you? Remember that when you getting hot under the collar and somebody says something to you and you want to hit back. Don't be so quick to get hot under

Sarah Ann Dupee

the collar. Cool it! If you can't hit back with something that's *good*, keep your mouth shut. You'll be the winner, honey, believe me.

'Cause they's too many kids of today doesn't know what is right and what is wrong 'cause they have nobody to teach them. If your parents is teaching you that which is right and which is wrong, honey, you are wonderfully blessed, 'cause there's too many parents in the world don't give a darn where their kids go and what they do. All they want 'em is off their back.

Sometimes I know you think your parents are nuts. I know you think that. They're too hard on you and all like that. Uh-uh! Obey your parents. You see, I got so many stories along in my life that will help kids. Can I tell you this story about obeying your parents?

My father told me once I couldn't go on a hayride. I liked to died! Well! I *liked to died!* I just thought that I was gonna go anyway, but my father said no, he meant that. You know what Satan can put in your mind? Peculiar things! You know what Satan was putting in my mind? Satan had told me to go in the house—it was near night, near time for this hayride—and

Sarah Ann Dupee, Billy Sperling, and Clarrisa Young

take your pillows and put them in the bed just like you were lying in the bed and cover it up just like you were there, you know, and when your father came to the door and peep in there, he wouldn't know that you had gone. But you see, I knew my daddy. He wouldn't come to the door and peep in. He'd come to the door and pull the cover down! But I didn't go. I liked to died.

And you know what happened to those kids? In this hayride down in Georgia, right down at Mars Hill Baptist Church—that was a white church there—and it was nothing but white sand all around this church and down the hill to this bridge where they had to cross. It was some pine trees on each side of the road and the shadow of those pine trees made those horses think that somebody was standing there with a stick fixing to hit [them]. That's exactly the way it looked. And the driver pulled the lines up for the horses to go on, and they rared up. And he hit them. And when he hit them, they lunged, and they hit the side of this bridge and down in this deep place—a little branch was down in there—the wagon, the horses, the driver, the everything fell down in there, and every child was killed. They had to shoot the horses because they was so broke up. Do you get the story now? What do you get about that story? What's the beautiful part about it? What can you see in that story now? If I had a-gone, I wouldn't be here today to talk to you kids. You see what I'm saying? The Lord plans your life out, and if you play your cards right, you'll fulfill the law. You get what I say?

About two o'clock, they came and woke up my daddy and asked, said, "Did Sarah go with those children?"

He said, "No."

They said, "Are you sure?"

He said, "Sure I'm sure because I told her not to go and I *know* she didn't go."

The Devil can make the biggest fool out of you if you're not careful. God knows I'm so glad you brought these children here, and you can tell this story—tell that an old lady told you that knew what she was talking about. I asked these eleven- and twelve-year-old kids in church class, I said, "I want you to tell me the truth, now. We're in God's house." I always have little children come in God's house with a smile. "Don't come in here with your mouth poked out! Come in God's house happy! And if you've got something in you before you get in the church, step back out and say, 'God, please let me go in with the right spirit.'" Will you all remember that?

So I told these children, I said, "I want every one of you in here to tell the truth. Have you ever been introduced to dope?" Did you hear me say what year I had? Elevens and twelves! *Every* hand went up! I said, "Thank you kids for being honest enough to tell the truth. Did you like it?"

Everyone said, "No, ma'm, Mrs. Dupee. It made me feel awful."

I said, "Now tell me this, children; why didn't you tell your principal or your teacher?"

Said, "We better not. They'd beat us up."

You see what I'm telling you? Don't get into it in the first place. Don't do it. And don't be afraid to tell somebody that can do something *about* it. The Devil *wants* to get you afraid. Don't *ever* be afraid. Don't *ever* be afraid. Keep the right spirit within you, and always want to do that thing which is right. Dope, dope is one of the main things that's got these children so shook up and frustrated! Tell the truth. Have you all ever seen it? Don't tell a story! Have you seen the dope? Have you ever been introduced to it? Have you ever taken any of it? Don't tell lies. [They indicate not.] Okay. I'm glad. When you *know* it's something that's wrong, you don't *need* to take it.

[There are lots of problems in this neighborhood.] People have offered to move me to better surroundings, but I stay here. What I enjoy most is that there's plenty of work to do. And I love that. There's so much work to be done here. You know, when you get to the place that you have nothing to do, then you in bad trouble. You in big trouble when the time comes you have nothing to do. But here, there's always something to do. Always somebody to talk to. Somebody you try to show them what it means to try to reach out and try to get aholt of something that will do something for you on the *inside*. That's what's wrong with our world, children, is that not enough kids know about God. And *that is it*. Get God on the inside of you.

Here about five years ago, there was three businessmen downtown. They had been discussing Dupee, and listen at this: they thought I was too nice to be living in this place here. And they had went out and found a beautiful little four-room apartment, and they said, "Mrs. Dupee, we think you're too nice to live down here, and we were just wondering if you would consider this. We'll make the down payment on the house"—listen at this—"and you'll just have to pay [the same monthly rent] as what you pay here. And we were just wondering how you would feel about that."

I said, "God bless you all. It's marvelous for people to think about you. There's nothing in this world that's any more precious than somebody that loves you well enough to think about you." And I said, "But let me tell you one thing, gentlemen. You're fine and God bless your heart. I appreciate that to the depths of my soul," I said, "but you know, I have learned this." I think then I was seventy-three. I'm seventy-seven now. "I have found this out in life. It's not where you live. It's *what you are* where you live. And I have made up in my mind they need me here, and I will be here." I said, "You know, life deals the cards, and it's up to you to play them the way they should be played." And that's exactly the history of Dupee. It's not where you live. It's what you are where you live.

"He started to stab the plane with his knife."

ELMER BALLOT

Elmer Ballot was born on November 13, 1913, in Selawik, Alaska, an Eskimo community three miles north of the Arctic Circle, ninety miles inland from the Bering Sea. His parents were Ahnacok and Ruth Ballot. Elmer has lived in Selawik all his life. His wife Lottie and he have six children. Elmer is a member of the Selawik City Council and president of the Health Council. He is a village historical researcher for Mauneluk, the regional native association based in Kotzebue.

Elmer came to school and talked to us in Eskimo about the Eskimos' first contacts with white men in Selawik. We translated it into English for this book.

—MARTHA RAMOTH, EUNICE RAMOTH, SARA KNOX,
ALBERTHA FOSTER, PEARL GREIST, ROBERT CLEVELAND,
CARL FOXGLOVE, HERMAN TICKET, BILLY TIKIK, ALICE KOENIG,
TILLIE HENRY, MARGARET SMITH, LYDIA RAMOTH,
ROMONA FOXGLOVE, ELVIRA STARBUCK, LINDA BERRY,
BONNIE SMITH, MIKE HADLEY, AND WILLARD COMMACK.
—GEORGE HARBESON, ADVISER, RIF PROJECT,
SELAWIK HIGH SCHOOL, SELAWIK, ALASKA.

FOR A LONG TIME the *Inupiat* [Eskimo people] lived alone in the Selawik area. When many years passed, the *naluagmi* [white men] came. That was the first time the Eskimos ever saw them; they were as pale as snow. The *anatkut* [medicine men], who always talked to the Devil and who could fly, got together and started to watch the *naluagmi* to see what their race started from and why they were as white as snow. The people could not even understand what the white people said. Neither could they see why they were so white. The *naluagmi* were not like the Eskimo race when it began. The people learned through the medicine men that the white people started from big white worms. And so it was after the Eskimo people lived for a while that the white people came to Selawik.

Some of the white people came in big boats with covers and inboard motors. You probably have seen those old boats in pictures before. The white people had with them tobacco. When *taataga* [father] Quasaq went to get the used cigarette he saw a white man throw on the water, he went into the water up to his chest and picked up the floating cigarette and tried to smoke it. When people really wanted to smoke, they picked up stubs from the ground just to smoke. Tobacco is not good to smoke all the time.

The first people who lived before us didn't know about things such as pieces of cloth. People had always made clothes with muskrat and weasel skins because there were lots of muskrats and weasels. The people who lived before us tried to make sinew with muskrats' tails and muscles. Rabbits' feet and tendons were used for sewing, done by the women. Not many caribou came here in those days so caribou hides we used later. Long ago there were no zippers in the jackets and no nylon. There were no white man's caps. There were no boots, combat boots or shoe packs. They came later. So did rubber boots. Everything's gotten a lot easier now, but a long time ago life was hard for us.

The white people always gave strange things to the Eskimos. They tried to give them flour, but the Eskimos didn't know what it was or how to use it. They didn't eat it because they didn't know it was food. One of the *naluagmi* gave an Eskimo woman fifty pounds of flour. She dumped the flour on the ground and took the sack for cloth. She really liked the sack because she wanted to make something with it. Cloth was precious but the value of flour not yet known.

One time one of the white men gave the Eskimos some tea. The people started to drink tea when they found out what it was. My *aanaga's* [mother's] relative, Illiaq, was given some tea in a wooden spoon. The people had no cups but only big wooden spoons. The *naluagmi* poured tea

Elmer Ballot

into the big wooden spoon and gave Illiaq some and said, "Drink some tea, Illiaq." After he sniffed the tea for a while he spilled it on the ground saying, "If I want tea, I will go to the muskrat lake and drink some." He said that because he didn't want to drink weak tea much. Illiaq lived many years after that happened. Just before he died he didn't want the weak, light tea of the white man.

There were no doctors to keep people alive in those days. When a person got a headache his *aanaga* always tied his head real tight with something like a bandanna, or he had to take off his parka hood outdoors and cool off

Back row (left to right): Martha Ramoth, Eunice Ramoth, Sara Knox, Albertha Foster, Pearl Greist, Robert Cleveland, Carl Foxglove, Herman Ticket, Billy Tikik; Front row: Alice Koenig, Tillie Henry, Margaret Smith, Lydia Ramoth, Romona Foxglove, George Harbeson, Elvira Starbuck, Linda Berry, Bonnie Smith, Mike Hadley, Willard Commack

his head. He was supposed to cool off even though he may have had a fever. If people had a fever, they went outdoors anyway. There weren't any dentists in the early years. When an old person died, he died with rotten teeth. Cure for a toothache was cutting the gums to let the tooth bleed. If the tooth still hurt, they tied sinew to the tooth and pulled it out. They didn't numb the tooth with shots then.

In those early days the men didn't have long hair like you boys have now. When a man had long hair, he always got a cutting board and put his hair down on it and cut it. There were no scissors and knives. The jade ax and jade *uluu* [woman's knife] was used for cutting. It was sharpened by splitting a piece of cottonwood in half and rubbing the cottonwood with sand. The dull blade was sharpened by cottonwood and sand. They often sharpened blades with rocks, too. Young ladies, like you students, didn't use pants like you do today. They didn't have pants or jeans, that's why. When they had cloth, they always made dresses and long parkas. Young girls and women didn't walk around like men when we were growing up. When a young girl had long loose hair, the old people always said that she was lazy. They said, "You're lazy. Why don't you braid your hair?"

In 1908, the people first started hearing about school and teachers. When school began in Selawik, the people young and old, all in one grade, started schooling in a mud house and not the log cabin which was later. When they first started schooling, my *aanaga* was one of those who went to school with the students. She learned how to sing the ABCs. That is what she learned a long time ago. When school started in Selawik, children didn't eat at school but at home. Later we had some oatmeal, sugar, salt, and hotcakes at school.

The school building I went to was in front of the present elementary school. Lawrence Jones's brother and I used to work as janitors. Every morning we went to school to build a fire in the stove. We and the person who rang the bell for the kids to go to school would work one week for a pencil. We tried hard to get pencils. When a student was bad in school, the teacher put him in a corner to lie down. He stayed there about two or three hours because he wasn't trying to learn what he was supposed to learn. Bad students had to put their hands out for the teacher to hit them with a ruler. If they didn't let the teacher hit them on the hand for punishment, then the teacher could take their clothes off and spank them. If they really didn't behave, the teacher put them in a small cellar. It had no windows and not much room to move around. The students could sleep there. They stayed about three or four hours in the cellar when they never behaved. That's the way school used to be a long time ago, but now it's not like that any more.

In the old days Selawik was not like it is today. We didn't have pool halls and we didn't have liquor. We didn't see anybody drinking in the village.

The first time we heard a drunk person was when we heard someone hollering and shouting. Many children went home because they were scared of the hollering person. There were a few of us that hid near the church and watched for the person who was drunk. His name was Kalotuk. When he came out of his house, he kept falling on the ground. That's the first drunk person we saw.

Once I was with a group of thieves. They told me there was home brew made in this house. I was the smallest person in the group. I must have been just a kid. The group and I planned to steal this liquor. We went to the window and took it out because the door was locked. It was a small window. The group pushed me into the house because I was a small boy. The older boys told me to take the liquor out little by little from the barrel.

When the boys pushed me in, I fell down on the floor. There it was—a barrel full of liquor. When I went to the cupboard I put all the jars and pails near the barrel and filled them and handed them out the window. The boys told me to drink from the barrel before I came back out. So I drank the liquor as fast as I could. I really didn't know how much it took to get drunk. I got drunk fast. When they were pulling me through the window frame, I broke it.

When the person who made the liquor came home, he told the people that someone went into his house and stole his liquor. He soon found out who had done it. I got so ashamed that I didn't come out of my house for a few days. It is not right to steal things from another person. It is better to ask the person when you want something.

Our parents taught us not to drink or smoke tobacco and not to steal anything from anybody. I was a bad person because I didn't obey my parents. I smoked, drank, and stole some things. Our parents, in the old days, told us that when we did these things we wouldn't have a good life and would feel ashamed of ourselves.

When a person drinks or steals his life is short. He dies early or he feels ashamed of himself. When you are young and steal, it may not bother you but when old age comes it will bother you a lot. It was told like this, "If you break or steal somebody's things, you will hurt yourself, and you and your family will still suffer for it." A person who told me this was true said he knew because he had learned his lesson. When he did something bad, he lied and said he didn't do it. Later when he wanted to confess, the people he wanted to tell had moved away or died and it was too late. So if you are guilty of something say, "Yes, I did it," and there will be nothing to bother you later. When you're young, your conscience doesn't bother you as much, but when you get old, it starts to bother you.

In the old days there was a person named Mauneluk. He was the man who predicted the future. You students must have heard about him before.

Mauneluk always said that in the future people would relax more than work. He said the people would have easier living with really good kinds of comfortable chairs. People, even his relatives, always told Mauneluk that he was crazy. They said it wouldn't be like that in the future. Mauneluk said that strangers would come from the wind directions of the Kobuk way [from the west]. The people said he was out of his mind because they thought they wouldn't be seeing the things Mauneluk predicted. Mauneluk said visitors would start coming when the weather was good. The people said he was crazy.

When the weather was good in 1927, Sig Wien came flying from the Kobuk way. Our grandfather Guunaq, Charlie Kiana's father, was there and saw the plane. That was the first time the people saw an airplane. People started crying and saying "Jesus is coming." Guunaq thought he was too late to repent. He and the others started crawling on the ground. Many were scared. Some of the people, when they saw the plane pass overhead, fell over backwards as they watched it go over it because that was the first plane they ever saw. When they saw the plane, they started praying because they thought that first airplane was Jesus coming. Lucille Kolhok's father, Uqitchuuraq, afterwards always said when the people saw the plane and started falling backwards, he saw that their necks were dirty, although maybe he didn't see dirty necks. Maybe he just *suglu* [joked].

The plane went to Kotzebue because there were no landing fields in this area at that time. The plane landed on a grassy flat place behind Kotzebue. One of the Kotzebue men took out his knife, and before anyone could stop him, he started to stab the plane with his knife. The plane had two wings on a side at that time and no top to cover up the pilot's head. Half of the pilot's body showed when he was flying around. The man stabbed the wings with his knife because he wanted to see how thick the wings were. That was the way the people were when the first plane came.

"I'm from out of the Beech."

STANLEY HICKS

Stanley Hicks and his wife live deep in the Appalachian Mountains of North Carolina. Like most traditional mountain families, they come from completely self-sufficient stock. Stanley's parents and grandparents made wagon wheels, wagons, chairs, churns, barrels, tubs, tables, baskets, cabinets, sleds, and many other essential items completely by hand from natural materials gathered in the surrounding forest, and they even made the tools they used to shape those items with. They also raised and preserved all their food, made their own soap, molasses (Stanley's grandmother had one of her arms ground off in their molasses mill by accident); and for a little extra cash they peeled and sold tanbark and dug wild herbs used in making early medicines, and packed it all out of the mountains to the closest towns.

In many ways, it was a desperate existence, but it was uniquely satisfying too; and despite the fact that Stanley has had jobs on the "outside," he keeps returning to it. Now, for example, he raises a little tobacco, raises enough food to get by on, and makes fine traditional banjos and dulcimers for sale to get what money he needs to pay his land taxes and expenses.

In that part of the country, he and his family have the reputation of being the finest traditional tale tellers and carriers of tradi-

tional ballads and songs anywhere around. The "Jack tales" that his brother, Ray, tells have been included in several collections of Appalachian folk tales. Their life is full of music and entertainment and high spirits and warmth. But they are well aware, too, of the problems facing the Appalachian people now and in the future; and they realize that they and their people may, in time, lose everything they now have to outsiders, and to economic pressures put on them by the outside world. And that thought colors all their days.

—RAY MCBRIDE, STEVE SMITH.
—ELIOT WIGGINTON, ADVISER FOR FOXFIRE.

WE HAULED all Dad's wood with steers. We had one yoke about seven or eight year old, and me and my brother would take them things to the woods, and when I tacked into the log, I'd holler at 'em and they was gone with it. Didn't need lines or anything. They'd take it right into the chip yard and stop. That's where we had a wood block. We'd have a wood block and braces put up where you put poles in them to saw them with a crosscut saw. We called it the chip yard, and that's where Dad done all of his hewing. Hewed his yokes out and wagon wheel spokes and hubs and his felloes. And he had his shaving horse there. He made everything he had. And I helped him hew out logs when he went and helped build log houses when I was a kid. That's what he done, but there was very little money in it. He mostly worked for fifty cents a day. Maybe he'd get up to a dollar. He'd just charge a dollar to sharpen both the rocks for a grist mill. It would take all day. He had his picks for that made in a blacksmith shop. I had some here that Dad had when I had a grist mill, but I got rid of them. Ought to have kept them, but the fellow that got the mill wanted the picks too.

And then Dad made barrels and churns and dulcimers and chairs. He'd turn out chair rounds with a lathe you pedaled [a treadle lathe or foot-powered lathe]. Then finally he got one run by a water wheel. He made his chisels that he turned with. Made all of his stuff. I mean there wasn't nothing you could buy. And if you could have bought it, there wasn't hardly any money to buy it with. Right here's a plane that he tongue-and-grooved with. And here's an old sawmill file that he made his bit out of. He put a peg in here to hold to, but it's lost out. Kids throwed 'em around after he died, and I just scrapped 'em up and picked 'em up where they'd throwed 'em away, and got 'em up and brought 'em home.

Another way we made a little money back then was stilling out birch oil

"I'm from out of the Beech."

and mountain tea oil and sassafrak [sassafras]. We'd still it [in much the same way people distilled moonshine] and sell it. We sold birch oil for twenty-five dollars a gallon. For sassafrak, we'd just use the roots, but birch we'd use the bark. We could get the bark anytime, but in the wintertime you have to beat it off with an old poleax or a maul. In summer we could just peel it with a spud like peeling tanbark. There's a white birch and a black birch, but the black birch is the one we peeled. And then this teaberry, or mountain tea, it has a red berry. We'd pull it anytime [of year] and still it out. And then we'd still penny-royal out—pull up any herb and still it to get the oil out. That was for medicine.

With trees like birch, the bark was all we used—and the twigs. Chop the twigs up fine till we could get them in the still. Then get in there and tromp it till we could get a lot in it. And then put water in. We wouldn't fill the still full. If you did, it would run over. You'd have to lack about six or eight inches of filling it to the top. And then we capped it down and put a fire under it. Same as making liquor—had the thump keg and all. Only difference is we had this in a wooden still—a big wooden still out of two-by-eights tongue-and-grooved together. It was about six feet long and three feet wide and about four feet deep. Had a metal bottom on it lapped up about four inches, and then it was set on a furnace just like you'd make sorghum. And then it had big two-by-fours that went across the top from one end to the other that we put wedges under to bind the top down till the steam wouldn't come out. Took about a day and night to run it out. Run out about four gallons. We'd fire it that morning—get it started running about ten o'clock, and then we'd run it all day and some of us would have to stay up with it all night till the next morning. We took a turn about. If you didn't keep it running, you didn't get your oil, you see. We'd run it in a half-gallon jar full of water and then this oil would drop in and send it to the bottom. See, the oil went to the bottom when the can was full, the water was gone and we had the can full of oil. And then Dad would send it to Johnson City [Tennessee] to sell it.

And then the backings [what's left in the still after it's been run], they come out. They're not very strong. You can drink them. Look right blue. And we'd drink them, you know. They was good to drink.

And then we'd use some of that oil ourselves. That birch oil—you use it for toothache. Use the mountain tea oil for toothache too. And then Mother would mix something with the mountain tea oil so it wouldn't be strong and rub it on for the rheumatism. And everybody used pennyroyal for medicine —use it for the little kids. When a little kid was born, they would take a drop and put it in water and sweeten it and give it to the kid till it was up a month or two months old.

And you know puffballs? Mash 'em and the smoke boils out of 'em? Well

Stanley Hicks

now they used that to stop blood with. If anybody got cut or anything, they'd grab one of them puffballs and squirt this dust in it and it would quit. My grandpa had some of them that he would save just for that. And my other grandpa was a preacher and stopped blood with a Bible verse. They called him from everywhere, and that's what he done.

And sheep sorrel—they used that for poultices. If you had a boil or something like that on you, they'd go and get sheep sorrel. Took the leaves and poured hot water over them and scalded them, and then took wheat bran from the roller mill and stir it in so it would hold and make a good poultice to put on these sores or a sprained ankle or anything like that, and it would really draw the soreness out. And where there was a boil, it would draw it in no time till it would be broke.

That's all they had then for medicine. We gathered everything here in the woods, and what we didn't use ourselves we had four big merchants that would buy it for medicines. Sometimes we'd pack it plumb out to Elk Park for them. We gathered shiny haw in the summer. These people that made medicine used that. And at the same time we'd gather mayapple roots and queen-in-the-meadow and quill weed and bamboo briar roots. And then we'd dig the burdock. And we peeled cherry bark—they used that. And Dad used to run out the cherry sometimes [on his still]. We called it cherry bitters. It *was* bitter, too. And then we'd pull galax—pull that mostly through the wintertime—and pull fern through the winter. Then we'd take these steers and have us a whole load of herbs and take it four miles to where the man bought it at and sell that and then we'd get some supplies— salt or soda or coffee—and put it on the sled and bring it back.

That mayapple was good for other things too. My grandpa, back when the ground squirrels and stuff would take up the corn, would go dig him some mayapple root and he'd boil it down and soak the corn seed in that, and when they ate that, it would kill them.

We picked up chestnuts. We'd sell them. And we raised October beans to sell. And then old people got a lot of stuff for their own use during the winter and dried that. See, they dried their beans, pumpkin, apples, peaches, huckleberries—all that. Dad had a dry-house with a metal bottom that you put a fire under. Had a little house built up and a furnace under it, and had drawers in here built like a beehive super only running across [from side to side]. And he'd fill this full of the stuff and shut the door and put a fire under here and dried it much quicker than it could if you put it out in the sun. The stuff down next to the fire would dry the quickest, so we'd take out the top drawer and shift 'em, you see. Just like an oven. Covered with shingles. We could dry two or three hundred pounds a week.

Then we'd sack it all up and hang it overhead in the house. And we dried our beef and hung it in the smokehouse in shoulders and hindquarters. And we'd smoke hog meat with cobs and hickory bark.

We lived rough, but we had good times, too.

There was lots we could do for fun. We'd make wooden bicycles—cut the wheels out of hollow black gum trees. And Dad made puzzles for us to play with out of wood. And some out of wire. There was one like a round pincushion—it was plugged together someway. You'd tear it apart and it was a *job* to get it back! It's perfect when it's together but it might take you two days to get it back.

And we used to play fox and goose. You've got two red foxes—you know, red grains of corn—and the rest of them is white. Play on a board like a checkerboard. And then the geese tries to hem these foxes up. Dad'd get 'em hemmed up and he'd say, "Que-e-e-e-e-e-e! Listen at her wheeze!" He'd say, "Watch her wiggle her tail, boys! She's a-dying!" It'd make us so cussed mad, you know. He was good on it. And then every time he'd jump one of our geese, he'd go "Quack!" Make like a goose a-hollering, you know.

And then we had another game we'd play to see who could jump the furtherest. And then we had stilts—go to the woods and make us a pair of stilts, and then we had a line marked off and we'd see who could walk in this line and not get out of it. It was a job, you know!

And we made wagons and snow sleds to ride in the snow with. I tried to make me a pair of snowshoes but they didn't work out. I didn't make 'em long enough. They tripped me and banged up my nose.

Then we'd hide stuff in haystacks and play horseshoes. Had another game we'd play—two lines facing each other [as in tug-of-war]. Two would get ahold of a stick and they'd line behind 'em and get ahold of their coattails and see who would outpull the other crowd. Sometimes you'd about stretch one in two, you know. They had all kinds of games like that, and they was good games, you know. Had a lot of fun out of it.

And then we'd shuck corn, and five hundred [points] was the game. A red ear was a hundred, and a speckled ear was twenty-five. We'd play that game to get the corn shucked out. When we wound up, the one that got the most games in a certain length of time, he got to rest up and didn't have to shuck no more corn. It was a sight to see the corn shucked! Maybe three or four hundred bushel in the pile—take three or four nights. And then the old people—they'd put a jug of moonshine whiskey in the bottom of the pile, and they'd say, "Now, boys, when we get shucked to this we'll get a drink of this whiskey." And you talk about shucking corn, son—they knowed it was in there and I mean they'd really lay to it to get to that whiskey!

And then we'd take and pond up water and we'd get a washing tub and two of us would get in it and we'd see who could get around the pond quickest. There was a lot of hard work to do, but we got a lot of fun out of it in ways.

I got to the fourth grade. We had to walk to school. We had to take a crosscut and cut our own wood for the schoolhouse. School only went about four or five months through the wintertime. It was pretty hard times with us when I was going to school. You know, they had these secondhanded stores. Dad went to get me a pair of knee pants, but they'd been here too long! I went to school in them, and you know how a young'un runs and plays. Well, they busted back here behind. And I didn't want to go in the schoolhouse, but the teacher come out and said if I didn't she'd whip me.

Well, I went in forwards—kept my hand back here—and got to my seat and sat down, and when I went out, I *backed* out, you know. I didn't want the young'uns to laugh and see my skin, you know!

So I got to the fourth grade. Later, during the war when they had a lot of work going on, I went up to Radford to the shipyard. A bunch of us went up there to get a job. Times was hard—you couldn't hardly get a job. We lined up in a big hall—I'd say fifty or a hundred feet long—all of us lined up a-signing up for jobs. And some of 'em had all kinds of education—had went up through high school and college. Well, we was going down the line, and they reached me a bunch of blanks and stuff to fill out, and I looked at them and I reached them back to the man. He said, "I want these filled out so I know what all you can do."

And I said, "Listen, I got to the fourth grade in school. I can do anything you've got—any kind of work you've got, I can do it. But I'm no college young'un. I can't fill out no blanks. I can't do that."

He said, "You mean you're up here for a job and you've only gone through the fourth grade?"

I said, "I'm up here for a job and I'll take anything you've got."

He said, "That's talking pretty big."

I said, "Anything you've got, I will take it and I will do it."

"Well," he said, "all right."

Well, they was seven of us went up there, and I'd say they was fifty more ahead of me, and the seven of us went and got an apartment. Went back the next morning and lined up down the lane. They called out if anybody had a job. Got down the line and called out, "Hicks."

And I said, "Here."

And the ones that went up there with me looked at me just like they would drop dead. They had gone through high school, and they looked like they was going to drop dead. Well, I stepped aside and they went on down, and I was the only one in the bunch that they called the name out.

"Well," he said, "I got you a job."

I said, "You have? Well, I appreciate it. I need it. What is it?"

He said, "You said you could handle anything."

"Well," I said, "I can. What have you got?"

He said, "Loading them big tires out of the warehouse."

I said, "I can do it."

He said, "You can?"

I said, "Yeah, I can do it."

And they had tires that went on these big r. .chines in there. They stood as high as that door. And I went in there and I looked at them things, and I didn't weigh but about 140. And they was another old big *husky* feller in there—big muscles—and he'd waller with them things and they'd just waller him down.

I'd bounce them things and put my shoulder against them and take 'em just as easy and roll 'em in the truck. Turn 'em over. Take that thing and roll another one and stack 'em up. They watched me a while. And one man, he come out there. He was driving a truck. And sweat was running off him—dripping off. Hot. And he said, "I want to know where in the name of God you're from."

I said, "I'm from out of the Beech Mountain."

He said, "Well, I've heard of that place."

I said, "That's near Boone."

"Yeah," he said. "I've heard of that." He said, "How long you been a-working at this kind of work?"

I said, "Today."

He said, "*Today?*"

I said, "Today."

I worked that week there, and these boys I went with never got a job and they left me. And I had to pay the house rent and had to pay all this. I couldn't make it.

I went back and told him, I said, "I can't make it. I've got to leave." ·

He said, "What's the matter?"

I said, "I've got no place to stay. I can't pay seven dollars a week rent *and* my board making a dollar and a quarter a day. I just can't make it."

He said, "I see your point." He said, "They've an old man and woman out here that might keep you and board you for fifty cents a day."

I said, "Well, I'll take it. But I ain't got no way of getting out there and back."

He said, "I'll run you out there anyway."

Well, he run me out there at quitting time. I talked to the old man and the poor old feller wasn't able to do nothing for himself; and the old woman, she was old and she wouldn't have been able to took care of him let alone waiting for somebody else. I looked the thing over, and I told him, I said, "Well, I'm sorry. I appreciate the job you got me—nobody knows—

Stanley Hicks and Eliot Wigginton

and I appreciate working here and all, but I believe I'll catch the next bus out of here."

He said, "Well, Hicks, we'll have to send your other check to you."

"Well," I said, "I'd like to have it now if I can get it."

"Well," he said, "all I can do is just pay the money out of my own pocket and when the money comes, you sign a blank so I can get it." I went in there and fixed it and he took me out to the bus stop and patted me on the shoulder. Said, "I hope to see you again." But I never did see him no more.

They pushed buildings down up there, it'd make you sick. You'd cry. They took them big dozers where they was building this powder plant and pushed buildings in. I mean crushed 'em and burnt 'em. *Nice* buildings. And they was an old woman—I can see her right now in my imagination. She was sitting on the porch and wouldn't get off and they carried her off the porch and pushed the house in and her a-crying.

It was hard to make it, and you had to have *some* money. I bought overalls like this when I was married for thirty-five cents a pair. Now they're ten and eleven dollars. But I can get ten dollars now quicker than I could get thirty-five cents then. I bought flour for thirty-five cents a poke and meal was thirty. Now flour's five dollars. Mother would buy cloth and make all of our shirts—buy cloth for seven cents a yard. What we bought for seven cents is now about three dollars.

During the tough times, Stanley's family got pressured economically into doing what many Appalachian families did at that time (and are still doing)—they sold their home. Therein lies one of the tragic continuing chapters of Appalachian history. Children with no land to hold them, and no jobs, moved by the thousands to cities like Detroit, Cleveland, Cincinnati, Dayton, Columbus, and Atlanta. Others, like Stanley, determined to stay in the area, began the long fight to find and pay for (at inflated prices) another piece of land within shouting distance of home, and dig in. Said Stanley, "I growed up in the mountains and I'll stay here till I die."

The pain of Stanley's struggle was not only the sale of the land, but also the loss of most of his father's tools and possessions:

I wish I could have saved all of Dad's stuff, but [the family] sold almost everything he had—give it away and sold it. I'd give anything on earth to keep his birch still, but my brother sold it for ten dollars. I wanted it so bad. Me and Dad worked on that thing for thirty days a-building it and fixing it. I wanted to bring it here to put up. A man from away from here bought it, and I went to buy it back from that man and he wouldn't even *talk* about selling it to me. He bought it just for an antique to keep. I offered him fifty dollars and said I'd go more than that on account of me and Dad built it. I said, "It's the last thing he built and I'd like to get it and take it home and set it up for people to see. I still know how to run it."

And he said, "Could I hire you sometime to come out here and operate it?"

And I said, "Yeah, you could, but I'd like to take it home." But no. He's got a great big thing—he's got wagons and buggies—and he won't let it go.

So it's all gone. I had to buy my own place. I bought four places before I come here. The first place, I bought when me and my wife first married. They charged me fifty cents to write the deed, and I barely had the fifty cents. Bought ten acres for a hundred dollars. And I told my wife, said, "I'm going to build us a little house." I paid fifty dollars on the land, then had a cow that had a calf that I sold for twenty-five dollars, and I scraped together the other twenty-five. Then I built us a little home on it. We stayed there two years and I told my wife, I said, "I believe we'll hunt a little better place than this." I sold it for three hundred dollars. The man paid me three hundred one-dollar bills. That's the way he had it saved up.

Well, I went and bought another place and got it for two hundred and fifty dollars, and timber was on it, you know. I cut the timber and took it to Ben Ward's sawmill and built my house out of it. We cleared up new ground and raised our stuff and all. Then I decided to pick up a little bit more land. Well, I found another place over on Beech Creek by mother. A preacher owned it, and I give him five hundred dollars for it—sold my other land for five fifty. And then I went and put me up a grist mill and run it for several years, and then I sold that for a thousand dollars. And then I give fifteen hundred dollars for the next place I bought down there and had to build me the barn and everything. It was just land, but it was good land. They was seventeen acres of it. And I sold that, then, for five thousand dollars and I come here and bought this. I don't like to go in debt too much, but I had to to get what I wanted. I finally got my land paid for two years ago. I come here in 1952 and times was hard. I disced up two acres of cabbage right over there. Couldn't sell 'em. No market. And I left another two acres down there to go to rot. Couldn't give 'em away. You couldn't *give* nobody that. I pulled my tractor under the barn and me and her pulled out and went to Burlington and went to working on a chicken farm. Worked down there part of two years to get back on my feet. I got back on my feet, came back here, and said the farming can *go*. Now I just raise my tobacco and enough garden stuff to do us. Took me twenty-one years to get this paid for and this is where we'll stay.

The families was selling the land off like crazy, and they still are, to these people that comes in from outside, and they don't care for you nor nobody else. And the young'uns, I don't know *where* they'll go to. They've got no place to settle down—they've got no place to make no home. I hope that they will quit. I think some of them has saw where they made their mistake and *will* quit. They've come here from everywhere now—they've come here from up in Vermont. I talked to one the other day—talked to him and his wife—and I said, "Why did you like to come here?"

And he said, "Well, I liked the people and I like the country." And he said, "It's a place I believe we can live in. But where I left at, it's come to a time where they don't care. They'll go behind you and stab a knife in you for fifty dollars." And he said, "I left there." He said, "Every day there's somebody getting killed there."

But they come here and don't mix—stay behind chain link fences. Look at the Beech where I was growed up at. Now if I go up to Beech Mountain, I have to pay a big entrance fee where I can go in there and see it, and I was borned and raised and worked in there where I growed up. I told them, I said, "You'uns just ruint my playhouse." Maybe it's helped a lot of people. It's brought a lot of money in, but it ain't brought *that* much, either. And they've run the mountain people off. This development corporation got all the land on the Beech they could get cheap—not over a hundred dollars an acre—and then they begin to come in and give this big money for these little nicks and nods and people just pitched it to 'em. Give it to 'em for a hundred, two hundred, three hundred an acre and the people would just pitch. Thought they was a-gettin' rich. But they was a-cuttin' their own throats and also their young'uns' throats and the generation's throat. But you couldn't tell 'em nothing. "Oh, I can take this money and I can do so and so." And the [developers] finally got down to where they've got it where they want it. They bought this place that my brother sold for five thousand and give twenty-four thousand for it, and now then they're selling it for forty thousand *a lot*. One man give 'em forty-five thousand for a lot that had a rock that he could put his car under! Cost him more for the land than it did to build his house.

But that's the way they done. They'd hire a man and they'd send him around. He comes here. See, I knowed all about the Beech. Knowed the whole works. And he come here and wanted me to show him around and said, "I'll pay you good."

I said, "What do you aim to do?"

He said, "I might buy me a little patch." And all the time he was working for *them*. He wasn't working for himself. See, this corporation would find out the friends of the people that owned the land, and they'd hire them to go and buy it, and then when the deed was made, that man would just turn it over to the corporation. And that's the way they got the whole works.

And now then I can't go up there myself unless I've got one of them stickers or something—or either pay 'em. I was growed up and raised in there and now I can't even go back. Got the gates closed. We wanted to ride our horses through there—just on the road—just wanted to ride through. "No. Can't go unless you want to pay."

My wife said, "Just tell 'em to keep it."

I said, "I've lived this long and I can live on." I said, "I growed up and was raised on this Beech. If I'd a-knowed it would a-wound out like it is, I wouldn't have helped." I said, "They didn't tell me straight." I said, "That's the way you'uns got a lot of this land. Now just take it and keep it."

Oh, it's a sight on earth what they've done up there. We cut haw in there and peeled cherry and went in there and camped—we'd go in there and stay for a week and get haw and pack it out of there.

Now most of the mountain people's just left out. Lot of them that owned it just left and went plumb out. The money that they got for it's gone now and they've got nowhere to come back to. Went out and had their big time off it, and now some of them say if they had that little piece of ground back, money wouldn't buy it. Young'uns have no place, you know, to go to. Can't even go now and visit and look at it.

[People don't care like they ought to. Land is sacred and we're throwing it away. Same with education. It's all mixed up.] Any of us need enough education to where if we need to go out here and fill anything out, we can do it. And have enough education to run a job. Then that's enough. They's no use just to keep a-goin' and a-goin' and a-spendin' and a-goin' on. They ought to learn 'em how to farm—how to work a hog up and work a beef up.

It's pitiful now. You can go to a college right now and pick out twenty students and bring them out in the country and I'd say there won't be five out of the twenty that can tell you or show you what to do. Well, how are they going to live?

I just got to the fourth grade, and this group of college boys and girls that was here [to learn how to make banjos]—they asked *me* things and I'd tell 'em and they didn't even know it and them finishing up college. Didn't know what a drawing knife was! The teachers ought to learn them that! When I went to school you learnt everything. I mean you learnt what I'd call jack-of-all-trades.

But I told those college kids that was here that I was proud to see some of them taking an interest in what I knew how to do. Course there was some of them that didn't care. They was four boys here—I liked them and all that—but they didn't *care*. And they was the first four that got their wood to make their banjos with, and they was the last four that left here, and [they left] with no banjos. All the rest had theirs done. All they wanted was a big time. Spend their daddy's money, I guess, or ever what they was a-doing. They was to be here at ten o'clock every morning, and I called the woman that they was staying with and she said, "They ain't got out of bed," and it was eleven o'clock. They hadn't got out of bed yet. "Well," I said, "tell 'em to stay in bed! I don't have the time to worry with 'em."

When they finally come in later, I told them, "I'm sorry to see you leave

here without your banjos made." I said, "I'm sorry, but you'uns ain't made *no effort* to do it and I can't make you'uns a banjo and *give* you." I said, "I've treated you'uns good, and I've done just as much or more for you as I have the rest of them," I said. "Now your time's up and you're just going back home without anything."

But the rest of them worked hard and got theirs done and I was proud of them. I was really glad they took interest in it. I'm about wore out and they'll have to carry on someday.

It's getting pretty rough. I'll tell you how I am. Now for me, I'm getting way up in age. For me, it won't bother me too much. But now look at the young people—the young generation—what in the name of the Lord's going to become of them? They ain't got no future. They ain't got nothing, see, the way they're a-doing. They got nobody to run nothing—to take care of them. I just don't know what in the world, I'll be honest with you.

Listen. One time me and my brother raised two acres of potatoes. We got five hundred bushel. I carried some of my half to Victor Ward's store and I sold 'em and got twenty-five cents a bushel. I sold seventy-five bushels for twenty-five cents a bushel and kept the rest of them to sell in the spring. And I bought a secondhanded cookstove for twelve dollars that me and my wife started out [housekeeping] with. I've studied that back over, boys, and I don't see how we made it. *But* we got along good and enjoyed it. And if we met anybody in the road, then we'd sit down just like me and you and the boy here are doing now and talk half a day. Now people's in a run. You see 'em and they're in a run. They won't stop and even speak to you. In a big hurry. Big time, I reckon.

But just as sure as we're a-livin', the big days is about over. It's going to get rough.